Foreword by Gilbert M. Grosvenor

Prepared by the Special Publications Division, Robert L. Breeden, *Chief*

National Geographic Society, Washington, D. C.

Melvin M. Payne, *President*

Melville Bell Grosvenor, *Editor-in-Chief*

Gilbert M. Grosvenor, *Editor*

LOWELL GEORGIA

In sunlight's ghostly glow, air pollution from automobiles, industries, and burning fields veils the San Joaquin Valley near Stockton,

AS WE LIVE AND BREATHE

The Challenge of Our Environment

California. Man, in his quest for progress, has blighted the air, the land, and the water.

AS WE LIVE AND BREATHE:
The Challenge of Our Environment

Published by
THE NATIONAL GEOGRAPHIC SOCIETY
MELVIN M. PAYNE, *President*
MELVILLE BELL GROSVENOR, *Editor-in-Chief*
GILBERT M. GROSVENOR, *Editor*
ROBERT PAUL JORDAN, *Consulting Editor*

Contributing Authors
RAYMOND F. DASMANN, RONALD M. FISHER, HAYNES
 JOHNSON, PHILIP KOPPER, H. ROBERT MORRISON,
 CHARLTON OGBURN, PAUL B. SEARS, HENRY STILL

Prepared by
THE SPECIAL PUBLICATIONS DIVISION
ROBERT L. BREEDEN, *Editor*
DONALD J. CRUMP, *Associate Editor*
LEON M. LARSON, *Manuscript Editor*
CYNTHIA RUSS RAMSAY, *Project Editor*
GORDON YOUNG, *Consultant*
MARJORIE W. CLINE, MARGERY G. DUNN, TUCKER L.
 ETHERINGTON, HELGA R. KOHL, ELOISE T. LEE,
 Researchers; PEGGY D. WINSTON, *Researcher and Stylist*

Illustrations
BRYAN D. HODGSON, *Picture Editor*
LINDA M. BRIDGE, *Picture and Legend Researcher*
WILLIAM L. ALLEN, MARGERY G. DUNN, RONALD
 M. FISHER, WILLIAM R. GRAY, JR., REX HARDESTY,
 MARY ANN HARRELL, ELOISE T. LEE, H. ROBERT
 MORRISON, *Picture Legends*

Layout and Design
JOSEPH A. TANEY, *Art Director*
JOSEPHINE B. BOLT, *Assistant Art Director*
URSULA PERRIN, *Design Assistant*
BETTY CLONINGER, JOHN D. GARST, JR., NANCY
 SCHWEICKART, MONICA WOODBRIDGE, *Diagrams*

Production and Printing
ROBERT W. MESSER, *Production Manager*
MARGARET MURIN SKEKEL, *Production Assistant*
JAMES R. WHITNEY, JOHN R. METCALFE, *Engraving
 and Printing*
MARTA I. BERNAL, SUZANNE J. JACOBSON, ELIZABETH
 VAN BEUREN JOY, ELEANOR S. MILUTINOVICH, RAJA D.
 MURSHED, DONNA REY NAAME, JOAN PERRY,
 SUZANNE B. THOMPSON, *Staff Assistants*
MARTHA K. HIGHTOWER, *Indexer*

Standard Book Number 87044-097-7
Library of Congress Catalog Card Number 74-151945

Page 1: Sign at a 1970 Earth Day rally in Boston singles out the source of environmental pollution. Binding: Water birds glide past smokestacks, evoking the disparity between nature and technology.

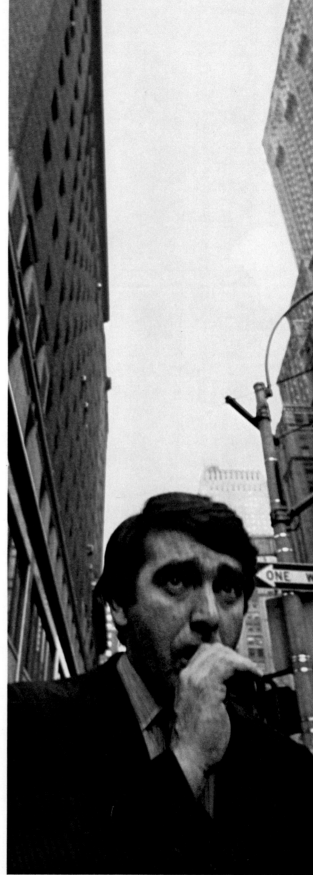

New York City's skyscrapers overshadow a tense pedestrian.

FOREWORD

The day was incredibly clear, perfect for flying. Below me, the Potomac River, sparkling in the brilliant sunlight, meandered through the rich countryside. On that morning, as I returned from Pittsburgh to Washington, D. C., I was struck once again by the immensity and the complexity of our environmental problems.

Riverbank outlets below cities and towns flush sewage into the historic waterway. Silt-laden tributaries pour their burden of soil from eroded farmland and housing- and highway-construction sites. Unseen, pesticides, fertilizers, and manure add poisons and nutrients to the water.

By the time the Potomac reaches the Nation's Capital, it carries large concentrations of chemicals, germs, and debris—enough to rank it as a health hazard. A Washington physician recently stated that water from the river that I swam in as a boy sometimes contains thousands of times the bacterial pollution considered safe by health officials.

Even boating, they maintain, can be dangerous: Water splashed into one's mouth may cause cramps, fever, vomiting, and hepatitis or other diseases.

But the Potomac is only a part of the environmental problem confronting those who live near it. From the suburbs encircling the Nation's Capital a network of highways carries long lines of car-borne commuters to and from their jobs. For many of them, rush-hour congestion has become a nightmare. And automobile exhaust fumes account for 80 percent of the city's air pollution.

These problems are hardly unique to the Washington area. Similar evidence of environmental degradation can be found almost everywhere, across the Nation and around the world. But there is real hope for the future: Perhaps for the first time in history we realize that man's survival upon this planet depends on how seriously, how consciously, he acts to preserve his environment.

The conservation and restoration of a livable environment is everyone's concern. Every citizen should become involved. We cannot afford to wait until tomorrow for someone else to act, for industries to clean up the air, for municipalities to purify our waterways. As individuals, we must be willing to make personal sacrifices—many of which will be time-consuming and expensive.

I believe that many Americans have begun to accept their ecological responsibilities. *As We Live and Breathe: The Challenge of Our Environment,* in its 240 pages, presents sound evidence to substantiate this belief.

Prodded by concerned citizens, state and local governments have joined in ambitious programs to clean up many of the Nation's waterways and to curb the pollution of our air. Congress has passed new and stringent antipollution laws, and the Environmental Protection Agency, established in 1970, is proving effective in enforcing them.

But many problems remain to be solved; to many environmental questions there are no simple or ready answers. Authorities often disagree about what causes ecological damage and how best to prevent it.

To present a balanced summary, the authors of this book have questioned dedicated experts and drawn upon a mass of information regarding the difficult, sometimes confusing, and often controversial issues facing us.

For years, the National Geographic Society has supported conservation, ecological research, and other projects of basic importance to our understanding of the earth. Through our publications we have presented the beauty of the natural world around us, from fragile snowflakes to the vast reaches of space.

When "Our Ecological Crisis" appeared in the December 1970 issue of NATIONAL GEOGRAPHIC, Society members expressed their support of our efforts with an unprecedented flood of mail. Many asked for more detailed information.

As We Live and Breathe represents part of a continuing response to these requests.

GILBERT M. GROSVENOR

Cars, trucks, and buses stream toward a maze of smokestacks and skyscrapers in New York City. Motor-vehicle and industrial

CONTENTS

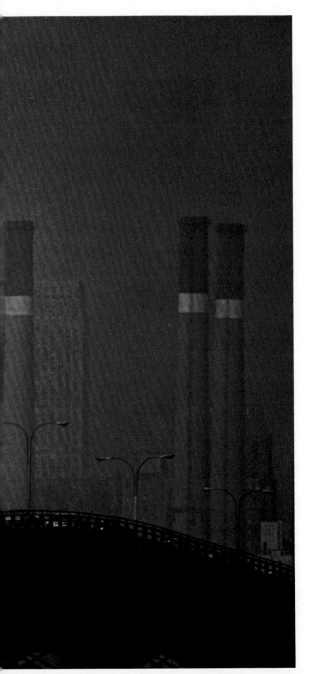

emissions place a heavy burden on the environment.

The road ahead shimmered in the heat. Withered stalks of last year's cotton crop and an occasional wind-contorted, leafless tree traced eerie patterns across the landscape in the bright sunlight. The view as we drove down the San Joaquin Valley past desolate fields, abandoned cars, and filling stations did nothing to cheer our spirits.

My wife and I were taking what we thought might be our last trip through California before moving to the East Coast. We had known the valley for most of our lives and had seen it change over the years.

It was a time of reminiscing—and of disappointment. The valley had always had its dust storms and its ground-hugging fogs, but now an unnatural pall of dirty air hung over the land. It blurred the sun and sky and enveloped us in a dreary, oppressive haze.

As I looked back from the Tehachapi Mountains, which separate the valley from southern California, all I could see was an endless cloud of smoke and gases. Ahead, below the blanket of brown haze, lay Los Angeles, one of the cities that made the word "smog" famous.

The valley had changed within my lifetime and now seemed an alien place. And so had the cities that I had known as a youngster. The charm and glamor of San Francisco, for example, still cast a spell on me, but the city was more fun and to me a far better place when we crossed the bay on ferryboats instead of on a bridge clogged with cars. It was more exciting to go to the zoo on the old streetcars that rocked past sand dunes than it is to whiz over the concrete freeway. In those days boys and girls could go almost anywhere, in daylight or dark, in safety.

I have seen many changes alter the face of California. In the springtime my family took Sunday drives to see the orchards south of San Francisco. I remember endless vistas of fruit trees in bloom—plums and pears, peaches and apricots. Today houses have sprouted where those trees once grew. Elsewhere, too, cities have spread relentlessly into farmlands.

The Spanish, who settled California in the 18th century, called the San Joaquin "Valley of the Tulares." But the marshes where the tall reeds, or tules, once grew are no more. They have been drained and plowed. The old lakes have disappeared; the rivers that fed them are now dammed, their waters trickling through ditches to irrigate orchards and fields. The wilderness had to go from some of the

DR. RAYMOND F. DASMANN, *an ecologist and an expert in wildlife and range management, is the author of* The Last Horizon, *among other works.*

"When the colonists came, they fell upon wild America as though it were a host of heathen enemy."

Victims of an offshore oil spill share the

A PEOPLE AT WAR WITH THEIR LAND

By Raymond F. Dasmann, Ph.D.

COMMON MURRE (URIA AALGE): LENGTH FROM BILL TO TAIL 17 INCHES, WINGSPREAD 28 INCHES. PHOTOGRAPHED BY ENTHEOS

solitude of an endangered California beach near Santa Barbara. Man's exploitation of earth's riches often imperils his environment.

valley. Herds of elk can't live in wheat fields, and coyotes aren't welcome in the suburbs.

Our farewell trip through the valley took place in 1965—in the decade when the fight against pollution became a popular cause. Pollution had been around a long time, but we accepted it as a price we paid for progress, for smoking factories meant jobs. "I like pollution," a lumberman from northern California once told me. "Those pulp mills have the good green smell of money."

But in the 1960's pollution became a greater problem and more widespread. Chemical pesticides not only killed insects and conquered malaria, but carried by wind, they also permeated the earth, accumulating in the soil, seeping into the rivers, poisoning our wildlife. Bloated fish—white bellies up—washed by the million onto riverbanks and the shores of lakes. In places brown pelicans, prairie falcons, and peregrines laid eggs with shells so thin they never hatched.

A threat to the oceans

In 1967 the oil tanker *Torrey Canyon* rammed into a reef off the coast of Great Britain, disgorging millions of gallons of crude. Spills and blowouts of offshore oil wells also fouled the Gulf of Mexico, the Santa Barbara Channel, San Francisco Bay, Long Island Sound, and the waters off Cape Cod.

Other hazards threatened the oceans. Scientists at the Scripps Institution of Oceanography at La Jolla, California, said they could find man-introduced radioactivity in a 50-gallon sample taken anywhere in the ocean. Water they tested also contained lead at seven to ten times the natural level. Another study revealed that ocean fish are almost universally contaminated with DDT and other pesticides.

Inland, ponds and the Great Lakes, brooks and rivers served increasingly as dumping areas for industrial wastes and sewage. During the summer of 1970, Government health officials warned thousands of Vermonters to boil their drinking water because of contamination. The oily, chocolate-brown Cuyahoga River, which drains the acids, oils, and wastes from Cleveland's industries into Lake Erie, burst into flame.

In the decade of the 1960's, air pollution, a problem most frequently associated with Los Angeles, also became a fact of life in other American cities. Sulfurous fumes from smelters and power plants fouled the once crystal-clear air of the Southwest. Smog stunted the growth of orange and lemon trees in California and mottled spinach leaves in New Jersey.

"Killer smogs" hit New York City in 1953, 1963, and 1966. During smog alerts, death rates rose and respiratory diseases increased. Was air pollution the cause? No one could say with absolute certainty.

It was in these recent years that the Smithsonian Institution surveyed the amount of sunlight reaching Washington, D. C.

The study showed that the amount of direct sunlight had declined by 16 percent since 1907, presumably because of air pollution. In other areas dust, soot, and aerosols were shading the earth and reflecting some of the sun's energy back into space. From 1900 to mid-century the burning of oil and coal had caused the carbon dioxide level in the atmosphere to rise by 11 percent.

Carbon dioxide lets the sun's rays enter, but it blocks the heat radiating from the earth's surface. Scientists puzzled over whether such a "greenhouse effect" might prevail and raise temperatures enough to melt the polar ice cap, or whether increased dustiness might bring on another ice age. Climatologists called for worldwide programs to monitor the atmosphere to find out what really was happening.

Those who knew the dangers of pollution voiced concern. In her book *Silent Spring*, biologist Rachel Carson warned in 1962 that the careless use of pesticides was upsetting the balance of nature.

All at once the whole Nation seemed to be awakening to an increasing, but neglected, menace. Newspaper headlines became more and more disturbing: "Dirty Air Forecast as a Houston Peril," "Virginia Is Warned of DDT in Shellfish," "Pollution Linked to Ills of the Young." Scores of new books and television documentaries analyzed the problems created by noise, industrial wastes, the population explosion, and power plants.

Thousands upon thousands joined citizens' groups to fight for clean air and water.

Congress created the Council on Environmental Quality to advise the President and coordinate federal environmental activities. Then President Richard M. Nixon established the Environmental Protection Agency, EPA, in a reorganization that brought programs scattered throughout the Government into one agency. EPA was charged with the responsibility to set up, monitor, and enforce federal antipollution standards.

An awareness spread through the country that it is not necessarily good to grow bigger, to produce more, to travel faster, if this means that the air will become unfit to breathe and the water too foul for human use. Pogo, the small, baffled philosopher possum of the comic strips, uttered his now famous words: "We have met the ENEMY and he is US."

We are all polluters. We drive cars when we can walk. We pay developers to drain marshes and pave over our parks. We buy more gadgets. We demand more throwaway bags, bottles, and cans. To change the situation ultimately, we will have to change ourselves. But, if we wait until each person reforms, it may be too late. Some of us feared that the human weakness and greed implied in Pogo's words could delay efforts to control pollution. In the meantime, we sought immediate ways to fight pollution. We wanted laws to protect the environment, and the power to enforce them.

"What is pollution?" a neighbor once asked me. "I know it is bad, but I really don't know what it is!" I couldn't answer him then, although I thought I knew quite a bit about the subject. Now I would tell him this: Pollution is the addition of any substance or a form of energy—heat, sound, radioactivity—to the environment at a rate faster than the environment can accommodate it. For example, sewage is not necessarily a pollutant. In small quantities it is quickly broken down, and processed into nutrients that nourish aquatic plants and the fish that feed on them. It is, moreover, useful fertilizer. But as the water becomes too rich in these nutrients, algae bloom in great numbers. As the overabundant algae die and decay, they consume the oxygen, making the water uninhabitable by fish.

But even if the water were somehow purified and the air cleansed, we would still have an environmental crisis. For man is more than just a source of pollution: He is a geological force that moves and shapes the surface of the earth. He destroys forests and other vegetation; he alters the courses of rivers; he directs the sprawl of cities and suburbs. Americans have misused their land and plundered its resources. Indeed, the history of the Nation reveals a people at war with their land.

What was America like before the Europeans arrived? How has it been changed? Ecologists have managed to construct the answer to the first question. The answer to the second lies all around us.

First there were the forests, enormously rich and diversified, extending from the shores of the Atlantic to the Mississippi and on to the Great Plains. In autumn trees of the eastern deciduous forest—oak and hickory, birch and maple—burnished the land with a blaze of color. In places the pines predominated; white pine and red, loblolly and shortleaf, spread over thousands of square miles. Beyond the Mississippi, grass took over,

Louisiana shooters fire into a cloud of passenger pigeons in 1875; within 25 years overhunting brought the species to extinction. Settlers, viewing the country's resources as inexhaustible, eventually depleted vast areas of land. Today, overgrazed Nebraska rangeland and overcut Washington forests bear witness to continuing despoliation of the Nation's landscape.

stretching for more than a thousand miles from Canada to Mexico. The tall prairie grasses in the east gradually gave way to the shorter varieties of the more arid high plains to the west. The great game herds roamed over the prairie and plains: the American bison, pronghorn, and elk. Here, too, grizzly bears disputed, for a brief while, the relentless push of the white man.

Westward, beyond the grasslands, lay the hot deserts of the Southwest and the rough, dry uplands of the Northwest.

Forests took root again in the western mountains. Trees rose in belts or life zones. Yellow or ponderosa pines grew in the lower bands, and spruce-fir forests in the higher region, giving way to alpine meadows at the timberline. Ptarmigan and marmot chose the alpine fields; puma and deer roamed the forest. In the mist-drenched valleys of the Pacific Coast the most luxuriant forests grew. There, the redwoods—tall, ancient, impressive—towered in cathedral-like groves above the other trees.

When the colonists came, they fell upon wild America as though it were a host of heathen enemy. The heroes were the men who conquered the wilderness—farmers and ranchers, loggers and miners. As settlers moved out from the eastern seaboard, the forests of America retreated before the onslaught of the pioneer. Great areas of precious woods vanished before the ax and fire of those who sought a place to farm. Where settlers found deep and fertile soil and plowed with skill and care, the lands remained rich and productive. Too often, however, pioneers cleared forests in areas with fragile soils. Rain quickly leached the minerals away. The earth itself washed or blew away, leaving only barren subsoil or rock behind.

The vast woodlands attracted the loggers and gave birth to America's lumber industry. The timber went into homes and factories, wagons and plows, wharves and ships, railroad ties and telegraph poles, and made possible the rapid spread of towns and cities.

For many years the woodsmen believed that the forests were inexhaustible, and they took no care. Fires sprang up—often started by a lumberjack's match or the sparks from an engine. Across New England into Wisconsin and into Minnesota, fire after fire burned through the woods.

By 1864 George Perkins Marsh, a Vermont lawyer and diplomat, had come to look with dismay upon the devastation of America. In his book *Man and Nature*, he deplored the fact that wherever man "plants his foot, the

harmonies of nature are turned to discords."

But in 1864 few were ready to listen. Yet, in that year, while the Civil War raged, a beginning was made far from Marsh's home, in the Sierra Nevada of California. The beauty of the Yosemite Valley—the spectacle of mighty granite mountains, sequoia forests, and flowery meadows—stirred the pride of Californians, and they succeeded in establishing Yosemite as a state "recreational reserve."

Only eight years later Congress passed another bill, and President Ulysses S. Grant signed it, creating the first national park in the world. The park reserved as a "pleasuring ground" the great land of the Yellowstone, remote in the mountains of Wyoming Territory. The concept that governments have responsibility to preserve wild nature for all people, for all time, had become a reality.

But in other areas the destruction went on throughout the 19th and into the 20th century. Forests were felled and burned, streams ran dry or roared down in flood upon towns or cities, grasslands were grazed into dust, and countless kills annihilated vast herds of buffalo and flocks of birds.

In 1813 naturalist John James Audubon recorded the flight of an immense flock of pigeons. They flew so close together that "the noon-day light was obscured as by an eclipse." He calculated that the one flock contained no less than a billion birds. By 1914 the last passenger pigeon had died, captive in the Cincinnati zoo.

Most shocking of all had been the slaughter of the buffalo. Millions were butchered in just a few years. Martin S. Garretson, secretary of the American Bison Society from 1917 until his death in 1951, described buffalo kills along the Santa Fe Railroad: "In the early 'Seventies one could have journeyed one hundred miles along the railroad right-of-way, without stepping off the carcasses of slaughtered bison."

The conservation movement received its initial major thrust when Theodore Roosevelt became President in 1901. He was determined to do something to conserve America's rich heritage of natural resources. He was influenced strongly by the views of Gifford Pinchot, the country's first professional forester.

"The natural resources must be developed and preserved for the benefit of many, and not merely for the profit of a few," Pinchot said. With proper cropping and management, the forests could provide timber and water, grazing and wild animal life, outdoor sports and recreation for everyone, for the long run, he believed.

Under Roosevelt's leadership the national

forest system of America took shape. But Roosevelt was shaken in an encounter with a man far different from Pinchot—John Muir, bearded crusader for the wilderness and founder of the Sierra Club. Muir believed that "mountain parks and reservations are useful not only as fountains of timber...but as fountains of life." He condemned modern man for asking, "What are rattlesnakes good for?" Muir felt passionately that snakes were "good for themselves, and we need not begrudge them their share of life."

Muir's passion for wilderness was lost on Gifford Pinchot, a man committed to the progress of civilization. Nevertheless, the ideals of Muir, and those of Pinchot, lived on, sometimes in concert, sometimes in conflict. Following the vision of Muir, the national forests and parks, and later the wilderness system of the United States, helped preserve wildness. Following the goals of Pinchot, the country's national forests also became world models for wild-land management, yielding timber, meat, wool, water, and recreation.

Once the rangelands with their millions of acres of free pasture had promised new wealth to men who could herd the Longhorns across the plains. As refrigerator cars, railroads, and steamships opened new markets for western meat in the 1860's, cattlemen raising Herefords and later the sheepherders grazed their stock in numbers too great for the semi-arid land, in a rush to make fortunes.

Grassland becomes desert

Overgrazed, its grass grown thin, plagued by drought after drought, the land that had supported a hundred steers could support fewer than fifty. Deserts overtook grasslands. Erosion became rampant. Rivers that once ran clear became seasonal in flow and clogged with silt. Weeds—worthless star thistles and poisonous Klamath—spread over great areas of federally owned land. Then stubborn homesteaders advanced into the plains, competing with ranchers—gun-toting cowboys and rough sheepherders—for the land.

They moved into the shortgrass country—portions of Kansas, Colorado, Oklahoma, Texas, and New Mexico. This tension zone between the desert and the prairie could build men's hopes when rains were right and dash them to the ground when they weren't. Thousands of acres, which had been covered by tough, drought-resistant buffalo and grama grass, were plowed under and planted to wheat. But in 1910 another drought forced many a farmer to abandon his land.

Beginning in 1914, as war raged over Europe, the demand for food increased. Once again the plow broke the prairie, and more and more land went from grass to grain.

Then in the 1930's farmers stared into a brassy sky looking in vain for the sign of a rain cloud. To catch and hold moisture for next year's crop, the land, powder dry, was plowed and left to stand fallow. But searing winds literally blew the farms away. "Two Kansas farms go by every minute," wrote a Nebraskan in his diary.

Streams of farmers moved west to California, following old pioneer trails—but too late to be greeted as pioneers. The migrants, hungry, harried, and confused, joined miserable crews of farm workers and groups of itinerant fruit pickers.

I met a migrant while traveling through the San Joaquin Valley in 1938. "I hate this country," he said. "There's cotton here and there was cotton back there; where there's cotton, there's poverty."

But it wasn't cotton, only misuse of the land, that created the Dust Bowl.

When the rains returned, the Dust Bowl was again cultivated. This time the farmers had the help of Government-supported programs to assist them in applying sound land-use principles.

The disaster of the Dust Bowl caused a rebirth of the conservation movement in America. The Federal Government formed the Soil Conservation Service to aid the farmer in the care of his land. It also established the Grazing Service, which was to become the nucleus of the Bureau of Land Management, to apply early concepts of "multiple use" and "sustained yield" to the Public Domain. The states began to assume a new responsibility for the conservation of wildlife.

The Nation's wild-land resources slowly started to recover. Pronghorn, deer, and elk reappeared; quail, foxes, and grouse became abundant throughout the land. Even the flocks of ducks and geese, herons and ibis, sandpipers and plovers returned to the marshes and the shores of the country.

A new land ethic gave birth to the National Wilderness System in 1964, which set aside many large areas for possible preservation in a roadless and undeveloped state forever. The Wild and Scenic Rivers Act of 1968 seeks to protect the last stretches of free-flowing primitive rivers. The wilderness represents a last chance to save not only unchanged vegetation; it also preserves a place where the sense of danger still survives. Only in the wilderness can man confront the raw, elemental side of nature and thus restore a contact with his long ancestry in the wilder reaches of the earth. It is wilderness that shelters the great beasts that cannot coexist with civilization, and protects those fragile or timid creatures that also need a world man has not disturbed.

Conservation was beginning to work, but a new kind of pollution crisis began to take shape, one born out of the need for energy to power new industries and better methods to move goods and people in and out of America's urban centers.

During World War II American industry geared up to help win the conflict. The long war years created a great hunger for consumer goods; industry later produced — in growing quantities — air conditioners and cars, plastic wrap and second homes, fiberglass helmets and electric curlers. Then more people demanded more goods as the population increased from 123 million in 1930 to 205 million in 1970. Industry set new goals and created new markets. Technologists and scientists expanded and revolutionized industry at a price that blighted the air, water, and land.

There was nothing really new about pollution. The situation in ancient Rome has been described by Lewis Mumford in his book *The City in History*. The accumulation of filth, garbage, and debris in this city of a million reached incredible proportions, and "as the increase of population created a demand for wheeled traffic in Rome, the congestion became intolerable."

Rivers of filth, pall of smoke

Historian Sir Arthur Bryant has described London in the 17th century:

"Rivers of filth coursed down the centre of the streets, and, at the time of the emptying of slop-pails, the passer-by nearest the wall had cause to be grateful for the over-hanging stories. . . . Smallpox and fevers, and more periodically bubonic plague, haunted the town. . . . visitors frequently noted a pall of smoky vapour, arising from the furnaces of the brewers, soap-boilers and dyers. . . . 'horrid smoke which obscures our churches and makes our palaces look old, which fouls our clothes and corrupts the waters.' "

In the growing cities of the United States things were not much better during the 19th century. In 1857 where Central Park now stands the land cleared for the site was, according to a history and guide to the park, filled "with squatters' shacks, bone-boiling works, 'swill-mills' and hog farms." A map reconstructing the Nation's Capital in Lincoln's day notes that from the canal behind the President's Park along what is Constitution Avenue today "70 separate and distinct stinks" rose from sewage, trash, and dead animals.

Why, then, was there no environmental crisis? The answer lies in part in the localization of the problem. London in the 17th century was a noxious place indeed, but England was a sparkling jewel of greenery, of fields and quiet villages where nature was fully capable of absorbing and repairing most of the indignities that man in his small numbers might inflict on it. In the mid-19th century Boston, New York, Philadelphia, and Washington could have their noisome aspects — but America was a wilderness land, sparsely peopled.

The growth of concern for public health, sanitation, and welfare that characterized the 20th century led to a cleaning up of the more obnoxious forms of pollution and virtually eliminated many of the more serious epidemic diseases. But although pollution became less virulent, the increase in the number of people and the spread of urban settlements created another environmental problem.

Conglomerates of cities and suburbs have concentrated the Nation's population in three regions: the Boston-Washington megalopolis on the East Coast, the San Diego-San Francisco corridor on the West Coast, and in a belt along the Great Lakes.

What had been acceptable in 1915, when the country had a population of 100 million, could present grievous hazards to a population of some 300 million by the year 2000.

The pollution problems of today are acute and accelerating in intensity, and, fortunately, so is public concern. Therein lies the hope for the future, but the problem is one of time. In the 19th century Americans ignored the havoc wrought on forests, wildlife, and rangelands. There was enough time then. Most of the damage could be repaired. Some species of plant, some kind of animal, was able to move back and recolonize the lands devastated and laid bare.

Today, however, in the United States and throughout much of the world, a large and rapidly increasing population is exerting an enormous pressure upon the land and upon nature. Can the damage be halted? Can the situation be repaired? There is still diversity in the world. We still have marshes, thickets, quiet beaches, primitive forests. Perhaps we will fight to preserve them. This is the great challenge to Americans and to the international community in the remaining decades of the 20th century. The survival of all humanity may well depend upon the answers we find.

MAN: A NEW GEOLOGIC FORCE

An Oklahoma farmer and his sons trudge past an outbuilding half-buried in dust.

The suffering endured by Dust Bowl farmers has eclipsed the cause of the tragedy: misuse of the land. For centuries tough grasses had anchored the topsoil of the southern plains through cycles of rainfall and drought. Then in the 1860's, herds of Longhorns and flocks of sheep overgrazed the land. Homesteaders arrived during cycles of rain, plowed the prairie sod, then left during the dry spells that followed. The demand for food during World War I coincided with a period of rain, but the drought of the 1930's transformed overworked farms into wasteland. Man continues to abuse his environment. Streams run foul. Lakes become unfit for fish. Fire and flood sweep mountain and suburb. Trash and litter offend the senses.

Torn asunder in the quest for coal, this area in western Kentucky lies scarred and barren after strip miners moved on. More than 1.5

million acres of land in the United States have met similar disfiguration and destruction.

Catfish lies dead at Lake Erie's edge.

Epitaph to summer fun stands before a Virginia lake.

The ruin of a lake

"I want people of Ohio, New York, and Pennsylvania to aid in a campaign for pure drinking water from the lake," said President Theodore Roosevelt of Lake Erie during a visit to Ashtabula, Ohio, in 1910. "You can't get pure water and put your sewage into the lake," he continued. "I say this on behalf of the children." The warning of the great con- servationist went unheeded. Municipalities around the lake poured sewage into it, and lakeside industries added other wastes. Such actions speeded the natural process of eutrophication—the overfertilization of the lake be with organic matter and nutrients.

This process creates an unfavorable environment fo animal life by consuming dissolved oxygen. Within th past 50 years, the dumping of wastes into Lake Erie ha produced as much eutrophication as would have occurre in an estimated 15,000 years without man's interference Today some 4,000 square miles of the lake contain s little oxygen that fish cannot live there. Similar problem imperil many of the Nation's waterways. A sewage trea ment plant overflowed into a stream flowing into Lak Accotink, Virginia, creating a health hazard (above). Swim ming remains banned, even after diversion of the sewage

Once-clear Fields Brook today carries industrial wastes into the Ashtabula River near its mouth at Lake Erie.

Smokestacks of an electric power plant loom beyond youngsters sieving algae from Lake Erie's waters.

U. S. Coast Guard helicopter stands by as a blaze rages out of control at a drilling platform in the Gulf of Mexico. Offshore oil-well

lowouts, tanker collisions, and spills during normal shipping operations threaten the ocean environment.

Plane discharges fire retardant onto a threatened hillside.

Continuing threats: fire and flood periodically plague Californians

Southern Californians battle desperately to save their communities from related threats: fires sweeping through drought-parched chaparral, fanned by winds of up to 7 miles an hour; and relentless rivers of mud, triggered by downpours that wash away fire-denuded mountainsides and canyon walls. Yet every year men build homes by the thousand on the slopes of the coastal mountains, in the very areas often laid to waste. "The southern California environment is hostile and tricky, and has been ever since the coast rose from the sea," said Dr. Martin L. Stout, professor of geology at California State College at Los Angeles. "Violent floods, landslides, erosion, the brush fires that help cause them—are all natural processes

Bulldozer clears a firebreak in the hills overlooking the San Fernando Valley.

CHARLES O'REAR; NATIONAL GEOGRAPHIC PHOTOGRAPHER BRUCE DALE (CENTER AND BOTTOM)

responding remorselessly to a pattern of feast-or-famine rains." The presence of man intensifies this pattern. By carelessness or arson, he starts fires that burn off vegetation. Later, winter rains may strip the bare earth from the hills, and the resulting floods and mud slides rampage through subdivisions.

In the winter of 1968-69, the heaviest rainfall in the area's recorded history transformed burned-out slopes into a Niagara of mud that took more than a hundred lives. Fires in the fall of 1970 left 11 dead and 350 injured. Experts estimated that the heat energy generated by the blazes approximated that of 12,500 atomic bombs of the size dropped on Hiroshima during World War II. Fires burned for more than a week, destroying 400 homes and consuming more than half a million acres of brushland.

As years pass new disasters strike, but in the interim expansion continues. Between 1960 and 1970, California's population zoomed past the 19-million mark, a gain of more than 20 percent that made it the most populous state.

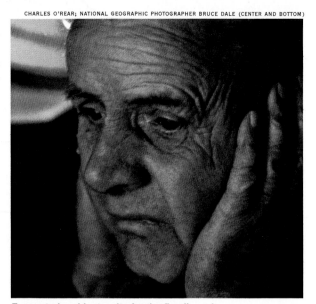

Evacuated resident waits for the flood's end.

Victim salvages belongings from his mud-choked house.

Torrent of mud churns past a helpless resident.

Exhaust-spewing jet thunders over the swimming pool of a motel in Miami, Florida.

Flotsam drifts amid green scum in a drainage ditch near Miami.

Trash clutters the edge of the Miami River.

The blight of conquest

Named in honor of *Pascua florida* — "flowery Easter" — the day in 1513 when Spanish explorer Juan Ponce de León sighted its lush shores, the Nation's ninth largest state bears the scars of man's conquest of the land. Ever-growing numbers of settlers, attracted by southern Florida's subtropical climate, create a demand for developed land.

Canals for flood control and irrigation drain swamplands for farms and subdivisions; as a result, water rushes seaward instead of nourishing the plant and animal life of the Everglades or replenishing underground freshwater supplies. Wells drilled to supply the needs of Miami and other coastal cities further deplete reserves.

Intensifying the extensive damage already wrought by man's interference, drought and fire during the spring of 1971 ravaged more than half a million acres of land. The thirsty Everglades National Park suffered severely.

Peeling billboard greets boaters on a Florida water highway.

25

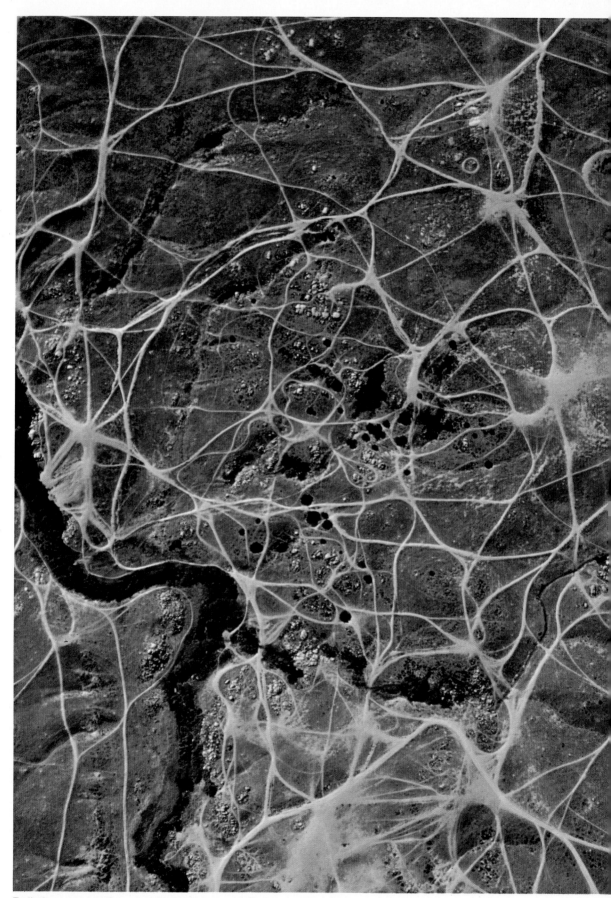

Trails from motor vehicles mar the landscape near Riverside, California.

Camper-laden pickup trucks head toward the desert, the destination of thousands of urbanites every weekend.

Folly in the desert: marks of man's passage

Once the domain of dusty prospectors and their burros, the Mojave Desert serves as a playground for a new generation. Thousands of California residents pour out of cities and suburbs each weekend—many of them in campers. Some carry motorcycles or minibikes, others tow dune buggies. They seek escape from the congestion, smog, and stress of daily life in the heavily populated Los Angeles basin. The sheer numbers—more than 100,000 on some holidays—along with a few vandals, threaten the fragile life of the desert. The wheels of their trucks and automobiles so compress the soil that the scarce rainfall runs off rapidly instead of soaking into the earth. Their motorcycles and dune buggies pattern the desert with tracks that may last more than half a century; scars left by armored vehicles during World War II training exercises remain visible today.

Desert wildlife, especially the rare, shy bighorn sheep, has retreated to shrinking enclaves as more and more visitors arrive. The delicate desert plants sustain heavy damage from vehicles. Battered and uprooted, their protective coatings broken, many die of dehydration. Of the more than 800 flowering species here, some 200 grow nowhere else in the world. Curiosity seekers pick clean invaluable archeological sites that might otherwise reveal information about the Indians who occupied them.

The thoughtless scratch their initials into the soft desert rock, defacing pictures left there untold centuries ago by Indian artists. Marksmen riddle signs and buildings with bullet holes. And varmint hunters upset the balance of nature by killing such predators as coyotes and foxes.

Bullet holes pepper the shell of an abandoned car.

Shifting dunes engulf homesteaders' cabins.

NATIONAL GEOGRAPHIC PHOTOGRAPHER JAMES P. BLAIR

Lunch-hour crowds cross Madison Avenue in mid-Manhattan.

The crowded city: too many burdens

Congestion chokes New York City. Trucks, buses, and automobiles inch along overcrowded streets. Pedestrians throng sidewalks and crossings. Subways transport rush-hour passengers jammed together in forced intimacy. Hulks of automobiles rest in jumbled stacks under a Brooklyn Bridge access ramp. This state of affairs results not only from the people who live in the city, but also from the 3.2 million New Yorkers and suburbanites who commute to the central business district daily.

More Americans live in suburbs than in the cities themselves, according to the 1970 census. Each evening commuters flee the central city, seeking to escape its problems —pollution, noise, crime. In the process, their automobiles create irritating smog. The highways they travel cost millions, while a lack of funds hampers the development of more efficient methods of transportation.

The influx of suburban residents creates a tremendous burden on the city, forcing it to provide increased supplies of water and electricity, greater numbers of policemen and firemen, and larger sewer lines and treatment plants.

The city, however, offers commuters much more than a place to work. They look to it for cultural amenities: concerts, museums, art galleries, zoos, restaurants, night clubs, and theaters. Urban leaders often point out that even though many suburbanites take advantage of the city's diversity, only a few communities, New York among them, tax nonresidents. Thus the threat of bankruptcy hangs over many municipalities throughout the country.

Rush-hour straphangers jam the Lexington Avenue subway.

Brooklyn Bridge rises behind a junkyard where New York City police deposit abandoned vehicles.

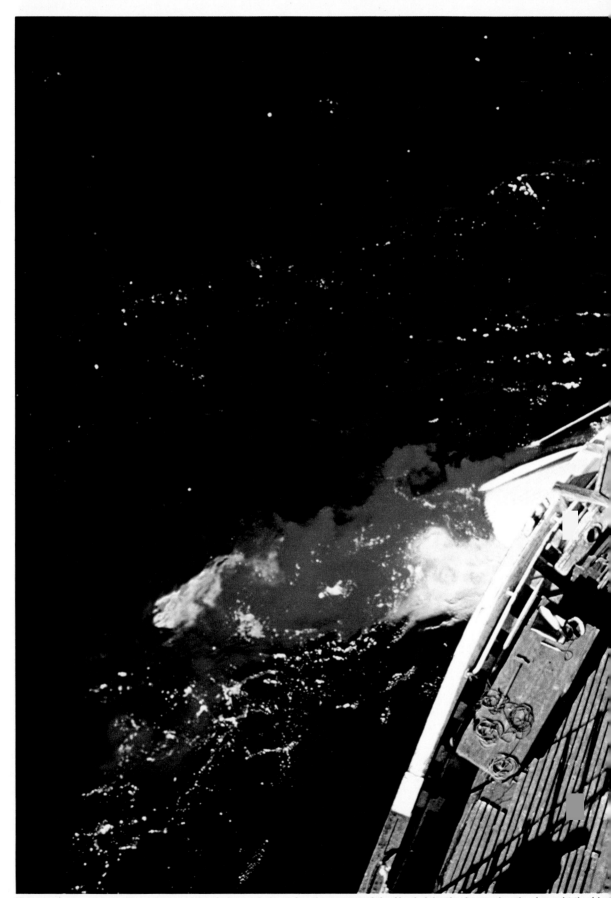

Victor and vanquished: Blood from a dying baleen whale stains the waters of the North Atlantic. As overhunting brought the blue

hale almost to extinction, whalers turned to lesser species, once considered too small to hunt.

Life, whether it be mold on a piece of bread or a weed on an abandoned road, exists wherever it can get a foothold. I have seen life flourish in unlikely places. On sheer cliff walls in the southern Rockies, gnarled piñons sprout from tiny rock crevices. Desert shrimp spring to life in temporary puddles from eggs deposited long before. White pocket mice and pale lizards skitter amid the drifting sands. Algae grow in the scalding water of hot springs.

In the course of some three billion years, life has emerged from shallow, primeval waters to cover the earth. Flowers bloom and the land supports life from the arctic tundra to the Sahara dunes. Creatures exist in the deepest, darkest abysses of the ocean. Caves, hard rock faces, and even cakes of salt support forms of life. But every kind of living thing—each of the known million and a half species of organisms that inhabit the earth—has conditions beyond which it cannot survive, limits beyond which it cannot pass. Plants and animals, giant to microscopic, gradually have evolved as part of a living system, related to each other and to the environment.

In the summer of 1946 I saw an example of how easily man can disrupt these natural systems. I was directing a small field class in ecology at Montana State University. We were working near West Yellowstone, and our goal was to learn as much as we could about living things and their environment.

We immediately noticed the spread of sagebrush into fine pasture land. The woody shrub with its masses of feathery, silver-gray leaves was replacing the native grasses. The sagebrush, we found, was getting its start in the mounds of loose dirt that small pocket gophers had pushed from their burrows, destroying the original sod. We wondered what had happened to trigger the population explosion of rodents, allowing them to run rampant on the grasslands.

Our search for an explanation led us to a forest ranger, who told us that ranchers had declared war on the coyote. He explained that cyanide guns, used to shoot the deadly poison into the predator's mouth when it touches the lure, had all but eliminated the coyotes.

Although studies of the coyote's stomach show that the animal's main diet consists of insects and rodents, and only rarely a weakened lamb or calf, the belief that the coyote is a dangerous pest dies hard. In this instance shortsighted stockmen traded good pasture

---

Dr. Paul B. Sears *is an eminent ecologist and former director of the Yale Conservation Program. His latest book is* Lands Beyond the Forest.

"Food and feeder, eater and eaten, all depend on each other in a tangled, complex web of life that includes the wind, the rain, the seasons."

Thirty-foot saguaro cactus stabs a suns

ECOLOGY, THE INTRICATE WEB OF LIFE

By Paul B. Sears, Ph.D.

...ky in Arizona. The harsh environment of the desert fosters its own network of plant, insect, and animal life.

for sagebrush to save a very few cattle and sheep—a poor exchange.

The hungry coyotes normally hold the population of rodents in check. Unless their numbers get out of hand, the gophers earn their keep and serve a vital function in the life of the prairie by mixing organic wastes and minerals that help form and enrich the soil.

In the deserts of the Southwest, nature through eons of evolution has fashioned a pattern of existence which succeeds in the face of drought and heat. Nature has found remarkable ways to endow the parched land with life.

Recently I revisited the Sonoran Desert of Arizona. Here plants with spines or tough leaves along with night-wandering animals have created an integrated, natural community called an ecosystem. The largest systems, such as the grassland, tropical rain forest, deciduous forest, and desert, represent great zones that vary in climate, known as biomes.

I walked out into the desert on the outskirts of Tucson, as the slanting rays of the sun cast mauve shadows in the fading light. Giant saguaros, fluted cactus columns weighing as much as three tons, towered some 30 feet above the sere brown desert floor. Below the surface these huge plants spread a network of long shallow roots that quickly soak up rain whenever it falls. The saguaro survives by storing water in fleshy tissue that swells when wet, shrinks when dry.

As I paused to pull a bothersome cactus thorn from my sleeve, a gila woodpecker in a flash of zebra-striped wings swooped down to a nearby saguaro. Three gaping black holes scarred the plant where in other days woodpeckers had dug to build their nests. When the birds tunnel a nest for themselves, they provide ready-built homes for purple martins or elf owls.

The late Joseph Wood Krutch, naturalist and longtime friend of mine who wrote of the austere beauty of the southwestern desert from his retirement home in Tucson, marveled at how the plants and animals made the best of the world as they found it.

"Thorns, prickles, and spines are everywhere," he once said. "Here and there one sees the armored paddle of a prickly pear half gnawed away by the wood rat who has made his nest among its roots. . . . In the cholla, fiercest of the cacti, both the cactus wren and the thrasher build their nests."

He considered the kangaroo rat, "a rodent which never drinks but is never thirsty," a desert dweller par excellence.

Other animals too—black-tailed jackrabbits, coyotes, and badgers—live in the thirsty land. They wait in the shade of plants or in burrows, postponing the search for food until the cool of evening.

Birds and bats, lizards and rodents live on insects and help control the insect population. Man's intrusions have brought surprising changes in this natural balance. For example, sprays used to control cotton and citrus fruit pests often drift beyond target, and some ecologists blame these insecticides for a serious decline in the number of Arizona's bees and bats. The bat population around Morenci, in southeastern Arizona, plummeted from 25 million to 30 thousand within five years. At one time these flying mammals destroyed 40 tons of insects each night. Now we can only wonder what happens to the insects; and we have no way to determine the full consequences of this near extermination of the bats. This kind of chain reaction is a real and pressing problem for the people of the Southwest.

"We know we're playing with dynamite when we disturb the natural vegetation and wildlife," said Richard A. Cantrell, one of Pima County's planners concerned with Tucson's rapid growth. Since my first visit to the city in 1955, it has grown from a community of 68,000 to one of 263,000, sprawling farther and farther into the desert.

"We have learned that a dune buggy rolling through an area of desert and leaving tracks can create a wash during the next heavy cloudburst," Mr. Cantrell added, giving an example of how easy it is to inflict damage on the desert.

"The planners of Pima County now realize," he continued, "that if you alter the vegetation of the desert, you alter the drainage. If you cut trees, there are no places for birds. Without birds to kill insects, you have to develop a tremendous spraying campaign to keep them from eating crops."

The grandeur of life

Food and feeder, eater and eaten, all depend on each other in a tangled, complex web of life that includes the wind, the rain, the seasons, and the minerals in the earth. Together they evolve into one pattern in the desert, another on the prairie; everywhere they are responsible for the grandeur of life.

Life maintains life, for the oxygen we breathe and the soil that sustains us is a product of living things.

The actual beginnings of life itself are lost, but we have some fossil record of what Loren Eiseley, the distinguished anthropologist and writer, calls "the long war of life against its inhospitable environment." At first the sun's rays bombarded the earth, burning fiercely on the barren rock, for the planet's primitive atmosphere of water vapor, nitrogen, carbon dioxide, methane, hydrogen, and other gases contained little or no oxygen and ozone to screen the ultraviolet rays.

Eventually the waters gave birth to a form of life capable of using the energy of sunlight to create simple sugar from the water and carbon in carbon dioxide, thereby releasing oxygen and—as new forms of green plants began to grow—creating a livable atmosphere.

"Only the green plant knows the secret of transforming the light that comes to us across the far reaches of space," writes Loren Eiseley. "There is no better illustration of the intricacy of man's relationship with other living things."

Men instinctively have known that all life depends on the sun. Generations of gardeners have come and gone realizing that while some kinds of plants tolerate or even require shade, no green plant can thrive without sunlight's magic wand. But it took a long time for science to acknowledge the fact.

When I was a student, I read of an experiment by the Flemish scientist Jan Baptista van Helmont, who lived from 1577 to 1644. He set out to prove that a tree gets the material for its growth from water.

Van Helmont planted a five-pound willow in 200 pounds of oven-dried soil, watering it daily. After five years he again weighed the tree and the soil. To his surprise he found that the soil had lost only two ounces, but the willow weighed just over 169 pounds.

Where did the tree get its weight?

He concluded that most of the material produced by the plant must have come from the water he supplied. Later, scientists discovered that more than half the dry weight of average plant material consists of carbon, an element which does not exist in water. Not until the discovery of oxygen, at about the time of the American Revolution, did researchers realize that the plant substance comes from invisible carbon dioxide in the air.

Joseph Priestley, an 18th-century English clergyman and chemist, found that in the presence of sunlight, green plants could change what he called "noxious air," which would quench a flame or suffocate an animal, into the good air we know as oxygen.

Years ago I tried a variation of one of Priestley's experiments. I placed a mouse and a potted sunflower plant on a marble slab under a bell jar. I moved the experiment into a dark cupboard, watching (Continued on page 40)

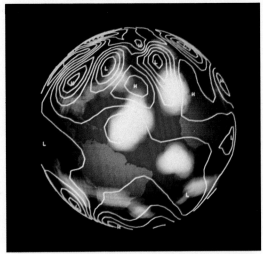

Whorls of air pressure (above) envelop the earth in a computer-produced model of weather patterns made at the National Center for Atmospheric Research in Boulder, Colorado. Computers and satellites help in developing weather theories and forecasts. Thunderclouds (below), photographed during the Apollo 9 flight, obscure the Amazon Basin. Man's activities can upset weather dynamics. Artificial lakes increase humidity; around cities, temperatures climb and wind currents change.

Estuary channel meanders through stands of cordgrass in a salt marsh at low tide on Sapelo Island, Georgia. Organically rich, sa...

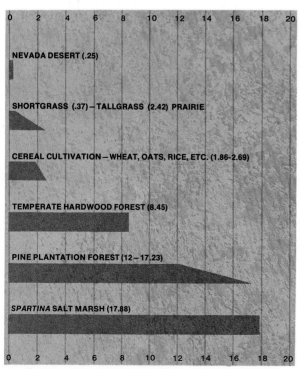

TONS OF ORGANIC MATTER PER ACRE PER YEAR

Chart bars:
NEVADA DESERT (.25)
SHORTGRASS (.37) – TALLGRASS (2.42) PRAIRIE
CEREAL CULTIVATION – WHEAT, OATS, RICE, ETC. (1.86-2.69)
TEMPERATE HARDWOOD FOREST (8.45)
PINE PLANTATION FOREST (12 – 17.23)
SPARTINA SALT MARSH (17.88)

Salt marsh: food factory on the coastline

Life abounds at low tide in the salt marsh of Sapelo Island, Georgia, one of scores of similar marshes that fringe North America's east coast from Nova Scotia to Florida. Cordgrass sways gently in the sea breeze and American egrets glide overhead, searching for food. Crabs scuttle across the oozy mud. Oysters, exposed by low tide (above), and ribbed mussels siphon bits of food from brackish water. Periwinkle snails creep up cordgrass stalks.

The salt marsh — an ecosystem like the desert or rain forest, which supports a variety of life forms — exists in quiet backwater areas on bays and estuaries separated from the open sea by sand dunes or a line of trees, protected from the destructive action of waves. Tides sweep in and out twice daily, washing minerals and nutrients to the sea and removing waste matter.

The marsh water, neither completely salt nor completely fresh, can support both sea and land life during its fluctuating tidal cycle. Dozens of species make their homes in the moist sand or mud of the marsh, and hundreds more — from deep-sea fishes to land-bound mammals — rely on it for food, shelter, or a breeding ground.

marshes support a vast variety of life—from single-celled phytoplankton to deep-sea fishes and large mammals.

At low tide, raccoons, mice, and terrapins forage; when the water rises, porpoises, squid, and shrimp swim in.

Because of its position between land and sea, and the constant parade of life through it, the marsh forms the most organically productive area in the world (opposite); it therefore supports more life. And such fertility contributes greatly to a balanced coastal ecosystem. Since Western man's settlement of North America, however, the number and quality of salt marshes have declined. Some, like those on Sapelo Island, remain virtually unmolested, but others have disappeared entirely.

Recognizing the economic and ecological importance of the marsh, some states have taken steps to preserve these vital shore areas. The Georgia Legislature passed a marshlands protection bill in 1970 designed to guard such areas against overdevelopment. But while lawmakers attempt to save marshes in one region, builders destroy them in others—Maryland has lost up to 10 percent of its salt marshes in the last 15 years to housing developments and industries. Maintaining only a part of the marshland along the entire shoreline, although helpful, may prove inadequate in the long run.

Eugene P. Odum, chairman of the University of Georgia's Institute of Ecology, who has studied the Sapelo Island marshes for 15 years, says, "Preserving a few marshes here and there will not be sufficient to save the range of wildlife that depends on finding them all along the coast."

Life common to the marsh: cordgrass, mussels, snails, and crabs.

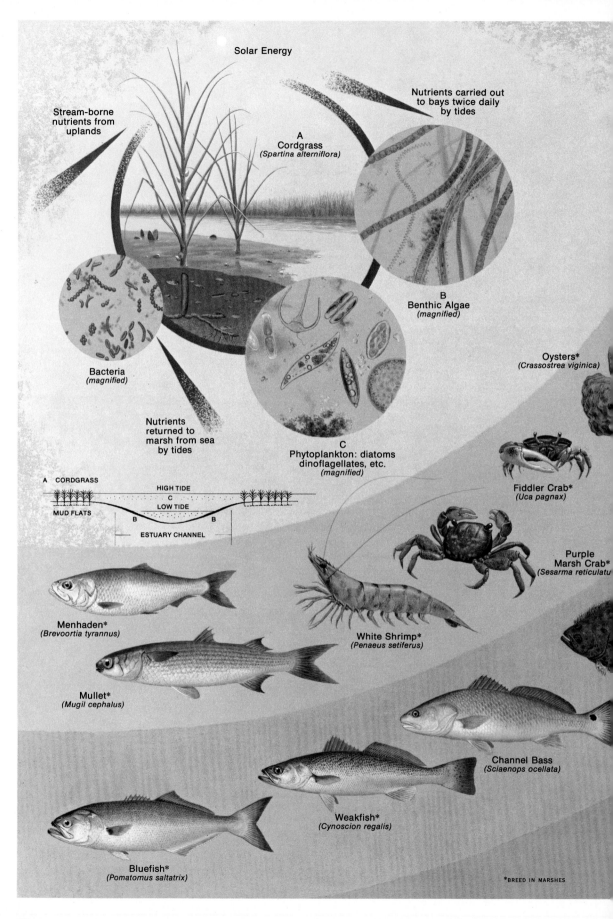

Solar Energy

Nutrients carried out
to bays twice daily
by tides

Stream-borne
nutrients from
uplands

A
Cordgrass
(Spartina alterniflora)

B
Benthic Algae
(magnified)

Oysters*
(Crassostrea viginica)

Bacteria
(magnified)

Nutrients
returned to
marsh from sea
by tides

C
Phytoplankton: diatoms
dinoflagellates, etc.
(magnified)

Fiddler Crab*
(Uca pagnax)

A CORDGRASS

HIGH TIDE

C

LOW TIDE

MUD FLATS

B   B

ESTUARY CHANNEL

Purple
Marsh Crab*
(Sesarma reticulatu

Menhaden*
(Brevoortia tyrannus)

White Shrimp*
(Penaeus setiferus)

Mullet*
(Mugil cephalus)

Channel Bass
(Sciaenops ocellata)

Weakfish*
(Cynoscion regalis)

Bluefish*
(Pomatomus saltatrix)

*BREED IN MARSHES

Sunlight provides the initial boost to the three basic units of life in the salt marsh—cordgrass, algae, and phytoplankton. Nutrients washed in from the sea by tides and transported from the land by rivers gather in the salt marsh, providing a further energy source.

All food manufactured in the marsh originates from these three basic forms of life, called the primary producers. Some initial consumers eat these producers directly—the marsh crab frequently munches on cordgrass leaves. But others wait for the cordgrass to decompose. When the plant dies, microscopic bacteria turn it into a soup of minute particles called detritus. This material, combined with bacteria and often algae, forms one of the essential foods of the marsh. Fiddler crabs sometimes scoop clawfuls of the mixture from the mud. Oysters and mussels sift it from the water.

The smaller creatures that consume the basic food, in turn, fall prey to larger forms of marine life which swim into the marsh during high tides. Eventually the bigger fishes return to the ocean and become food for offshore and deep-sea life. Man reaps abundant financial and recreational benefits from the entire chain.

SOME INITIAL MARSH ANIMAL CONSUMERS

SOME ADDITIONAL MARINE FINFISH CONSUMERS

SOME COMMERCIALLY IMPORTANT OFFSHORE AND PELAGIC FORMS DEPENDENT UPON THE MARSHES

Marsh Periwinkle*
(Littorina irrorata)

Ribbed Mussel*
(Modiolus demissus)

Shad*
(Alosa sapidissima)

Scup
(Stenotomus chrysops)

Striped Bass*
(Morone saxatilis)

Summer Flounder
(Paralichthys dentatus)

Swordfish
(Xiphias gladius)

Blue Marlin
(Makaira nigricans)

Bluefin Tuna
(Thunnus thynnus)

Blue Crab*
(Callinectes sapidus)

Quahog Clam*
(Mercenaria mercenaria)

Scallop
(Pecten irradians)

Surf Clam
(Spisula solidissima)

it from time to time. After about an hour the mouse passed out. Then I placed the setup on a windowsill in bright sunlight. In a matter of minutes the little animal revived and began to run around, as lively as ever.

So exact was the balance that by simply moving everything a foot or two into shadow and back again, I repeated the whole performance one more time. That was enough; recalling my own feelings when coming out of anesthesia, I sympathized with the mouse and ended the experiment.

Plants use the mysterious green substance chlorophyll to harness the energy of the sun as they take the fundamental step in the production of food. Then when plants decay, their remains help to build the soil. On field trips I used to show summer-school classes of teachers in Connecticut how soil is formed and plant life progresses.

On granite surfaces we saw the process which transforms raw rock into fertile soil. Crusts of lichens, black through gray-green to brilliant orange, brightened patches of bare rock. I explained that lichens produce acids that corrode the surface and loosen the less soluble material. The students saw this for themselves when they scraped the lichens off with pocket knives. Lichens also work on the rock by sticking to it like a drop of glue on the back of one's hand. Swelling when wet, they shrink when dry and pull up any bits that may be loose, as drying glue pulls on skin.

We also studied the stages in the birth of a forest. In pockets of soil we saw that woody shrubs and vines had found lodging. Nearby, these had given way to an oak forest—the home of birds, squirrels, and other animals. Tough tree roots forced their way into crevices, often prying the rocks apart and exposing more of the rock surface to weathering and the action of lichens. Decaying leaves, dead trunks, and animal droppings littered the forest floor, adding organic material as the soil developed.

From the weathered rock also come mineral nutrients necessary to plant and animal life. As farmers and gardeners know, soils vary a great deal, and often we must add nutrients that our fields or flower beds lack. The familiar NPK on fertilizer sacks stands for nitrogen, phosphorus, and potassium. Besides these, there are some 20 or more trace elements, such as iron and boron, that are needed for the plant growth that supplies human needs through food chains.

A steer eats grass and grain. We eat beef. But that is only the ascending part of the scale; there is also a descending phase in which fungi and bacteria convert wastes back to simple raw materials.

Going up the food chain, we find that, on the average, at least ten pounds of forage are needed to produce one pound of rabbit, and ten pounds of rabbit produce one of coyote. We could diagram another food pyramid of many worms, fewer robins, still fewer hawks.

As the food chain descends, successive waves of scavengers take over until the waste materials—manure or carrion—return the elements to the soil and air, ready to enter once more the great wheel of life, death, and decay. Plants bring nonliving matter to life, then, with the aid of animals, fungi, and bacteria, convert it into raw material again.

No waste in nature

There is no such thing as waste in nature —no beer cans on the beach, no junkyards piled high with refrigerators, no disposable products made of indestructible materials. Wastes from industry, farms, and cities pouring into the sea and air and accumulating on the land have created a situation foreign to the biological world. The orderly cycles of nature with their simple economy cannot manage such vast quantities of man-made waste. The micro-organisms of decay don't know how to deal with many of the synthetics and chemicals new to evolution.

One of the pleasures of my school days in Ohio was to collect flowering plants from the few patches of forest protected from grazing and cutting. When I returned each year, I observed the slow decay of a log in one of my favorite areas. As it broke down into rust-colored punk, ferns and herbs took root in its cover of lichens and mosses. I could lift the log and see the insects, worms, and fungi hastening the work of decomposition. Of course, the bacteria also did their share. In the end only a patch of rich earth remained, straddled by the roots of a young tree.

There amid the trees, where the air hung heavy with the earthy smell of the woods, I brushed away the topmost layer of brown leaves on the forest floor to get to the lacy skeletons of older leaves, their soft parts eaten away or rotted out. Still deeper in this shallow layer, I found the black spongy material called humus, the final stages of decay of all that had accumulated on the forest floor. But less than a foot below the surface, the dark, rich layer stopped abruptly, giving way to brown or gray mineral subsoil.

This forest soil, rich when newly cleared, quickly loses its fertility as the leaf mold is used up. By the early 1830's New England farmers had cut much of the forests, exposing the thin, top layer of rich soil to the wind and weather. Today nature has reclaimed a great deal of that land, for 75 percent of those fields lying abandoned over the years have reverted to forest.

But only a small portion of our food comes from forest soils. The bulk of our cereals, for example, is produced on the grasslands. I first saw the prairie in 1913 when I went to the University of Nebraska to study botany. Much of Nebraska's grassland by then had yielded to the plow, but enough was left to impress me with its beauty and variety and with the depth of its rich, black soil.

I remember how road cuts had exposed a layer of topsoil which extended three to five feet. I could see the network of fine fibrous roots that held the soil and supplied food for countless tiny organisms which in turn would nourish new generations of plant life.

I remembered, too, how from early spring until frost, flowers created changing waves of color—bursts of purple, red, or gold as each of the many plants came into bloom with the passing seasons.

In this variety lies the secret of how the prairie can survive in an environment too harsh for many trees. Plant life, rooted in the prairie sod, is adjusted to sudden changes of temperature, strong winds, hot sun, and the inevitable drought years. The plants come up from this underground system and thrust out few or many new shoots as conditions permit. They can even lie dormant for a while. Unlike the fields planted in acres of corn or miles of wheat, where the outcome depends on a single crop, there is no chance for complete failure in undisturbed grasslands.

Monocultures, with just one crop on thousands of acres, do not exist in nature.

I talked about this with David M. Gates, director of the biological station at the University of Michigan, and a respected colleague. "Nature," he observed, "maintains a diversity for good reason.

"We know, for example, that in the course of cultivation many varieties of corn have been developed, differing in their relation to temperature, moisture, and disease.

"But with the growth of mechanized farming and the development of monocultures, we are in real danger of losing some of these varieties," said David. "We are narrowing the options or alternatives that we may need in case of emergencies," he added. We both wondered what would have happened if farmers throughout the country had not been able to

Scuba-diving scientist from the University of California at Davis checks a monitoring station 70 feet below the surface of Lake Tahoe. The instrument package records water movement, temperature fluctuation, and light penetration. Dr. Leonard Myrup (below) observes a model of Lake Tahoe he developed to study the natural actions of the lake. Artificial light simulates solar lumination and heat, wire mesh creates waves, and dye traces currents. Some 64 studies probe Lake Tahoe, monitoring variations in the natural order as man's penetration endangers the fragile lake system.

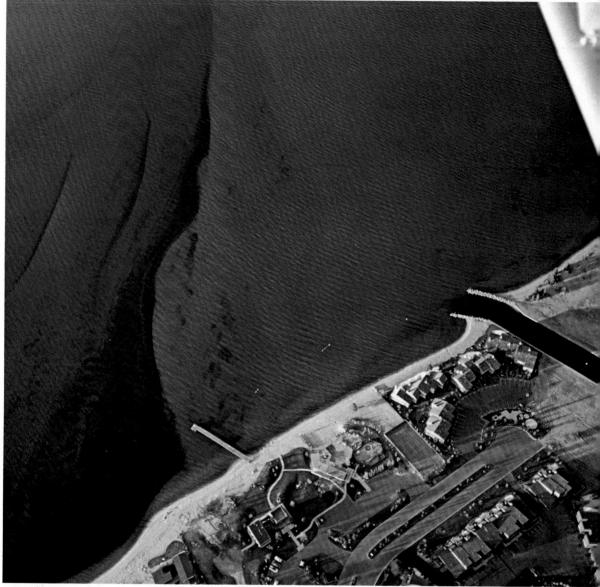

Fed by siltation from housing developments, algal bloom discolors Lake Tahoe's crystal-blue waters.

Pollution perils Lake Tahoe

"I thought it must surely be the fairest picture the whole earth affords," mused Mark Twain in the 1860's after a visit to Lake Tahoe, an azure jewel cradled among 10,000-foot peaks in the Sierra Nevadas of California and Nevada. Today road cuts and ski runs score the mountainsides, casinos and luxury hotels line the southern lakeshore, and pollutants from motorboats and housing projects foul the waters. Lake Tahoe plunges to a depth of 1,645 feet, contains 40 trillion gallons of water, lies 6,225 feet above sea level, and yet has a small watershed.

These factors, combined with slow drainage, create a problem: Once dumped, pollutants tend to stay. "In the natural geologic aging process," says Charles R. Goldman, of the Division of Environmental Studies, University of California at Davis, "lakes tend to become more fertile and their basins gradually fill with the material eroded from their watersheds and with the remains of dead aquatic plants and animals," a process called eutrophication. The less productive a lake, the bluer its color, he explains. The richer the chemical content and the more abundant the plant life, the greener the water becomes.

Lake Tahoe, a highly infertile body of water, would retain its pristine clarity for thousands of years under natural conditions. But when man interferes with nature by accelerating erosion and defoliating a lake's watershed, allowing minerals from the soil to run into it, eutrophication speeds up. Today such pollutants nurture diverse forms of algal growth (opposite) in Lake Tahoe.

"Man's potential for destroying the great natural beauty of Tahoe and other lakes must be recognized and controlled," Dr. Goldman contends, "or lakes containing clear blue waters will soon be only a matter of historical record."

nobryon sociale and *Fragilaria crotonensis* (262.5 times life-size)

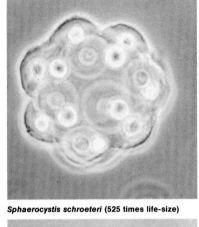

Sphaerocystis schroeteri (525 times life-size)

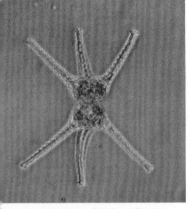

taurastrum paradoxum (345 times life-size)

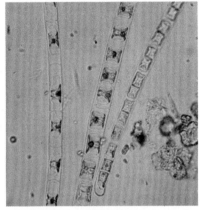

Ulothrix aequalis (172.5 times life-size)

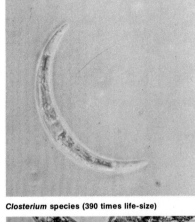

Closterium species (390 times life-size)

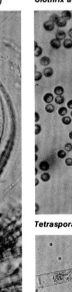

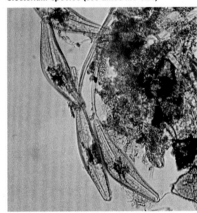

Tetraspora gelatinosa (172.5 times life-size)

Cymbella lanceolata (180 times life-size)

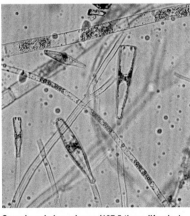

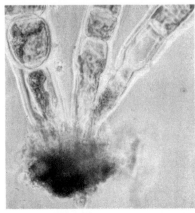

alothrix parietana (262.5 times life-size)

Gomphoneis herculeana (187.5 times life-size)

U. aequalis with holdfast (345 times life-size)

43

substitute other strains of corn quickly for the kind affected by the corn blight in 1970.

"Monoculture is costly in other ways," David continued as we discussed the changing character of the American farm. "With more fertilizers, more chemicals, water, and machinery, we are able to get good crops; but I am convinced that if we add all the costs of maintaining our farm systems, we will find agriculture becoming increasingly expensive."

Department of Agriculture statistics indicate that it cost less to produce a bushel of wheat in 1971 than it did in 1961. But this does not count such long-term costs as the leaching of surplus fertilizer into our waterways and the alteration of soil texture by huge farm machines.

To find out just what is happening, whether we are actually improving the stability and the productivity of our land, a new breed of ecologist equipped with an array of electronic instruments and armed with computers is investigating the prairie with a thoroughness far greater than we could achieve when I was at work in the grasslands.

"We are trying to learn how man affects the land by such stresses as grazing, plowing, irrigation, and the heavy use of chemical fertilizers," said George M. Van Dyne, director of the U. S.-International Biological Program studying the grasslands. He talked about the work at project headquarters in Colorado State University's Natural Resource Ecology Laboratory, in Fort Collins.

Nature's cafeteria

"Since this program began in 1968, we have observed that the grassland is very much like a cafeteria where a great number of creatures come to feed. We have just begun to learn how many there are in the line, and what they are putting on their trays," he said.

He then spoke of a fascinating discovery at their Cottonwood Site in South Dakota. "We found a scale insect about the size of the head of a pin that lives on the sap drawn from the stems and leaves of prairie plants. Our initial calculations show that this little pest may actually be the most important herbivore—the greatest consumer of plant life in this part of the prairie."

Dr. Van Dyne hastened to add, "We need to understand what has kept the population of this insect within limits." What a calamity it would be if something upset the balance of nature and removed the natural controls on the population of this hungry insect.

The balance of life in the Great Lakes was upset drastically by the building of the Erie Canal and the Welland Canal in the early 19th century. The canals opened the way for the slow but deadly invasion of the Great Lakes by the eel-like sea lamprey, a parasite which attaches itself to a victim and drains its body fluids. By the mid-1950's, lake trout—formerly the mainstay of the fishing industry—had fallen prey by the million to this parasitic intruder.

With the decline in the predatory trout population, alewives, which had also found their way into the Great Lakes, multiplied unchecked. But many adult alewives could not complete their full life cycle in the freshwater environment, and since the 1870's, have died in vast numbers. As recently as 1967, for example, thousands of tons of alewives washed up on the shores of Lake Michigan in decaying windrows, ruining the beaches and creating a stench around the entire lake.

Today a control program has killed enough lamprey larvae to permit the stocking of the lakes with Pacific salmon and lake trout. Biologists hope that this move will reduce the number of alewives.

I recently learned of a remarkable experiment which offered further evidence of the effect of transplanting a sea creature from its own ecosystem into a natural community where it was a stranger.

Researchers at the Smithsonian Tropical Research Institute in Balboa, Canal Zone, tested the reactions of Atlantic Ocean fish to the venomous black-and-yellow sea snake, which coexists with fish in the eastern Pacific. The Pacific fish—even when starving—avoided the sea snakes as food. But the Atlantic fish—strangers to the Pacific sea snakes—ate them and died from their deadly poison.

Plants also must adjust to local conditions or perish. Early pioneers planted peach trees in the prairie. The trees grow very well indeed if not caught by frost; but in the prairie, spring spells of balmy weather entice a peach tree to bloom too soon. Then, savage cold often returns, killing blossoms or young fruit. Yet the cottonwood, oak, and wild plum, native to the prairie, do not fall victim to these false alarms.

The life of a lake shows how plants and animals meet the challenge of change. I once studied the plant life bordering a marsh in Sandusky Bay on the south edge of Lake Erie. Plants grew in zones of increasing height, from those submerged in open water, through cattails, to a wet meadow of tall reed grasses. Gradually, willows invaded the marshy meadow to be followed eventually by swamp forest.

Clearly enough, these zones represented

the marching order of vegetation invading and filling in the bay with an enrichment known as eutrophication. I have seen this in scores of lakes since. Unless renewed by some geological event, such as the melting of vast continental glaciers, lakes are doomed to fill in and die. When very young, they are nearly sterile, without much in the way of life; but as silt and nutrients wash in from the land, the lakes develop their own aquatic life. Man, by dumping in even more nutrients, hastens this natural process which eventually converts a lake to dry land.

Ecosystems in lakes, on land, and in the oceans have developed and operated through millions of years, modifying the environment, slowly adjusting to change, and generally increasing the capacity of the earth to sustain life. These systems have made the planet livable for man. They have cushioned the raw forces of environment, screening out murderous rays of the sun, creating soil, regulating the flow of water, and stabilizing land forms. In addition to all of this, they have provided food, and recycled their own wastes with a beautiful and efficient economy.

To this system man is a newcomer. If the record of our planet could be inscribed in a book of about 4,700 pages, each covering a million years, only the last page would include the account of *Homo sapiens*. The whole story of his life as a farmer and city dweller could be told in the very last line of the last page. Four centuries of science and technology would be contained within the period at the end of that line.

But even though man is a newcomer, he has enormous capabilities for modifying the environment. He possesses, by virtue of his nimble fingers and highly developed brain, both the physical means and the mental disposition to dominate his world.

What we cherish, we take care of. But where the land and the seas are looked upon as chattels for immediate profit, both man and his environment suffer. From the air, one has only to look down at the barren, bulldozed landscape of housing developments to recognize the value of our trees.

Beyond this, man must begin to question the morality of ruthlessly destroying organized patterns of life that had operated long before our advent and indeed helped to make the earth habitable for us. Only as we learn to see and appreciate for ourselves the systems of living communities will we begin to respect and cherish them. We must learn to share the landscape with those that inhabit the earth with us.

Crane hoists a 10-foot-wide core of earth from the shortgrass prairie of northeastern Colorado. Scientists will attach instruments to measure the weight and moisture loss of the 4-foot-thick, 45,000-pound sample, studying it as a representative section of the prairie. At sunset (below), biologists track jackrabbits equipped with transmitters to follow the animals' daily pattern of activity. These projects, part of a grasslands biome study headquartered at the Colorado State University Natural Resource Ecology Laboratory, help to define the prairie environment and man's impact on it.

Raised net of an insect quick-trap cart looms over the prairie.

Dissecting a prairie

Braking to a halt, a peculiar contraption drops its long, spindly arm, capturing insects under a quick-net trap. Entomologists, part of a team of scientists studying Colorado prairie ecology at the Pawnee Site Project, vacuum the insects into a net bag and later count them. One finding from this research involving the number of insects and their diversity: Insects daily devour 1/10 as much foliage per acre as cattle. Part of the International Biological Program studying the world's ecosystems, the project centers on a 115,000-acre prairie near the Natural Resource Ecology Laboratory of Colorado State University at Fort Collins.

"In this investigation of the grasslands," explains George Van Dyne, project director, "we are trying to find out how man affects the land by grazing, plowing, irrigation, and the heavy use of chemicals." According to Dr. Van Dyne, the research involves four components: plants—the food producers; animals—the consumers; bacteria and fungi—the decomposers; and soil, climate, and water— the nonliving factors.

Armed with sensitive electronic devices, 85 scientists from 28 universities dissect the grassland, compiling information on all aspects of its existence. They feed the data into computers to produce a mathematical model of a prairie. "With these models," says Dr. Donald A. Jameson, Pawnee Site director, "we can use the computer to manipulate an ecosystem and immediately find what impact man's activities will have on it."

The Colorado investigation seeks to determine relationships between all forms of grasslands life—larks, pronghorns, prairie dogs, grasshoppers, plants. The results may apply to grasslands around the world. "This and other biome studies," Dr. Van Dyne says, "could provide some answers to the very disturbing problems facing man today concerning the preservation of environmental quality."

tomologist John Leetham vacuums insect life from the Pawnee Site in northeastern Colorado.

. Leetham separates insect species.

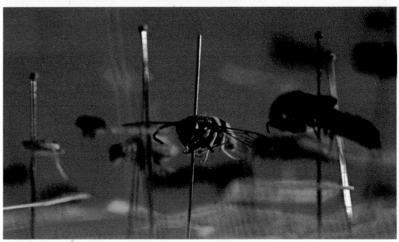

Specimens from grasslands census await classification.

Modifying weather

Buffeted by Colorado's winter wind kites bearing sensitive monitors penetrate massive clouds to collect ice crystals on special film. As part of the U.S. Bureau of Reclamation Project Skywater, scientists meet in the San Juan Mountains near Durango to test the feasibility of seeding clouds with silver iodide in an attempt to increase snowfall, thereby yielding greater spring runoff. Project Director Archie Kahan expects the seeding to produce 16 percent more snow over the 3,300-square-mile test area, and to add needed water to the Colorado River system.

As beneficial to man as weather modification programs may prove their impact on ecology remains virtually unknown. Therefore, during the four-year experiment, scientists from three Colorado universities will examine the effects of the increased snowfall on a wide cross section of indigenous plants and animals, carefully observing the toad—the animal most sensitive to changes in snow cover. Paleoecologists—researchers of the ecological past—will try to determine the historic balance of life in the area and to ascertain the effect of past weather changes on nature

Lofted on frigid winds, a kite rises toward snow clouds to record ice crystals.

Scientist checks film before a kite flight

LOWELL GEORGIA; TAKESHI OHTAKE (BOTTOM)

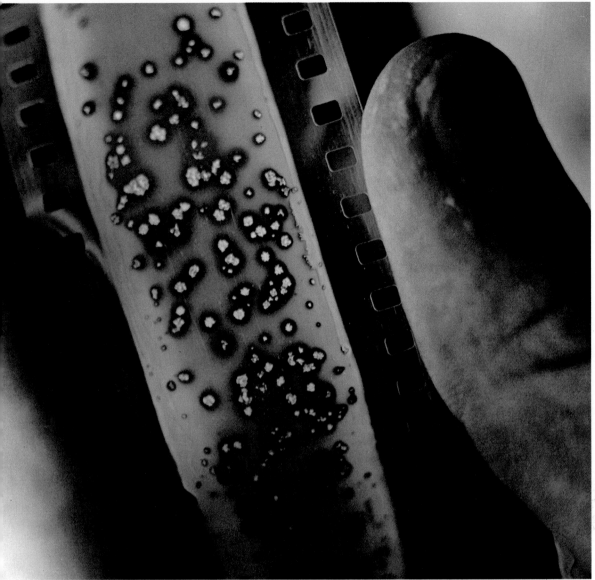

prints of ice crystals speckle plastic-coated film in part of a Colorado study to test cloud-seeding effects on weather.

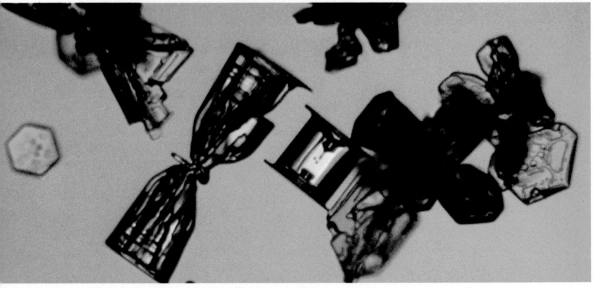

versified shapes distinguish ice crystals magnified 65 times actual size.

Man revives an ecosystem

Once threatened with destruction by spiny sea urchin giant kelp forests now thrive in Pacific Ocean waters of southern California, harboring many forms of life—alga fish, mammals, crustaceans—in a balanced ecosyste Forming a traditional food chain, sea urchins fed on th kelp, controlling its population, and sea otters preyed o the urchins, keeping their numbers in check. Man ups this delicate system, however, when he began killing th otters for fur. With their natural enemy all but eliminate bottom-grazing sea urchins multiplied, inundating th kelp beds. Nutrients from pollutants dumped into the se also supported urchins, further increasing their number

The animals chewed through the lower parts of the ke plant where it attaches itself to the sea floor. The remain der of the strand, often 200 feet in length, drifted to th surface. Great numbers of sea creatures—from perc bass, and rockfish to lobsters, abalone, and scallops lost their shelter and food source, and departed. Ma began to forfeit a valuable cash product; the chemic algin, used in the manufacture of such diverse items a paint, fertilizer, and toothpaste, comes from kelp. The fe hundred remaining sea otters had no impact on the in flated sea urchin community until man came to their ai

Marine biologists, under the direction of Dr. Wheel J. North of the California Institute of Technology in Pas dena, California, discovered the reason for the dwin dling kelp forests. By killing vast concentrations of se urchins with quicklime and crushing the survivors wit hammers, the scientists reduced the population to reasonable number.

The kelp forest eventually reclaimed much of its fo mer territory, and the diminished sea urchin communi could easily sustain itself on the number of naturally dyin kelp plants. Marine life has returned; the kelp beds onc more teem with life; and the kelp industry, which funde much of the research, again harvests a substantial cro

Sea otter darts to surface with a sea urchin under its forepaw.

Fishes swim past drifting kelp.

Gas-filled bulbs buoy kelp fronds toward sunlight.

Wheeler J. North kills sea urchins off San Diego, California, with a hammer after their rapid spread threatened giant kelp forests.

ight-hued sea slug glides among kelp streamers. Marine life once more abounds in the underwater ecosystem.

After subjecting a poinsettia plant to smog at the Statewide Air Pollution Research Center in Riverside, California, horticulturis

Tobacco plants show damage from exposure to smog.

Healthy green turnip leaves contrast with smog-injured ones.

O. Clifton Taylor and an assistant check its leaves for damage.

Dr. Taylor examines a smog generator in operation.

Smog: a poisoner of plants

A fumigation chamber (above) at the University of California in Riverside tests the effects of air pollutants on plant life. Horticulturist O. Clifton Taylor explains that exhaust gases from automobiles and industrial stacks can retard growth, make leaves wither, and cause bleaching and pigmentation. Creating photochemical smog (above right), Dr. Taylor can study its impact on vegetation.

Smog injury ranges from house plants to forests — car gases have damaged over one million ponderosa pines in the San Bernardino National Forest, 80 miles east of Los Angeles. In California alone, crop losses due to air pollution reached 25 million dollars in 1970. Dr. Taylor hopes to find species and strains of plant life that can resist smog. Crop selection and plant breeding, he believes, may protect against an agricultural disaster.

Air pollution pits and scars a grapefruit.

Newly hatched brown pelican peers from its nest.

Biologist Robert W. Risebrough examines a deformed egg.

Pesticide threatens pelicans

Brown pelicans nesting on uninhabited Anacapa Island 15 miles off the coast of southern California show effects of an accumulation of the pesticide DDT potent enough to cause drastic changes in their reproductive cycle. Hundreds of pelicans migrate to the island almost every year to nest. Recently, however, few young birds have appeared. In 1969 five chicks, at the most, hatched; the following year observers noted one hatchling. Robert W.

Risebrough of the University of California's Institute Marine Resources explained the reason for the unbelie ably low birth rate—females produced eggs with shells s thin that they either shattered immediately or broke a the mother attempted to incubate them. The cause: DE and its compound DDE, Dr. Risebrough concluded.

Washed from croplands or borne on the wind to the se and there supplemented by factory effluents, DDT work its way up the food chain, accumulating in pelicans ar other fish-eating birds. The brown pelican appears doome to extinction in California, Dr. Risebrough believes, "ur less DDT levels in the sea decline over the next few years

DDT, magnified 65 times by a polarized-light microscope, shows the pesticide's crystalline formation.

W. GORDON MENZIE (BELOW AND UPPER RIGHT, OPPOSITE)

Broken egg in an empty nest reveals the effects of DDT compounds, a threat to the brown pelican of California's Anacapa Island.

55

Dead ahead, a fireball sun edged above the Florida horizon, burning away mist in the orange groves. Beneath our helicopter, lakes and ponds glinted in the pale light, and white egrets stalked their shores. From a cloud of mist half a mile ahead, our sister ship ascended, then wheeled away toward a nearby grove. As we circled to watch, a fog ejected by the helicopter's spray boom drifted down among branches of the orange trees. Back and forth the chopper went, swooping and turning, nearly brushing the tops of the trees, leaving a wispy and impermanent trail: a trail of pesticide—a substance as controversial as it is misunderstood, as pervasive as it is invisible, as insidious as it is miraculous, as life-giving as it is death-dealing.

I was flying with crews from Helicopter Spray, Inc., of Lake Wales, Florida, as they applied dioxathion to groves managed by Waverly Growers. My pilot, Bob Pharo, dipped to treetop level to follow the applicator ship, and my apprehension nearly erased my interest in the citrus red and rust mites we were after.

Mites—spiny, minute invertebrates related to insects—appear initially on citrus foliage, destroying the leaf tissue, and then go on to attack the green twigs and the fruit itself. An infestation can wreck a grove's productivity in a single season. Manufacturers report that an application of dioxathion "totally blocks the mites' nerve impulses," and they die.

But what of the insects among the orange trees, ones like ladybugs that man calls beneficial? And what of the egrets? And fish? And the pickers who harvest the crop? Such are the questions raised by ecologists and scientists who understand that in nature's delicate balance, the destruction of any one species may have far-reaching consequences. In this particular case dioxathion would do relatively little damage to organisms other than mites, but this cannot be said of many pesticides.

Struggling to wrest sustenance from the earth, man often seems more gladiator than grower. His arenas span the Nation, from the citrus groves of Florida and the truck farms of Delaware to the rolling cornfields of Iowa and the melon rows of the Imperial Valley of California. He copes with early freezes and late freezes, hailstorms and windstorms, too much rain and not enough rain, marauding insects and rampaging blights—any one of which can spell disaster. And as he plants, often he pollutes.

RONALD M. FISHER, *who learned about agriculture firsthand as a youth on an Iowa farm, is a member of the National Geographic Special Publications staff.*

"Struggling to wrest sustenance from the earth, man often seems more gladiator than grower. His arenas span the Nation."

Sprinkler system drenches a vineyard i

AGRICULTURE: THE PRICE OF PLENTY

By Ronald M. Fisher

PHOTOGRAPHED BY HARRY CULLUM AT ALMADÉN VINEYARD, PAICINES, CALIFORNIA

alifornia. U. S. agriculture, although plagued with environmental dilemmas, excels in productivity.

He cultivates his land, and if he is not very careful he turns his creeks and streams silt-brown in the process; by volume, silt pollutes more surface water than any other single source. He enriches his soil with millions of tons of inorganic fertilizer a year. In runoff this may stimulate algae growth in his rivers and lakes. He fattens his livestock on huge feedlots, and in doing so creates serious problems of animal-waste disposal. He uses poisons to rid his crops of enemies, and sometimes kills insect friends in the bargain.

War on pests

Pesticides, I learned, have been with us for hundreds of years. Marco Polo may have brought pyrethrum—a poison-yielding chrysanthemum—to Europe from the Far East. By 1763 Frenchmen were killing aphids with ground-up tobacco; its deadly ingredient—nicotine—was isolated in 1809. In the 20th century more powerful pesticides emerged from chemical laboratories.

We have never lacked targets for pesticides. A pest, we say, is any creature or plant that interferes with our health or comfort, destroys our belongings, or robs us of food and fiber. Chemical compounds to combat them include insecticides, herbicides, fungicides, rodenticides, and miticides.

Certain insects are among the hardest pests to control. After some 250 million years, insects have evolved biological defenses that have defied most of man's or nature's weapons. A vertebrate species can be destroyed almost inadvertently, even while we work to save it; but despite our best efforts we never have been able to eradicate a single insect species, except in local situations—and then often only temporarily.

The most common insecticides are the organophosphates and the organochlorines. The former deteriorate relatively rapidly once applied and thus lose their power to kill. The latter, also called chlorinated hydrocarbons, persist in the environment and may accumulate in food chains.

Present-day productivity of farm goods depends on monoculture—specialization in one crop or kind of livestock—a practice that tends to stimulate "boom-and-bust" cycles of pest populations. With adjacent fields planted to the same type of crop, insect pests can spread virtually unhindered.

And so can disease. The corn blight that struck the country in the 1970 season was helped along by the absence of resistant hybrid strains in vast acreages of corn. Total production dropped 10 to 15 percent as a result.

The single family farm—like the one I grew up on—is another casualty of monoculture. In an earlier day farms functioned as more or less independent units. My parents survived the Great Depression not in comfort, certainly, but with less privation than most, because their farm provided most necessities. And they did it without big doses of chemical pesticides.

While pesticides without question do much good, there is also no question that they have done, and are doing, harm. Every chemical pesticide is a poison to some living thing, and no poison has yet been found that will affect only one kind of insect or weed.

"In practically every spray operation," says Dr. William A. Niering, professor of botany at Connecticut College in New London, "thousands of nontarget insects are killed; many of them may be predators on the very organisms one is attempting to control.

"For example, in the campaign against the gypsy moth, one of its natural enemies, the *Calosoma* beetle, also has been affected."

The battle against the imported fire ant, whose wasplike sting proves painful to people, also illustrates how nontarget organisms may be victimized. A native of South America, the fire ant was first noted in the United States shortly after World War I.

In an attempt to eradicate it from the 126 million acres it then occupied in nine southern states, the U. S. Department of Agriculture in 1957 began applying heptachlor, an organochlorine. Soon after treatment, fish and wildlife began to die.

The late Rachel Carson, who first alerted the Nation to the dangers of pesticides in her book *Silent Spring,* singled out the fire ant program as "an outstanding example of an ill-conceived, badly executed, and thoroughly detrimental experiment in the mass control of insects. . . ."

That was in 1962, when amid a public outcry, the USDA halted the use of heptachlor. Today the campaign against the fire ant continues, this time with corncob grits and soybean oil treated with mirex, an organochlorine currently approved by the Environmental Protection Agency for such purposes.

Most famous of the organochlorine family of insecticides is DDT, for dichloro-diphenyl-trichloro-ethane, a war baby that grew up like Frankenstein's monster to turn on its creator. Swiss chemist Paul H. Müller discovered its insecticidal properties in 1939 and won a Nobel Prize in 1948 for developing it. The world at first hailed it as a panacea. DDT stopped a typhus epidemic in Naples in 1943, saving many thousands of lives. It has brought malaria under control in much of the world. The World Health Organization, maintaining that if DDT is bad, malaria is worse, advocates its continued use in many nations until more effective alternatives can be found.

The danger of DDT and its derivatives lies in their tendency to move up through the food chain, concentrating in animal fats. A classic case occurred at Clear Lake, California. Vacationists, bothered by large swarms of annoying gnats, had the lake treated in 1949, 1954, and 1957. The insecticide was DDD, a close relative of DDT, which supposedly would not harm fish. But eventually the western grebes feeding on fish from the lake began to die.

Analysis of the birds' fatty tissue showed residues of DDD of up to 1,600 parts per million. Since the poison had been applied at no more than 1/50 of one part per million, how had the deadly levels built up in the grebes? Analysis of other life in the lake showed the answer: Plankton had accumulated 250 times the applied concentration, frogs 2,000 times, sunfish 12,000 times, and grebes up to 80,000 times as much. According to Miss Carson, "It was a house-that-Jack-built sequence, in which the large carnivores had eaten the smaller carnivores, that had eaten the herbivores, that had eaten the plankton, that had absorbed the poison from the water."

Some bird species with high DDT residues produce egg shells too thin to protect embryos; many of our birds of prey—pelicans, ospreys, bald eagles—lay eggs that fail to hatch, and their numbers steadily decrease. Alexander Sprunt IV, research director of the National Audubon Society, says flatly, "Unless we ban DDT, the American eagle will become extinct." Dr. Sprunt announced that researchers had found an eagle nest on the shores of Lake Superior containing "the ultimate"—an egg without a shell. The peregrine falcon is another victim: The California Fish and Game Department counted only two nesting pairs in 1970, compared to a hundred in 1946.

In 1969 the Conservation Foundation in Washington, D. C., revealed a potential danger to other birds as well: "When leaves from a sprayed elm fall, they are eaten by earthworms. The DDT doesn't harm the worms; but it accumulates in their tissues. When robins eat the worms, they accumulate it in ever larger and finally lethal doses." The USDA no longer recommends using DDT against Dutch elm disease.

Scientists have only begun to study some of the synergistic (Continued on page 64)

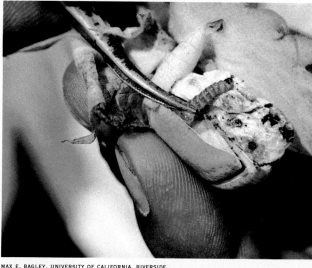

MAX E. BAGLEY, UNIVERSITY OF CALIFORNIA, RIVERSIDE

Chewing through cotton lint to feed on seeds, the pink bollworm (top) cost Arizona growers an estimated 12 million dollars in 1967. Although insecticides remain in heavy use, scientists have begun to seek alternatives through biological controls. In California's San Joaquin Valley, the release of one million adult moths sterilized with radioactive cobalt may prevent pink bollworm infestations. Entomologists at the University of California, Riverside, study native predators like the ambush bug (above) that attacks pink bollworm larvae.

Farmer-executive Earl Blaser pilots his own plane to inspect crops on his 2,300 California acres — and looks for new tracts to buy

One machine and 36 people package 200 cartons of field-fresh lettuce hourly.

From the good land

With mass-production techniques th
make U. S. agricultural workers t
most efficient in the world, toda
American farmer provides enou
food and fiber for 45 people — fo
times his achievement just 30 yea
ago. Businessman in denims, he reli
on geneticists to develop high-yie
grains or fruits and vegetables suit
to mechanized harvesting. He co
sults computers for analyses of co
and profit margins. He invests in au

ase for additional planting.

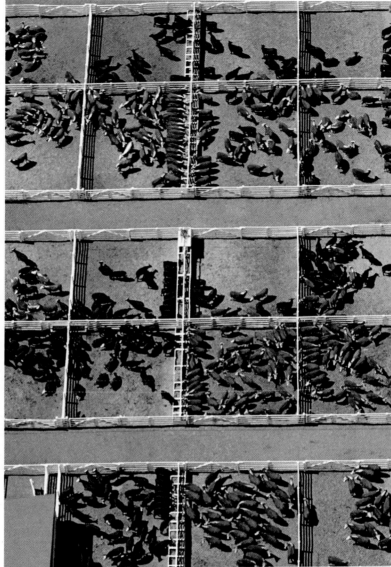

Cattle in Colorado holding pens await shipment to slaughterhouses.

ation to help gather eggs by the mil-
n in block-long hen houses, or fat-
n cattle by the thousand in feedlots.
But innovations may create prob-
ms. In the 1930's free-grazing steers
ached slaughter size in 30 months;
eir droppings enriched pasture or
nge. Now feedlot steers mature in
months; but the waste matter pro-
ced by a lot of 20,000 cattle, com-
ring roughly to the sewage load of
city of 200,000 persons, poses a
mendous disposal problem. Ques-
ns of consumer health arise over
e of antibiotics and growth-stimu-
ing hormones in livestock rations.

Egg City, California, produces a million eggs a day from two million hens.

A Chicano—Mexican-American—migrant worker and his son stand outside quarters provided by a farm owner.

tonio del Buono, fluent in Spanish and English, offers legal assistance to farm workers.

Protecting farm workers

Farm workers face increasing occupational dangers through exposure to pesticides. Risks to laborers from highly toxic substances figured in union bargaining for the first time in 1970, when Cesar Chavez' United Farm Workers Organizing Committee negotiated a contract with California table-grape growers. The pact set controls on the use of pesticides, and established minimum-wage standards, equal employment practices, and medical benefits for union members.

Growers turn from organochlorines, such as DDT, to organophosphates, such as parathion. Although these compounds decompose more rapidly than organochlorines, some have a toxic strength 300 times greater. Of 132 recorded cases of pesticide poisoning during 1970 in North Carolina, 55 stemmed from organophosphates.

According to Dr. Thomas H. Milby of the California Department of Public Health, "We are beginning to recognize a new kind of hazard from organophosphates because of the residue buildup on foliage after application. In one instance, 90 peach pickers were poisoned while working in orchards subjected to unusually heavy parathion spraying over a period of several months."

Government and industry officials attempt to alert farm laborers to the dangers of pesticides, particularly through warning labels printed in Spanish and English and pictures to reach those who cannot read. In spite of such warnings, workers and employers often fail to observe precautionary measures or to use protective equipment.

ket's sign announces *huelga* — strike.

Demonstrators keep all-night vigil for jailed union leader Cesar Chavez.

63

effects of insecticides, in which the interaction of two compounds results in a combination more toxic than the sum total of the originals. For example, the synergism that takes place in an insecticide combining DDT and toxaphene—another organochlorine—makes it effective against boll weevils, which had become resistant to toxaphene alone. At least 50,000 pesticide formulations are currently available; no one knows how many will react with each other, or in what ways.

Unfortunately, pesticides don't always stay where we want them. Penguins in Antarctica show traces of DDT. Eskimos in the Arctic have smaller residues of DDT in their bodies than many Americans, but it's there. Pesticides may run with rainwater off farmers' lands and into the rivers, which in turn deposit the poisons in the sea; and winds carry them literally everywhere on earth. Most Americans have 8 to 10 parts per million of DDT in their fatty tissues, although this level shows signs of decreasing. DDT in significant amounts persists in mothers' milk. Federal authorities found it necessary to impound 8,000 pounds of kingfish, caught within 20 miles of the California coast, for excessive DDT content. And farmers in the Northwest have had to step up importations of honeybees to pollinate their crops after applications of other insecticides greatly reduced the local bee population.

A protracted controversy rages between those who would drastically limit the number and amount of pesticides used and those who insist we cannot survive without them.

"Field tests and careful studies show that no commercial crops of apples, peaches, cherries, sweet corn, grapes, strawberries, cranberries, raspberries, potatoes, tomatoes, carrots, kale, mustard, collards, spinach, and other common foods could be grown in this country without chemical insecticides and/or herbicides," says Parke C. Brinkley, president of the National Agricultural Chemicals Association.

If this is so, Charles F. Wurster, biologist at the State University of New York at Stony Brook, wonders how we managed to grow commercial crops before pesticides came along. He terms Mr. Brinkley's statement a "very serious exaggeration."

I asked Joseph J. Crowley, vice president of a Delaware vegetable growing and processing firm, if he could continue in business without chemical pesticides. "Absolutely not," he said. "Most of our products wouldn't begin to meet the standards of either the Federal Government or the housewife. The Food and Drug Administration says there can be no worm cuts on processed lima beans, for instance. We couldn't meet that requirement without pesticides. And women today expect to buy perfect produce. There's a cost factor, too. To harrow fields often enough to control weeds would be prohibitively expensive. And that's what we'd have to do, without herbicides."

Secretary of Agriculture Clifford M. Hardin cautions that "the benefits chemicals yield by enabling the farmer to produce more food on fewer acres with less labor must be weighed . . . against the dangers they present."

Many scientists believe that an overwhelming reliance on chemical insecticides has created its own shortcomings and failures. Robert van den Bosch, a biologist at the University of California's Agriculture Experiment Station near Berkeley, points out that we have more insect pest species than ever before, and that some 250 of them are resistant to increasingly costly insecticides. Houseflies in America, for example, developed resistance to DDT as early as 1948, and have since adapted to many other pesticides aimed at them. Dr. van den Bosch told me about a highly promising alternative—"integrated control."

"This concept," he said, "combines chemical, biological, genetical, and agricultural methods to provide effective pest suppression at minimum cost and with minimum environmental impact. We're not simply killing pests; we're learning how to live with them, as long as they don't compete too seriously with us. We've had great success here with such crops as cotton, grapes, and alfalfa."

A change in direction

To find out more about integrated control, I spent a busy day at the Entomology Research Division of the U. S. Agricultural Research Service in Beltsville, Maryland, and came away impressed with the progress being made.

C. H. Hoffmann, the acting director, explained the change in direction that the research of his division has taken in recent years. "In 1955, two-thirds of the program was involved with conventional insecticides; now barely 16 percent is. We're looking for more selective chemical and nonchemical methods to control major insects, particularly those pests requiring heavy doses of insecticides year in and year out. We don't expect to be able to find biological controls for all insect pests—so we're concentrating on the two or three dozen most important ones.

"And while trying to control these, we're also working to protect beneficial insects," Dr. Hoffmann added. "For instance, pollination of about one billion dollars' worth of crops each year depends on the use of honeybees, but many bees have become victims of chemical pesticides."

Dr. Hoffmann led me to his colleague, William E. Robbins, who told me about tampering with the processes controlled by insect hormones. "Insects rely upon hormones to regulate their growth, feeding, mating, reproduction, and diapause—a state akin to hibernation." Disrupting the hormone-regulating machinery, he said, can cause an immature insect to stop developing, grow too fast, or mature into a monster. Nearly all of these effects kill the insects.

"We can condemn some female insects to an unproductive life," Dr. Robbins explained. "Using hormonal chemicals, we can interfere with the ovaries and either keep the insect from producing eggs or cause it to lay eggs that will not hatch. Synthetic hormones or antihormones that will jam the lock, so to speak, and prevent the insect from developing and reproducing, could provide us with a safe, selective means of insect control."

It seemed ironic to me that the next man I visited—Horatio C. Mason, who was working on the problem of controlling *Drosophila* flies on tomatoes—had a flyswatter hanging on the wall within reach, but I didn't mention it. "*Drosophila*, which we also call a vinegar fly, lays its eggs in fresh cracks in ripe tomatoes," Mr. Mason explained. "They hatch into little maggots in 24 hours or less. The fly population can increase enormously in no time. The FDA's tolerance for insect contamination of processed tomatoes is zero.

"In 1969, working with the Campbell Institute for Agricultural Research and the New Jersey Department of Agriculture, we undertook a program of releasing sterile flies on a 75-acre field of tomatoes. The sterile males compete for mates in the natural population, and less fertilization takes place.

"Between June 24 and September 4 we released 50,000 flies per week per acre—about 40 million in all. We obtained reductions of up to 81 percent in *Drosophila* eggs laid in cracked tomatoes, compared to untreated fields we checked against."

Encouraged, I moved along to the office of Roger H. Ratcliffe, leader of the alfalfa weevil investigation. "Adult weevils rob alfalfa of its nutritional value by feeding on the leaves," said Dr. Ratcliffe. "The weevils may severely reduce crop yields and cause millions of dollars of damage in the United States each year.

"Agricultural Research Service entomologists have been working on various control

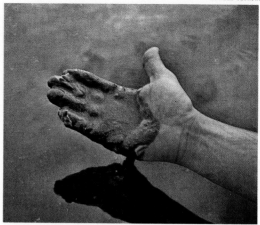

Thriving algae coat the hand of a sanitary engineer at a test site simulating a high-rate-growth pond for the proposed San Joaquin drain, part of the California state water plan. Ecologists believe that nutrient-rich, subsurface agricultural waste water could foster algal bloom in the drainage system and its receiving waters, such as San Francisco Bay. One solution: Grow algae to assimilate the nutrients, then separate the algae from the water, and thus remove the offending pollutant. Below, dust clouds the air as a farmer plows dry peat soil near Stockton, California. Dust, an increasing source of air pollution, also may add nutrients to waterways when it settles.

California Aqueduct snakes through the southern San Joaquin Valley with water for industrial, agricultural, and domestic use.

Pipes 12 feet in diameter will carry water over the foothills of the Tehachapi Mountains.

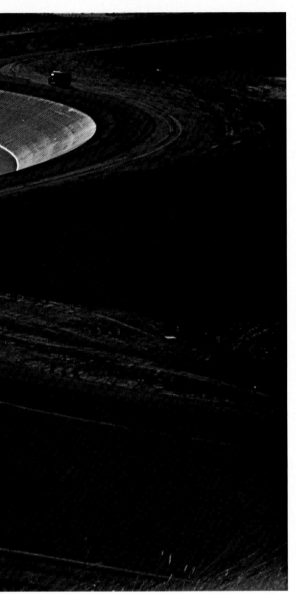

Work proceeds on Edmonston Pumping Plant near Bakersfield.

California canals: boon or bane?

sweeping concrete canals and mountain-conquering pipelines divert water from northern California to semi-arid central and southern regions of the state. Most of the flow will supply industrial and domestic users; less than a third will serve agriculture directly. Scheduled for completion in 1973, the State Water Project—a vast, man-made river complex containing 685 miles of aqueducts built or begun—will cost at least 2.3 billion dollars.

In concerted attacks on the project, environmentalists charge that a proposed peripheral canal east of San Francisco Bay would reduce the flow of the Sacramento River to a dangerously low level. This reduction, they argue, would imperil the bay's environment, impeding natural flushing action that cleanses the estuary and permitting salt water to enter—and contaminate—fertile lands.

Walls of the canal near the pumping plant dwarf workmen.

methods. One of them involves the introduction of natural enemies of the alfalfa weevil into infested fields—the most important of these are small wasps brought from Europe. The adult wasp lays its eggs in the body of the weevil; the developing wasps then feed on the weevil, eventually killing it.

"Researchers have also bred a new strain of alfalfa with partial resistance to the weevil. It took ten years of research," said Dr. Ratcliffe, "but it should be a good step in the direction of better weevil control. When an insect feeds on the growing tip or terminal of the new strain, the plant is able to put out side branches and thus tolerate greater weevil feeding."

Large black-and-white photographs of viruses—some rod-shaped, others like doughnuts, building blocks, and marbles—papered the walls of the laboratory of Arthur M. Heimpel, the division's principal insect pathologist. In his library he talked with me of killing insects by infecting them with their own diseases.

Dr. Heimpel defined for me the ideal microbial insecticide: "It should, of course, be infectious, preferably for several different kinds of insects. It should be easily and inexpensively produced, storable, and safe for use around man and other animals."

Do such microbial insecticides exist?

"Yes," said Dr. Heimpel. "There are several. Among the most familiar is *Bacillus popilliae,* the milky spore disease that is used against the Japanese beetle. Another is *Bacillus thuringiensis,* which attacks moth and butterfly larvae. When you use these, you are engaging in microbial control."

Troubled waters

The growing and processing of food also have other profound effects on our environment. Robert L. Coughlin of the EPA points out that "west of the Mississippi, agriculture is the principal source of water pollution. In the Great Plains nearly 30 percent of water pollution is attributable to agriculture, as opposed to about 15 percent from municipal sewage."

A farmer who fails to follow sound soil-conservation practices contributes, directly or indirectly, to the siltation that clouds our waterways. And a farmer who uses large amounts of inorganic fertilizers may also contribute in certain areas to the growing eutrophication of the Nation's lakes, rivers, and streams; nitrates dissolve readily in water, and thus become highly susceptible to leaching.

A related problem of agricultural pollution confronted me during a visit to the Group 21 feedlot near Sutherland, Iowa. From a centrally located grain elevator and barn, acres of cattle pens sloped down two sides of a hill. Paul J. Geuther, the amiable young veterinarian-manager, showed me around. Aberdeen Angus cattle, their tails turned to a brisk December wind, watched with melancholy eyes as we drove through. Confined in pens, they seemed less spirited than the freely pastured cattle of my Iowa youth.

"Feedlots the size of ours are a relatively new phenomenon," Dr. Geuther explained. "We have a potential capacity of 12,000 head here."

As I pondered that, we drove to the crest of a ridge that bisected the lot, and stopped. Dr. Geuther pointed to a thin stream meandering across the valley floor. "That's Waterman Creek. It runs into the Little Sioux River, which runs into the Missouri. We maintain a distance equal to two feet per head of cattle from the creek, but left alone, waste still would be washed into it by rainfall and end up heading toward Sioux City. To avoid a pollution problem, we catch the runoff before it reaches the creek."

Carefully terraced troughs, downhill from the pens, channel waste into a collecting pond where bacterial action breaks it down. Solid waste is periodically collected from the pens and used to fertilize cornfields—also owned by Group 21—that provide all the silage for the cattle. The system works so well that the local Izaak Walton League chapter awarded the feedlot owners a silver cup saluting their contribution to clean water.

Unfortunately, many operators have not solved the problem of waste disposal so completely. Farm animals in the United States create some two billion tons of waste a year, and an appreciable amount finds its way into lakes, rivers, and streams.

Extensive funds will be required to halt this damage to our environment. "Terracing, troughs, and holding ponds cost money," Jim Greenfield, another Iowa feedlot manager, told me, speaking from experience. "The Federal Government presently pays 50 percent of the cost of pollution-control projects up to a maximum of $2,500." But that, I found, represents only a small fraction of the true cost of such programs.

Man traditionally has valued manure as a fertilizer. Why not sell it? Economics interfere. A commercial fertilizer can be manufactured and marketed less expensively than manure can be gathered, processed, packaged, and distributed to points of sale. But some manure goes to good use.

A firm near Seattle, Western Sawdust Products, Inc., buys sawdust from the lumber industry and manure from dairy farmers and packages a 50-50 mixture for sale to gardeners and nurserymen.

Others take a more radical approach. Chicken manure, for example, is extremely high in nitrogen, which livestock readily can convert into protein. In one experiment a mixture of cattle manure and hay has been fed successfully to sheep and steers. Broad-scale use would require not only approval of the FDA but also a change of attitude on the part of the American public.

While the farm belt copes with too much waste, California tries to solve the problem of too little water. Actually, it's more like too much water in some places and not enough in others. The State Water Project seeks to correct the imbalance. The project will divert water from rivers in northern California to the central and southern parts of the state for industrial and domestic use. The water also will irrigate what some agricultural experts consider economically marginal farmland in the San Joaquin Valley.

Ecologists say that the project could reduce the annual flow of the Sacramento River into San Francisco Bay by more than 80 percent. This in turn could impair the ability of the estuary system to dilute sewage and agricultural drainage containing sizable amounts of insecticide residues and nitrogen, and increase the natural incursion of salt water.

No two experts seem to agree on what this ultimately will mean. Both the director of the state department of water resources and the Army Corps of Engineers insist the effect will be small, maintaining that tidal action is by far the most important factor in purging pollution from the bay. Many biologists disagree. They believe that freshwater inflow is vital to the flushing of the bay.

Predicts one ecologist: "Algal blooms and water plants will increase, threatening the natural life of the bay. From an environmentalist's point of view, the State Water Project may well become one of the major disasters of all time for northern California."

The country awoke to another kind of threat to the environment in mid-January 1970, with the tragic story of the Huckleby family of Alamogordo, New Mexico. Ernest Huckleby had fed his hogs with waste seed grain that had been treated with a fungicide called Panogen, a methyl-mercury compound.

A dye added to the fungicide treatment, as a Government-required safety measure, had tinted the seed red to show that it was poisonous, but Mr. Huckleby felt the danger was exaggerated. He mixed (Continued on page 74)

Flourishing at the age of 38 days, a summer squash plant spreads above strips of aluminum foil that repel disease-carrying aphids. New Jersey farmer John Mastrobuono and Norman J. Smith, a Rutgers county agent, inspect its leaves and find them healthy. A control plant of the same age and hybrid strain exhibits stunting caused by the experimental application of mosaic virus. Flying aphids transmit viruses from plant to plant, but shun the reflection from aluminum-covered fields. In tests and commercial plantings, the foil has reduced virus infestations by 90 to 98 percent—without the use of pesticides—and has increased squash yield fivefold.

Whirring over an orchard in the State of Washington, a helicopter spreads pollen on blossoming apple trees.

igil from the sky

FRANKLIN E. MANZER AND GEORGE R. COOPER

though helicopters sometimes substitute for honeybees
er orchards and fields, crops worth about one billion
llars a year still depend on bees for pollination. And
es succumb quickly to the popular insecticide carbaryl,
ss dangerous to mammals than DDT. With early warning
plant damage, precise spraying on pinpointed targets
n replace the blanket spraying that endangers bees.
ickily, infrared film reveals disease in plants before the
aided eye can detect it, since sick leaves take on a col-
different from healthy ones. Below, aerial photographs
om tests in Maine record the ravages of potato blight.
uch remote-sensing devices may someday help in the
mpaign against blight or pest incursions, with aircraft
satellites relaying data to computers on the ground.

Potato blight becomes evident to the unaided eye.

ealthy potato plants appear scarlet on infrared film.

ilm reveals checkered patches of induced blight and shows adjoining areas of plants withered when sprayed to hasten ripening.

71

Antennae of the male gypsy moth (seven times life-size, in laboratory rack) can detect the scent of a female a quarter mile away

ummer bleakness of a Cape Cod forest demonstrates the voracity of gypsy moths: One larva can eat three oak leaves a day.

ntrolling the gypsy moth

1970 gypsy moths defoliated 800,000 acres of trees in e United States: three times the damage of the previous ear, six times that of 1966. Use of DDT to control the est declined in the late 1950's in response to warnings at it, and a number of other organochlorines, may ac- umulate in nature's food chains, thus endangering the urvival of certain species as well as man's health. For ix decades scientists had tried using the gypsy moth's natural enemies to control it, but with very little success.

A new method utilizes the fact that the flightless female moth attracts males for mating by her scent. U. S. Depart- ment of Agriculture chemists Barbara A. Bierl, Morton Beroza, and Carroll W. Collier have isolated, identified, and synthesized this attractant. In 1970 their artificial "disparlure" drew more males to traps than did the natural female attractant. Males have flown a quarter of a mile to just four-billionths of an ounce of natural lure.

Disparlure probably can be produced commercially for $40 an ounce; if so, it may prove an economical way to concentrate male moths for trapping or selective spraying.

cented, sticky trap holds male moths.

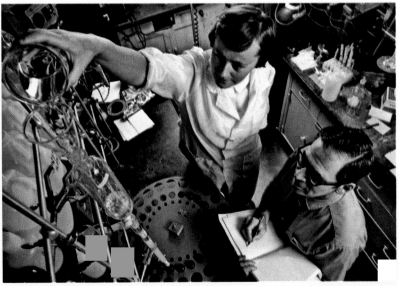

Barbara Bierl and Morton Beroza analyze scented attractant by chromatography.

the seed with garbage and fed it to his hogs.

In eating the contaminated pork, his family soon paid a dreadful price for the misuse of the waste seed grain.

Mrs. Huckleby was pregnant at the time. A son, Michael, born that spring, is blind and retarded. Another son, Amos Charles, is blind and suffers a lack of coordination. One daughter, Ernestine, can neither walk, talk, nor see. However, another daughter, Dorothy Jean, who had the highest accumulation of mercury ever recorded in human hair, has been almost completely rehabilitated.

The Huckleby tragedy was an unusual accident. Eventually it led to the suspension of sales of methyl-mercury fungicides in the United States. It also alerted the American public to another danger—mercury poisoning, whose initial symptoms include tunnel vision and irritability. And suddenly the deadly substance seemed to be everywhere.

I asked Warren C. Shaw of the Department of Agriculture about mercury fungicides for treating seeds.

"When you put seeds in the ground, fungus may attack them," he said. "Mercury fungicides, developed many years ago to protect seeds, proved so effective that there was too little incentive to develop alternatives. Now most mercury fungicide compounds may be withdrawn from the market. We still use some, but in minute amounts. When you plant treated seeds, the mercury you add to the environment will total only about three grams per acre—less than occurs in nature. The danger is to birds or other animals that might eat treated seeds."

I also asked about another possible danger: that mercury applied to seeds might find its way into fruit of the mature plant, and from there into our food. Wheat seeds, for instance, are treated before planting. What happens after planting?

"It's a dual process called absorption and translocation," Dr. Shaw explained, "and there is some evidence that mercury fungicides applied as seed treatment may be absorbed and translocated upward in minute quantities into seedlings. But the amounts are barely detectable. By comparison, the amounts translocated by plants from naturally occurring background levels in some soils would be as great or greater."

In the mid-1960's, however, a Swedish study revealed that barley and oats grown from treated seed had a concentration of about .03 parts per million of mercury, whereas crops from untreated seeds had less than half that. And hens eating grain grown from treated seeds laid eggs with two to three times the mercury content of eggs from chickens whose feed came from untreated seeds.

Harold G. Alford, acting director of the pesticides office of the Environmental Protection Agency, cites contradictory data and says, "Test results we have seen give no indication that mercury will come through in the crop grown from seed treated with a fungicide containing mercury."

Everyone agrees on only one thing: The subject needs considerably more study before final answers can be determined.

If it's true that "you are what you eat," then Americans might think they are, in large part, sodium nitrate, monosodium glutamate, oxygen interceptor, fumaric acid, calcium carbonate, and artificial flavoring. Virtually every American eats about three pounds of food additives a year. Most of them have unpronounceable names.

Precooked, prepackaged, ready-to-eat foods —convenience foods—require emulsifiers, coloring agents, preservatives, and flavoring agents. Some chemicals aid thickening or foaming or firming; some prevent these actions. Others increase or decrease moisture content, and still others serve as ripeners or inhibit ripening.

Problems plague the FDA

Since 1958 the FDA has been charged with approving all new additives in our food. But problems familiar to all bureaucracies have beset agency officials. Short of funds and understaffed, the FDA generally relies on research done by industry or universities to determine the relative safety of new chemicals.

In recent years, food technology has advanced so rapidly that it threatens to outstrip the agency's capacity to regulate it. There are, for example, more than 2,000 food additives currently on the market.

Some critics feel the FDA has become overly protective of the food industry, pointing to seemingly lax standards of consumer protection. The World Health Organization describes an artificial food coloring called Red 4 as "dangerous," but maraschino cherries still contain it. The food industry argues—and the FDA agrees—that nobody eats enough maraschino cherries at one time for the ingredient to do any harm.

Sodium nitrite preserves color and prevents spoilage in meat products like hot dogs, smoked ham, and bologna. The problem is that chemical compounds in the stomach may transform sodium nitrite into nitrosamines, which in turn may cause cancer. The FDA permits up to 200 parts per million of sodium nitrite in preserved fish and meat; Dr. William Lijinsky, a University of Nebraska cancer specialist, for one, believes this standard should be reduced drastically.

Other chemicals may be added to our food while it's still on the farm. Back at the Group 21 feedlot I watched a farmhand drive a dump truck into a big grain elevator and stop beneath a hopper, from which a ton of cattle feed descended. The feed, mostly corn and molasses, also contained antibiotics to reduce infections and hormones to stimulate growth. Antibiotics have been added to cattle feed since the 1950's; experimental evidence indicates these antibiotics accumulate for a time in an animal's blood and muscle tissue.

Since 1958 withdrawal periods have been established for medications fed to livestock. Drug manufacturers and meat producers urge that animals be taken off drugs at specified times prior to their being sent to market. The Animal Health Institute in Washington, D. C., coordinates their efforts through a national animal drug certification program. And the FDA has taken legal action against violators. The agency also has a task force investigating potential effects on human health of drugs used in animal feeds.

Dr. Emil M. Mrak, biologist and Chancellor Emeritus of the University of California at Davis, told me, "The situation regarding safety-testing methods is completely chaotic. It seems that anyone studying, say, the effects of pesticides or additives may use any procedure he wants, whether it is sound or not."

FDA officials do not agree, contending that testing methods have been recognized and revised for years. They see the problem as one of updating these procedures with the most recent scientific knowledge. An FDA-EPA biological laboratory, which will aid in accomplishing this, is scheduled to go into operation at Pine Bluff Arsenal in Arkansas by 1972. Says Acting Director Dale R. Lindsay: "We want to get industry's scientists involved; this will help us gain lead time."

My look at how we produce our food left me with disturbing questions: Have we poisoned our world, contaminated our food, and forgotten the principles of careful farming? Or have we now begun to reverse a trend, to forgo the arrogance that led us to dominate nature and attempt to mold it utterly to our will?

Only time will tell, but it seems unlikely—given any other alternative—that we would choose to leave our grandchildren the legacy of a toxic, ruined land.

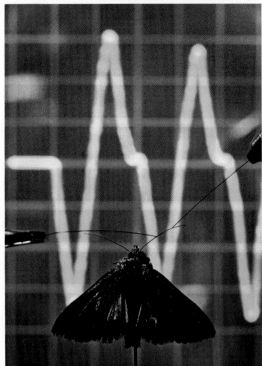

Delicate electrodes monitor the response of a male cabbage looper to the attractant scent of a female, while an oscilloscope (background) records his reaction for a research project now ten years old. Entomologists at the University of California, Riverside, have found that male moths become too confused to mate when the female's scent is diffused over whole fields. One of the most difficult insects to control by conventional measures, the cabbage looper ranks among the five most serious farm pests in California, and among the ten most serious in the entire United States.

Tragedy reveals mercury's dangers

Suffering with symptoms of damage to the central nervous system—from failing vision to coma—three children in the Ernest Huckleby family of Alamogordo, New Mexico, have focused world concern on the perils of mercury contamination. In autumn 1969 they had eaten pork from a hog fed on seed grain treated with the fungicide Panogen, containing methyl mercury. When stricken, they carried high levels of mercury in hair, urine, and blood. Yet four other members of the family also had high concentrations but no ill effects. Physicians worked six weeks to reach a diagnosis. Reports of similar tragedies in Japan, where more than 200 people have met disability or death from contaminated seafood, and in Guatemala, where poor families ate mercury-treated seed, finally helped identify the illness.

For more than half a century, farmers have used mercury compounds against fungi that attack the seeds of cereal crops. Growers spray orchards and vegetable fields with mercury fungicides, and sometimes apply them directly to the soil. In the 1950's and '60's studies showed that some plants absorb and translocate small amounts of mercury. Sweden banned methyl mercury in 1966. The U.S. Government forbids alkyl-mercury sales, sets a zero tolerance on mercury-pesticide residues in foods, and continues to investigate other agricultural mercury compounds, seeking less toxic alternatives.

Most scientists believe that the principal risk to humans from mercury-treated seed lies in its accidental consumption by such food-producing animals as the hogs of Alamogordo. As the Huckleby tragedy showed, human susceptibility to mercury poisoning varies, for unknown reasons. Mercury compounds—like many others now discharged into the environment—challenge agricultural experts to reconcile plenty with safety.

On the road to recovery, Dorothy Jean walks with crutches.

Learning speech again, Amos Charles remains blind.

...nded, mute, her hearing and powers of movement severely impaired, Ernestine Huckleby clings to life.

...rcury on seed grain glows pink in ultraviolet light.

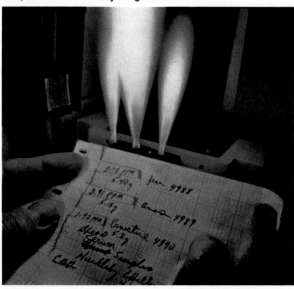

Spectrophotometer measures mercury in blood samples.

ENERGY: A CRISIS IN THE OFFING

By Henry Still

Giant shovel at the River Queen coal mine in Kentucky rips away 125 cubic yards of dirt and rock with each bite. Nearly 40 perce

"The Nation has developed a relentless hunger for enormous amounts of electricity."

U. S. coal comes from strip mines.

My guide was a Navajo Indian named Hugh Cleveland. His face was quiet, etched by wind and time on the barren mesas of the Southwest. His strong hands were quiet, too, but they had learned the ways of modern machinery.

"Look," Hugh said proudly. "I'll show you something." A blunt finger pressed a button on the console of a computer. An automatic typewriter clattered briefly.

"*Ya-at-hey,*" it wrote—"Greetings" in Navajo. "Welcome to Four Corners, largest coal-fired power plant in the West. At full load we will produce over 2,000 megawatts of power. To reach full load we will require 24,000 tons of coal each 24 hours. We hope your visit with us is enjoyable. We invite you to come again."

Hugh Cleveland's magic machine had taken a moment from its job of monitoring steam-powered generators and rumbling furnaces busy converting powdered coal into enough electric power to serve customers in Arizona, New Mexico, Texas, and southern California.

The Four Corners project at Fruitland in northwestern New Mexico, more than a hundred miles from Albuquerque, represents a new trend toward locating generating stations away from large cities, where pollution makes them increasingly unwelcome, and close to a source of fuel.

Five other huge power installations—one in operation, two under construction, and two proposed—in Nevada, Arizona, Utah, and New Mexico eventually will transform these wide-open spaces of the Southwest into a gigantic network supplying electricity hundreds of miles distant.

Power plants devour vast quantities of coal or oil and pump millions of tons of ash and sulfur dioxide into the atmosphere. Natural gas, a much cleaner fuel, is already in critically short supply. And we have nearly exhausted the possibility of additional hydroelectric projects, which dam rivers and flood large tracts of land. As the power industry turns to energy locked in the atom, we face the perplexing problems of controlling man-made radioactivity and abating thermal pollution, the heating of our waterways.

The Nation has developed a relentless hunger for enormous amounts of electricity. We need power to drive the wheels of industry and transportation, to heat in winter and cool in summer, to operate computers, and to light our homes, streets, and shopping centers.

HENRY STILL *is a science writer specializing in environmental subjects. He is author of* Will the Human Race Survive? *and* In Quest of Quiet.

The United States has doubled its production of electricity each decade since 1940. In 1970 the power companies produced 1,529 billion kilowatt-hours of electricity. (A kilowatt-hour of electricity will light ten 100-watt bulbs for an hour.) The Federal Power Commission predicts that by 1980 we will generate 3,086 billion kilowatt-hours per year, more than twice the 1970 output.

"Such growing demands for energy must be considered in context with our desires for clean, healthy communities," said Roger S. Carlsmith, an associate director of the National Science Foundation's environmental program at Oak Ridge National Laboratory in Tennessee. He was one of many experts I consulted on a wide-ranging journey to discover the environmental price the Nation pays for its fuel and electricity.

Strip mining today

I turned first to coal, the fuel of the Industrial Revolution and the largest single source of electrical energy today, producing 46.4 percent of our total output. To get a picture of strip-mining practices, I flew over the hills of Kentucky and parts of eastern Ohio. I saw scars of raw earth where hillsides had been ripped away to get at the shallow coal, leaving deep benches across the highlands. Bleak high walls—the naked bluffs left after miners have cut away most of the mountain—loomed above the silt-clogged streams. Below the benches, I saw lagoons of orange- and rust-colored water, tainted by acid formed when mining exposed iron sulfide to air and water.

Harry M. Caudill, Kentucky lawyer and journalist, describes what happens to the mined land in his book, *Night Comes to the Cumberlands:* "The overburden is scraped off and the coal is scooped out.... When the strippers move on, once level meadows and cornfields have been converted to jumbled heaps of hardpan, barren clay from deep in the earth...years elapse before the yellow waste turns green again...."

In the past several years the power boom has created new, profitable markets for coal. Meanwhile, the introduction of more stringent safety regulations in tunnel mines has required heavy investments in costly equipment. This, coupled with a growing shortage of skilled labor, has caused many operators to turn to coal beds lying just below the earth's surface. In 1970 nearly 40 percent of the Nation's coal came from these low-cost operations—an increase of 12 percent in one year. Strip mining for coal alone has torn up about 1.5 million acres—an area the size of Delaware.

Some mine operators accept their responsibility to reclaim the land. Larry Cook, executive vice president of the Ohio Reclamation Association in Columbus, showed me how reclamation can work. Bulldozers level the spoil banks to fill the cuts and contour the earth to gently rolling terrain. Then grass and trees are planted.

"We depend on nature to help us," Mr. Cook said. "The animals and birds come back in to perpetuate the forest."

"But how can you reseed a huge rock cliff shot away and left bare by the strip miners?" asked Rufus M. Reed, an angry resident of Lovely, Kentucky, as he discussed the problems of land restoration in mountainous regions. "How are you going to reset uprooted oak trees? And how are you going to keep the silt back? Our streams flow thick with mud and debris."

Also, acid from abandoned surface and underground coal mines pollutes 20,000 acres of lakes and 10,000 miles of creeks and rivers in the United States, often imperiling fish and plant life. Most states now require mining companies to neutralize the acid in their drainage water but, even so, communities in the Appalachian region must spend millions to make their water fit to drink.

Another type of change is taking place in the desert country of the Southwest—one that to me eloquently dramatizes the conflicts which come into play as the Nation seeks to keep pace with energy demands.

In northwestern New Mexico the Utah Construction and Mining Company operates one of the country's largest strip mines. I visited the tract of barren land, leased from the Navajo Indians, which supplies coal to the power plant at Four Corners.

The road to the Navajo mine led between shaly mesas and low hills sparsely grown with brown clumps of grass. Tumbleweeds rolled slowly with the breeze. In the distance a faint plume of gray smoke streaked the clear blue sky. I crossed the San Juan River onto the Navajo Reservation past the century-old trading post of Fruitland where Indians still come for supplies.

James H. Olsen, mine superintendent, showed me the operation. We drove past sand and boulder spoil banks 50 feet high. The road led down into a man-made ravine where the coal was being blasted free and loaded into 120-ton trucks bound for the Four Corners plant five miles away.

Woody Diswood, a Navajo, operated the controls of a huge dragline that scooped 45 cubic yards of spoil with each pass. "It don't take too long to move a mountain," Woody said impassively.

When the coal is exhausted in one area, other machines go to work to begin reclaiming the land.

At the power plant smoke and sulfur dioxide, an acrid, invisible gas, billowed out of giant stacks. The smoke, like that from other plants using fossil fuels, consisted of small particles of fly ash—the unburnable mineral residue—and traces of unburned carbon.

At maximum operating load, the five huge coal-fired boiler units pour 350 tons of fly ash a day into the air over that vast sun-drenched land—more than that emitted into the air of New York and Los Angeles combined. Technically it is possible to make precipitators that can attract, under ideal conditions, more than 99 percent of these particles on electrified plates. However, few precipitators perform at this efficiency.

Spurred by the New Mexico Citizens for Clean Air and Water and other groups, the management agreed to cut fly-ash emissions to 30 tons a day by improving their precipitators and by installing ten million dollars' worth of wet gas scrubbers. They will collect ash in a high-pressure mist of water and empty it into a disposal area.

As coal burns it also releases sulfur, which combines with oxygen to form sulfur dioxide. I learned that coal and oil used to generate electrical power account for about half of the sulfur dioxide emitted into the air.

What, I wanted to know, does breathing sulfur dioxide do to us?

Many doctors and scientists, I learned, are convinced that air pollution plays a major part in the spread of respiratory diseases. Still, the air contains such a variety of gases, chemicals, and smoke that no scientist can point conclusively to any one ingredient as the villain. In laboratory experiments, however, researchers can observe the pollutants separately and in combination.

Dr. Mary Amdur, a toxicologist at Harvard University's School of Public Health who has studied the effects of sulfur dioxide since 1948, has found that when she exposes guinea pigs to sulfur dioxide, their breathing changes only slightly. But the addition of particles of metallic salts to the water vapor in the air converts some of the gas to sulfuric acid mist, several times more irritating than the gas alone. Sulfuric acid mist constricts the bronchial tubes, making the animals' breathing labored. This multiplier effect represents a classic example of synergism.

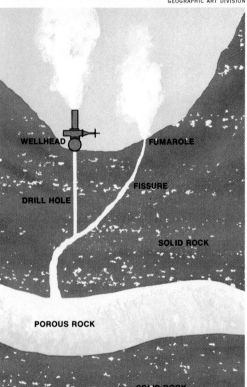

WELLHEAD — FUMAROLE — FISSURE — DRILL HOLE — SOLID ROCK — POROUS ROCK — SOLID ROCK — MAGMA

Plumes of steam reveal a vast reservoir of geothermal energy that powers an electric generating plant at The Geysers, California (top). Western states possess large reserves of this relatively pollution-free source of power. In the illustration above, magma, or molten rock, heats a solid layer. This in turn heats a water-filled porous region resembling a giant sponge. Some of the scalding water changes to steam and escapes through surface cracks, or fumaroles. Steam intercepted by wells drives the plant's turbines.

Sulfur dioxide combines with water vapor to form sulfuric acid droplets in atmospheric samples collected at the South Pole.

At full capacity, Kentucky's Paradise Power Plant burns 24,000 tons of coal daily and emits 1,400 tons of sulfur dioxide. At right, stea

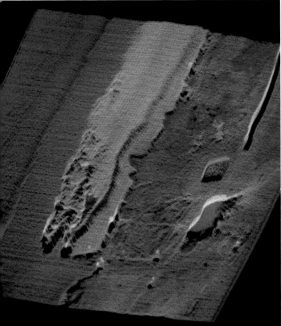

ared photograph shows temperature variation of river water.

ows from the plant's 440-foot cooling towers.

Power plant emissions: a major source of pollution

Coal-burning generating plants, such as the one below left, produce almost half of the electrical power in the United States — and constitute a major source of pollution. Fly ash, soot, and sulfur dioxide pour from their smokestacks. Even with increased availability of "cleaner" nuclear power, the Nation will have to rely heavily on coal to meet needs for electricity in the next 30 years.

Sulfur found in coal oxidizes during combustion, creating sulfur dioxide (SO_2). In the atmosphere SO_2 combines with water vapor to form sulfuric acid, which kills vegetation, corrodes stone and metal, and causes respiratory problems in periods of severe air pollution. About half of the polluting sulfur dioxide emissions come from coal- and oil-fired power plants; they pump 20 million tons of sulfur into the air each year — an amount equal to that mined annually throughout the world.

Industries seek ways to reduce SO_2 emissions. One method, spraying magnesium oxide into smokestack gases, captures the SO_2 for use in the production of sulfuric acid, a chemical much in demand commercially.

Another resource currently discarded — the waste heat from power plants — could heat homes. Researchers also have experimented with using the heat to prolong growing seasons in cool climates, and to warm water in controlled areas for raising fish and oysters. About 60 percent of the heat from any fuel now goes to waste because of inefficient generating processes. Water used to condense steam in the turbine returns heated to rivers and lakes with effects not fully understood. Some power companies call the process thermal enrichment; some environmentalists call it thermal pollution.

In naturally warm waters, as in Biscayne Bay, Florida, a slight rise in temperature may cause damage to marine life; in a swiftly flowing, cold river such as the Columbia, the heat dissipates more rapidly. An infrared photograph, color-coded by temperature levels (above left), aids scientific studies of heat effects on river ecology by showing a plutonium-producing plant's discharge into the Columbia River. Orange and yellow indicate the hottest parts. Underground pipes release water in the middle of the river, creating heated mountainlike areas with cooler green plateaus. Colder water appears purple.

Water not returned to lakes, rivers, or oceans must cool before reuse. Giant towers, similar to those at left, capable of cooling the water for a plant producing enough electricity for a city of 1.5 million people, would cost about 40 million dollars. But the heat escaping into the atmosphere wastes energy. In addition, a ten-percent loss of energy occurs in the distribution of power to customers; new techniques for reducing the temperature of transmission lines could conserve this.

Until engineers find other ways of producing and transmitting electricity, two out of every three tons of coal mined will go to waste through inefficient use of its energy.

Like most scientists, Dr. Amdur does not directly relate the results of her experiments with animals to humans, but she believes that they do give clues to how man may react: "Such chemical interactions could help explain the extra deaths, especially among the young, sick, and aged, during air-pollution episodes."

Several thousand persons have died in such disasters. On the gray cold morning of October 26, 1948, a fog settled over Donora, a bleak factory town in Pennsylvania. A temperature inversion held the fog over the city while factories and mills continued to pour gases and ash into the darkening sky. In this inversion a lid of warm air aloft prevented the normal circulation in the atmosphere and trapped the pollutants beneath it. Before rain cleared the air six days later, 20 persons had died and nearly half the population of the town had fallen ill.

In 1952 a "pea-soup" fog shrouded London. An inversion trapped the fog over the city and with it a brew of fumes and ash. The smog triggered an epidemic of bronchial ailments which pushed 4,000 people, many of them heart patients, to a premature death.

Extensive studies of industrial smog in New York City by Cornell University Medical College from 1962 to 1965 show that as many as 13 excess deaths a day may occur when the levels of sulfur dioxide increase beyond the average daily concentration. This relationship implies guilt by association; nevertheless, many researchers are convinced that breathing air polluted with sulfur dioxide and minute particles creates a health hazard.

"Any facility that still emits plumes of smoke and ash—the shortest plane ride reminds us all how many there are—is clinging to a 19th-century environmental ethic," says William D. Ruckelshaus, Environmental Protection Agency administrator. "No matter what the current status of state, local, or federal laws affecting their actions, not to clean up smoke is inexcusable."

We have had the technology to remove particles of fly ash from the air for at least 35 years, but we have lagged behind in developing effective measures to curb sulfur dioxide emissions. According to the EPA's air pollution control staff, these emissions continue to increase year after year, even though many cities—New York and Chicago among them—have instituted new regulations prohibiting the use of fuel with more than 1 percent sulfur.

I visited the Union Electric Company in St. Louis, one of the first utilities to try to remove sulfur from stack gases. Ray Hurt, a mechanical engineer, told me of the company's experiment with powdered limestone to convert sulfur dioxide into particles a wet scrubber can trap. "We tried piping the limestone directly into the furnace, but that hasn't worked effectively. Now we hope to try a process which will put the limestone directly in the scrubber."

Still another method uses a slurry of water and limestone to remove sulfur. But in most cases the companies will end up with a throwaway residual product that creates a disposal problem as well.

Catalytic oxidation, a process being tested by other plants, employs a variety of chemicals to extract and recover sulfuric acid, a useful industrial commodity.

It seemed clear to me that to provide clean power from coal would require intensive research. Scientists have begun to work on the technology that would convert coal into a cleaner liquid or gaseous fuel economically. The petroleum industry already is reducing the sulfur content of fuel oil, making it less polluting than coal. A plant in Venezuela and others in Caribbean countries now supply East Coast markets with this oil, and many public utilities have begun to use it.

Reckoning with oil spills

Oil, however, has an impact upon the world's environment beyond that of sulfur and smoke. Spilled oil has destroyed thousands of seabirds, and may prove a threat to other forms of marine life.

A team of scientists at the Woods Hole Oceanographic Institution in Massachusetts had an opportunity to study a spill of fuel oil in September 1969 not far from their doorstep on Cape Cod. Immediately after the accident dead fish, crustaceans, and marine worms washed up into tidal pools. A year after the accident the waters looked clear, but when Dr. Max Blumer tested the sediments, he discovered that oil was still present over large areas of the sea bottom. Moreover, the shellfish continued to harbor harmful chemical elements of oil, a possible public health hazard.

George R. Hampson, a member of the Woods Hole team, observed that the oil had distorted the behavior of many species of marine life. "I could catch a flounder with my bare hands, and fiddler crabs did not scuttle away as I reached out for them," he told me. Mr. Hampson believes that oil may confuse animal behavior, blocking the creatures' chemical receptors, which direct their food finding, homing, and mating. New England fishermen learned long ago to confound lobsters by using kerosene-soaked bricks as bait.

The wreck of the tanker *Tampico Maru* in an isolated cove off Baja California, Mexico, in 1957 spilled 7,000 tons of heavy diesel oil and destroyed the entire marine population along two miles of coast. Some species began to return within two months, but sea urchins and abalone were still greatly reduced in number four years later.

At last observation, 10 years after the accident, several forms of marine life had not returned, leading to a distorted ecology. Sea kelp, for example, grew unhampered in huge beds, undisturbed by the sea urchins which normally fed on it.

Spills have increased as petroleum companies drill more offshore wells into continental shelves and new supertankers transport mammoth cargoes of oil. Nearly 3,000 drilling platforms dot the coasts of the United States, posing a threat of blowouts in the biologically productive off-shore waters. The world's fleet of tankers numbers about 4,000, and the traffic of oil across the oceans has reached almost a billion tons per year.

I had seen the spill at Santa Barbara, California, in 1969 and had watched the mass of greasy fluid, iridescent in the slanting sunlight, creep toward shore. Breakers turned muddy black. A well six miles out in the channel had ruptured and covered 800 square miles of ocean and 40 miles of beach with black, sticky crude.

Some people were at work trying to sop up the oil. Others struggled in an effort to wash the glutinous substance from seabirds.

An oil-soaked bird is a pathetic sight. It cannot swim or fly. Oil mats its feathers, destroying its insulation, so that it dies of overexposure, if not starvation. Most attempts to rescue such birds have failed. Very few—usually fewer than 3 percent—survive after treatment. By giving them intensive care and keeping them in captivity for as short a period as possible, biologist Philip B. Stanton has been much more successful in rehabilitating birds at his center in Upton, Massachusetts. He has achieved up to 90 percent recovery.

Crude oil gushing from the tanker *Torrey Canyon* in 1967 spread slicks over the ocean and washed onto beaches in the English Channel, claiming possibly 25,000 seabirds. The British Government tried using detergents to disperse the oil; the French used hydrophobic chalk to sink it to the bottom. The detergents actually did as much harm to marine organisms as the oil itself, and chalk just plunged the problem to the bottom of the sea.

In the United States, industry, Government, and independent researchers are seeking ways to clean up oil spills more effectively. A variety of skimmers and vacuum pumps can collect it, but they experience difficulty in rough water. The Pittsburgh Corning Corporation is working with tiny glass beads to serve as wicks to burn surface oil.

Edward N. Azarowicz has evolved a combination of microbes which eat crude oil, breaking it down to carbon dioxide, water, sugars, and proteins, thus restoring nutrients to aquatic life. "The microbes get to like the stuff," he said in his office at Bioteknika International, Inc., in Alexandria, Virginia.

Dr. Azarowicz has placed these microbes in tidal waters off the Virginia coast during summer and winter, but he has not tested them in an actual spill in the open sea.

For the present, using straw and sawdust to soak up the oil remains the standard cleanup procedure, but prevention of spills is still the obvious solution. Some are accidents, but at least two-thirds occur in routine operations as captains flush ship bilges and tanks with sea water. Several ports have set up cleaning stations to comply with federal regulations against harmful discharges.

Oil also may threaten the fragile ecology of the tundra. Plans to lay a pipeline from oil fields on the North Slope of Alaska south across the tundra and mountain ranges to the ice-free port of Valdez have pitted environmentalists against oil suppliers and those who say the Nation needs more petroleum. Walter J. Hickel, formerly Governor of Alaska and subsequently Secretary of the Interior, has said, "I believe we have room to set aside just 15 square miles, to be taken up by the entire right-of-way for an 800-mile pipeline. . . ."

Some experts raise questions of potential earthquake damage to the pipeline, and others reckon with the danger of oil spills, looking toward the day when tankers begin traveling between Valdez and ports in Washington. Oil persists longer in cold waters, scientists point out, magnifying its destructive impact on marine life many times over.

While the demand for oil surges, an even greater controversy rages around the fledgling nuclear power industry. Ushered in by the holocausts that leveled Hiroshima and Nagasaki near the end of World War II, nuclear energy now promises vast new quantities of power without producing ash, smoke, or sulfur dioxide. For many Americans, however, nuclear power has raised the fear that radioactive emissions might contaminate the earth. When atoms split, they release enormous energy. This nuclear fission also releases radiation; exposure to it *(Continued on page 90)*

Exhausted strip mine in western Kentucky erodes rapidly even though graded and reseeded. Acid runoff taints the ponds.

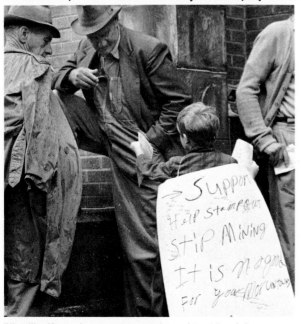

Pikeville, Kentucky, youngster seeks end to strip mining.

Strip mining scars heal slowly

Contour strip mining rips away a mountain in layers, producing mounds of spoil banks that disfigure the land and
threaten homes—and sometimes whole towns—with mud-
slides. A rising demand for electrical power sharpens the
need for fuel. Miners have stripped an area the size of
Delaware to reach coal, leaving a desolate landscape.
Dirt and acid runoffs pollute waterways, some of them the
only source of water for many communities.

Mine owners, spurred by stricter state laws and criticism
from aroused citizens, have stepped up rehabilitation of
the scarred land by grading and reseeding. Some of these
projects have proved successful; others have not. In the
reclaimed area above, acid and orange iron hydroxide
continue to drain into man-made lakes.

The misspelled message at left urges support of John
Ray, a resident of Pike County, Kentucky, who fought in
court to stop coal operators from strip mining in his area

BILL STRODE, LOUISVILLE COURIER-JOURNAL; NATIONAL GEOGRAPHIC PHOTOGRAPHER JAMES P. BLAIR (OPPOSITE TOP)

aring destruction of her home, Mrs. Ollie Combs, 61, stops a bulldozer from stripping a hillside in Knott County, Kentucky.

attling the bulldozer

ust want to live out my life in my hollow and be left one." The yellow bulldozer had threatened to destroy r hill and the little hollow of Honey Gap in Knott County, entucky, where her home stands. So 61-year-old Ollie ombs threw herself in front of the machine, and stopped e blade from tearing into the hill for coal until the sheriff rried her bodily down the mountainside. For days she d climbed the hill, walking stick in hand, to challenge the bulldozer—to her and other mountain people the creator of cascades of muddy topsoil that roll down hillsides during spring and fall rains. Mud and acid, the twin ravagers of mountains and their streams, had wrecked other hills and other dwellings, but, if Ollie Combs could help it, not this time.

When she violated an order to keep away from mining operations, officials charged her with contempt of court. She spent 20 hours in jail. Her determination prompted the governor to hasten application of more stringent mining regulations. But most important of all, at least for a little while, the mountain stayed, and the bulldozer went away.

e eats Thanksgiving dinner in jail.

Law enforcement officers arrest Mrs. Combs.

John Pawlus (center), victim of black lung disease after working in coal mines for nearly three decades, awaits retirement with his wi[fe]

Turning away from the mines

"There'll be no more coal miners in this family," says John Pawlus (foreground above), who has spent 27 of his 57 years working underground. "I lost my right foot in 1941," he explains. "They gave me a total of $2,800 —monthly compensation for three years. That was it. So I got a wooden leg and went back into the mine. Now they tell me I've got the black lung."

He lost his foot in the same mine that claimed his father's life in 1917. His wife Rose, 54, lost her father in a mine disaster in 1927. Her brother died of black lung and emphysema at 55, "so weak at the end that he could only crawl, not walk," she recalls.

In his tragic family history, Mr. Pawlus characterizes many of the 125,000 men who dig the Nation's coal. Mine accidents have killed 80,000 men in the past 60 years; respiratory diseases, emphysema and black lung (pneumoconiosis)—a disease caused by inhaling coal dust— have disabled hundreds of thousands

more. Mr. Pawlus probably will colle[ct] disability payment for his lung d[is]ease, yet Congressman Carl D. Pe[r]kins of Kentucky has noted that a[d]ministrators in his state turn down [__] percent of the applications for su[ch] benefits. Workmen's compensati[on] covers black lung, but not emphyse[ma] —two diseases virtually indistinguis[h]able with regular diagnostic metho[ds]. "The only sure way to diagnose bla[ck] lung is to conduct an autopsy," stat[es] Dr. Donald Rasmussen of the Appa[la]chian Regional Hospital in Beckle[y,] West Virginia.

A miner visiting Dr. Rasmussen

...ose and son Steve.

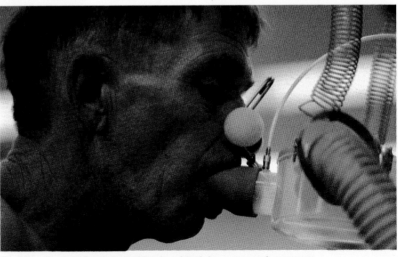

Layer of tissue shows effects of inhaled coal dust—black lung.

...inic in a black-lung research project walks a treadmill and breathes ...rough a mouthpiece (right), while ...chnicians monitor his heartbeat, ...spiration, and blood-oxygen levels, ...nd measure the carbon dioxide con... ...nt of exhaled air. Dr. Rasmussen ...opes to use the data to establish ...rm diagnostic standards for the ...sease. Meanwhile, Mr. Pawlus con...iders himself fortunate to have sur...ved to draw his pension, and even ...ore fortunate that his sons John, ...r., 32, and Steve, 22, will not work ...elow ground. "Let them go into the ...ines? I'd break their arms first."

Machine checks miner's breathing in a black-lung research program.

can cause leukemia and other forms of cancer, stillbirths, a shortened life span, and deformities in offspring for generations to come.

Man is exposed to many different forms of radiation, from medical X-rays to nature's cosmic rays and background radiation emitted from elements in the earth's crust. A Roentgen, or R, named for the discoverer of X-rays, Wilhelm Konrad Roentgen, measures a unit dose of radiation. For example, a single dental X-ray generally produces a local dose of .5 to 1R, and a chest X-ray, from .015 to .45R, depending on the equipment and technique used. Natural background radiation exposes the body to an average of .1R a year.

After years of nuclear weapons testing in the atmosphere, scientists were appalled to discover that the fallout of radioactive substances—primarily strontium-90 and cesium-137—haunted the earth with new sources of radioactivity, accumulating in food, lodging in the bones of our children, lurking in water. By comparison, nuclear reactors emit relatively low levels of radiation.

We know that a single dose of 100 to 200R reaching the whole body will cause radiation sickness—nausea, anemia, and fatigue. A dose of 500R kills. The amount of genetic and physical harm done by radiation depends on the areas of the body exposed, the potency of the total dose, and the rate at which it is received. But no one has been able to determine with certainty if small amounts of radiation can build up in the body and reach a harmful level. Scientists find themselves embroiled in a profound controversy over this question. Some believe there is a threshold point below which no damage occurs. Others say that no threshold exists and that even minute doses of radiation can accumulate, possibly causing damage to genes, or death.

Radiation in perspective

John H. Gibbons, director of the National Science Foundation's environmental program, argues: "Let's put radiation from atomic power plants into perspective. Nuclear power now and until the year 2000 is expected to add no more than 1/100 of the exposure we get from natural background radiation.

"This is not to say that *any* radiation is good," Dr. Gibbons hastens to add, "but we should be concerned about all sources. Almost all of the man-made increase in radiation comes from X-rays, and there's equipment available that could cut exposure to less than 1/10 of what most patients get now, with no sacrifice in the quality of the X-ray."

Government scientists set industry standards for emissions from reactors based on biological information regarding human tolerances. "The maximum radiation exposure that you would get if you were sitting on a fence post at the boundary of a modern nuclear plant for a year," said Floyd L. Culler of the Oak Ridge National Laboratory nuclear division, "would be about 1/10 to 1/100 of the dose from a single chest X-ray."

In June 1971 the Atomic Energy Commission proposed stringent new standards on emissions of radioactive effluents from nuclear power plants, limiting radiation exposure for persons living nearby to 1 percent or less of current federal levels. All nuclear power plants presently in operation, as well as the 94 additional ones under construction or being planned, will be required to comply with the new standards, says the AEC. Fearful of radiation hazards from long-term exposure, a number of scientists—among them Dr. John W. Gofman and Dr. Arthur R. Tamplin of the Lawrence Radiation Laboratory in Livermore, California—had been pressing for even stricter emission limits for nearly two years.

I arrived at the large, modern nuclear power plant at San Onofre, California, on a clear day with the sun glinting on the ocean. A 140-foot, light blue sphere contained the reactor. Offices and grounds were spotlessly clean with no sign of fumes or smoke. The plant was silent, and the automated control room gave no hint of the tremendous nuclear forces at work. H. L. Ottoson, the station superintendent, told me that monitors located at the edge of the 85-acre property had never detected radiation above normal background levels.

The reactor core holds tons of uranium in tubes containing pellets about 1/2-inch long and 3/8 of an inch in diameter. One load will operate a reactor for several years, for the plant consumes only about a pound of uranium a day. A nuclear reactor uses fuel in such a way that makes an explosion virtually impossible. However, it is possible for a heat buildup to melt the fuel and release radiation; in fact, some melting has occurred in experimental models. Nevertheless, San Onofre engineers assured me that numerous safeguards in plant design minimize such a danger.

I recalled what Karl Z. Morgan, director of the health physics division at the Oak Ridge laboratory, had told me: "Any worthwhile enterprise involves accepting certain risks. The choice seems to be between the small hypothetical risks of nuclear accidents and the very real hazards of a smog-polluted environment or the crisis of a power shortage."

From the problem of accidents I turned to the vexing issue of radioactive wastes. The residue from power production is still small, but the United States has accumulated large quantities of waste from the production of plutonium for nuclear weapons.

AEC officials at the Atlantic-Richfield Hanford Company at Richland, Washington, showed me the bleak desert land where steel tanks store high-level radioactive wastes beneath the earth. Small sheds and vent pipes mark these tombs, some still boiling with radioactive heat. A few tanks have leaked up to 70,000 gallons, but the liquid radioactive material presumably was absorbed by the desert soil before reaching the water table.

A geological survey of the Hanford area in 1966, however, revealed fault zones—signs of weakness in the earth's crust—raising nightmarish questions of what might happen to these tanks should an earthquake occur.

Other geologists, however, countered that the possibility of the Hanford facility not riding out an earthquake "is so remote that it can safely be disregarded."

Hugh Warren, head of operations and waste management at Hanford, explained a plan for the final disposal of the nuclear wastes.

"We are experimenting with binding the most toxic wastes—including strontium-90—into cement or rock and then burying the mixture in layers of basalt thousands of feet below the Hanford reservation. For the past three years we have been reducing radioactive liquid to solid salt cake."

If safe, efficient means of packaging and transfer can be developed, radioactive cakes from commercial power plants may eventually be stored in an abandoned salt mine near Lyons, Kansas, a primary AEC disposal site for less-potent atomic wastes. "Nature gave us dry salt covered by layers of tight shale under Kansas with solid rock extending for thousands of feet below the salt," said Floyd Culler of Oak Ridge.

A team of scientists from the University of Kansas vigorously protests this proposal. William W. Hambleton charges that the AEC has not looked fully into the effects of high temperature on the structure of salt and rock.

"If you're going to bury something that will remain deadly for 500,000 years," Dr. Hambleton says, "you'd better be sure you know what you're doing."

Earlier, at the San Onofre plant, I also had become aware of the problem of thermal pollution associated with large power plants. San Onofre's cooling water comes from the ocean, 350,000 gallons per (Continued on page 96)

Project Rulison scientists in 1969 set off a nuclear explosion 1½ miles beneath the Colorado landscape (below) to release natural gas by shattering oil-bearing rock. Equal to 40,000 tons of TNT, the blast made it possible to recover fuel at a much faster rate than from conventional wells. A sign (above) warns of radiation released by gas burning at the well.

Oil spreads around a Santa Barbara drilling rig in 1969.

U. S. Coast Guard system pumps oil from disabled tankers.

Polluting the oceans

Oil surrounds the grounded tanker *Torrey Canyon* (opposite) and a leaking drilling platform near Santa Barbara, California (above) — two incidents that aroused public concern over oil contamination of the ocean. But day-to-day operations, such as pumping out ships' bilges and flushing holds of tankers at sea, may create far greater damage. More than 7,500 instances of oil pollution occur annually. Dr. Max Blumer of the Woods Hole Oceanographic Institution estimates that losses in shipping amount to 3.5 million tons a year; oil pouring into seas from all sources may reach 10 million tons.

In the two-month cleanup battle with the *Torrey Canyon* spill, British and French crews used sawdust, straw, chalk bombs, napalm, flamethrowers, and detergents; still the oil spread onto beaches. The Santa Barbara accident released only a twelfth as much oil as the *Torrey Canyon* spill, yet crude covered 800 square miles of ocean.

One means of combating spills employs an air-droppable device (above) to contain the oil. Bioteknika International, a Virginia research firm, proposes using microbes to rid water of oil. The microbes would enter oil droplets, devour them, then die, becoming food for marine life.

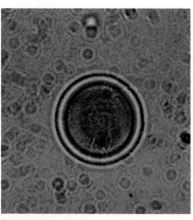

Drop of oil magnified 1,000 times

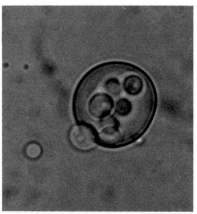

Oil-eating microbes enter droplet.

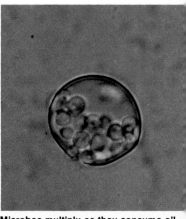

Microbes multiply as they consume oil.

UNITED PRESS INTERNATIONAL; N.G.S. PHOTOGRAPHERS BRUCE DALE (OPPOSITE LEFT) AND JAMES P. BLAIR (OPPOSITE RIGHT); VICTOR R. BOSWELL, JR., N.G.S. STAFF (OPPOSITE BELOW)

American tanker *Torrey Canyon* breaks up in 1967 off England's southwest coast, dumping 119,000 tons of crude oil into the sea.

Alaskan oil strike stirs controversy

Exploitation of a 10-million-barrel oil reserve on Alaska's North Slope awaits construction of a controversial cross-state pipeline. Extending southward from Prudhoe Bay to the ice-free port of Valdez, the line would carry two million gallons of crude a day. At Valdez a 48-inch Japanese-made pipe spans a storage area (center).

Environmentalists contend that the pipeline will harm the fragile arctic ecology. Oil spilled in the cold climate would persist for years, they argue, damaging plants and destroying wildlife; hot oil in the pipe would thaw the permafrost, causing the pipe to sink and rupture; a single break in a 15-mile section of pipe could allow seven million gallons of oil to escape; the 350 rivers and streams crossed by the 790-mile line could carry spilled oil over large areas; earthquakes could snap the line; construction would damage tundra. And some fear that a tanker accident could release oil along the Alaskan or Canadian coast with devastating effects.

The oil companies have offered reassurances: Electronic monitoring will warn of any defect in the line; construction techniques and the kind of pipe used will allow the line to survive an earthquake as great as any in Alaska's recorded history; strategically placed shut-off valves will minimize oil loss; the ground under the pipeline will remain stable even after thawing. Test plots of grasses (upper) will help determine types to use in replanting along the construction route to prevent erosion.

Seemingly undisturbed, caribou amble by an oil camp (right). Designers plan crossing points for the caribou in places where the pipeline will run above ground. Oil companies maintain that modern tankers and strict control procedures, including one-way traffic at some points, will reduce chances of accidents at sea.

Markers identify snow-covered plots used to test more than 100 varieties of grass

Sections of pipe for the line that would link the Arctic oil fields with Valdez, on the G

Caribou pass an oil camp near Prudhoe Bay, in Alaska's far north. The pipeline wou

termine the best ones for reseeding areas disturbed by pipeline construction.

Alaska, lie stacked near the port.

ss routes followed by the animals on their seasonal migrations.

minute, and discharges go back to the sea in a half-mile circle around the discharge point.

"People have caught bonita, halibut, bass, and yellowtail all around here," the superintendent told me. "There's no adverse effect on the aquatic life as far as we can tell."

Some fish, however, are more sensitive to temperature changes than others. Salmon and trout cannot tolerate water heated beyond 60° or 70° F., but carp and catfish are more flexible. Generally, each species of aquatic and marine animal can survive and reproduce only within certain narrow temperature ranges.

Thermal pollution from two conventional fossil-fuel plants has disturbed 300 acres of algal and grass beds extending out from the shore of Florida's Biscayne Bay. Clams, snails, crabs, and worms, as well as some game fish, have disappeared completely.

The water temperature in the bay is naturally high—approaching 90° F. in some shallow areas. "When it gets to 92°, there are definite kills," says Lee Purkerson, an EPA biologist.

Lake Michigan shares with Biscayne Bay some of the physical characteristics which make thermal effects so harmful. Shallow, near-shore waters reach temperatures of more than 80° F. during summer months, and the entire lake circulates slowly. Yet Lake Michigan will have seven nuclear plants along its shores by 1976. To date only two of these are scheduled to use cooling towers, but environmentalists are pushing for installation of cooling systems for the other five plants as well.

AEC officials at Hanford told me of their experiences with thermal pollution. The Hanford reactors have discharged more waste heat into the Columbia River than reactors have released into any other stream in the world. "We've worked with the federal Fish and Wildlife Service," said Bill Devine, an AEC technician. "Staff members have stated that there have been no detrimental effects on salmon, the most vulnerable species of the fish world. Of course, we're blessed with a cold, high-flow river. Our heated discharge increases the temperature only one-half a degree on the average. The sun on a warm summer day raises it four times that much."

Many power companies are now diverting heated water away from the rivers into cooling towers or ponds. But Sam E. Beall, director of the reactor division at Oak Ridge, sees thermal waste as a valuable resource for the future. "Problems arise when plants get so big that they cause local sources of thermal pollution," Beall said. "So how do we use the heat?"

He suggests piping the hot water to homes and buildings. "One actually could design a power plant to heat and cool a city, and supply its electricity as well. We've also looked into heating huge greenhouses and farm buildings to hasten growth of vegetables, poultry, and pigs." Other suggestions for using waste heat range from irrigation of crops in cold climates to controlled fish farming.

While some scientists struggle to reduce air and water pollution from energy production, others work toward better ways of generating electricity. As nuclear plants increase in number, they threaten to exhaust the limited reserves of uranium. The AEC is counting on a breeder reactor to rescue the atomic power industry from a critical shortage expected some time between 1980 and 2000.

When perfected, the breeder will produce power and generate more fissionable material than it consumes. In seven to ten years, a breeder reactor would produce enough surplus fuel to operate a second reactor. Some scientists believe, however, that the AEC is pushing development of a fast breeder reactor too rapidly, and have warned of a danger of release of radioactivity.

Energy from fusion

Fission splits atoms; fusion combines them, and in the process unleashes stupendous amounts of energy. But to produce a fusion reaction requires temperatures of hundreds of millions of degrees. At these enormous temperatures, matter acquires such special properties that it is neither solid, liquid, nor gas; in this state it becomes plasma.

For a generation scientists have struggled to achieve the temperatures needed and the means of containing this plasma long enough in a magnetic field to sustain the fusion reaction. If controlled fusion proves possible, most scientists agree it would take from 30 to 50 years to put a commercial power generator into operation.

The great advantage—beyond a limitless supply of cheap fuel—is that a fusion reactor would produce only small amounts of radioactive wastes, except for tritium, a hydrogen isotope, which scientists plan to recycle into the reactor. "But if it should escape into the atmosphere, it's going to stay there," says Dr. Ernest C. Tsivoglou of the Georgia Institute of Technology in Atlanta. He fears that in the long run tritium must be regarded as a serious contaminant.

One possible source of power without pollution lies buried in layers of magma, or molten rock, beneath the surface of the earth. In certain areas these layers heat local underground water, and steam escapes to the surface via vents or geysers.

In recent years geothermal power plants have been constructed to harness this steam to produce electricity. One such plant is in operation in California.

Another method of producing power, called magnetohydrodynamics (MHD), uses high-temperature gas moving at supersonic speed through a magnetic field to generate electricity directly. The MHD process, which can employ either fossil fuels or a reactor to heat the gas, will be able to utilize fuel more efficiently than any type of power plant currently in use.

The process also permits recovery of sulfur and nitrogen oxides and produces less waste heat. Still to be tested are ways to build generators strong enough to deliver large amounts of power for long periods.

Looking to the future of the system, Dr. Arthur Kantrowitz, director of AVCO Everett Research Laboratory in Massachusetts, where the first working MHD generator was developed, says that he is "firmly convinced that we can have the power we need, without degrading the quality of our environment, by the decade of the eighties."

In other laboratories scientists are studying ways to convert the sun's rays into electrical energy at an affordable price. As employed in the U.S. space program, solar power costs roughly 2,000 times more than conventionally generated electricity.

My travels had introduced me to the multitude of pollution problems that result from the production of power. There seemed to be no way to escape the dilemma created by the profound commitment our society has made to the use of energy.

One Government official who has been speaking out on this subject is S. David Freeman, director of the energy policy staff in the President's Office of Science and Technology. Summing up the problem, he says:

"Energy is vital for many essential purposes, but all of the present sources damage the environment. We greatly need to intensify the research and development effort in the electrical power industry to find less-polluting methods of producing power. In the meantime we must begin to examine ways to cut down on our use of energy.

"We should practice conservation, not just pay lip service to the word. This means we will be faced by a series of complex and difficult choices. No matter how hard we try, our real needs for power will grow; but we can reduce materially the rate of growth and the pollution that goes with it."

In an abandoned salt mine (below) a thousand feet underground near Lyons, Kansas, technicians from the Atomic Energy Commission test methods to dispose of radioactive wastes from commercially operated nuclear power plants. Circular vaults in the 300-foot-thick salt deposit would hold the condensed wastes. Some scientists question the safety of placing highly radioactive material, dangerous for 500,000 years, into the mine without extensive study. Radiation changes rock salt (above left) into deep blue, energy-storing crystals.

Reactor Containment
Building

Turbine Generator
Building

Administrative and
Control Complex

Fuel Handling
Machine

Fuel Transfer
Cell

Steam
Generators

Fast Reactor Core

Fast breeder nuclear power plants, such as the one designed by Atomics International (above), will create more fuel than they us

Fuel from fission

Nuclear power plants use energy from atomic reactions to produce steam and drive turbines, emitting far less pollution than coal-fired generators. In a water-cooled reactor (right), atoms split, or fission, in a self-sustaining chain reaction that releases vast quantities of heat, but uses up a scarce form of uranium, U-235. A more plentiful form, U-238, some from reactor wastes, absorbs neutrons and becomes plutonium-239, a fissionable fuel, when wrapped around the core of a fast breeder reactor. Efficient use of

neutrons would create more plutonium-239 than the actor could consume, providing enough in ten years to fuel itself and another of similar size. It would operate lower pressures and higher temperatures than curre reactors, but would discharge 40 percent less waste he

A favored method of cooling (below) employs liquid s dium to carry thermal energy from the reactor to a h exchanger; there the sodium gives up its heat to a seco loop and returns cooled to the reactor. Controversy s surrounds the problem of difficult-to-handle radioacti wastes created by nuclear reactors, and some scienti also question the ability of engineers to cope with pote tial heat and radiation hazards posed by the fast breed

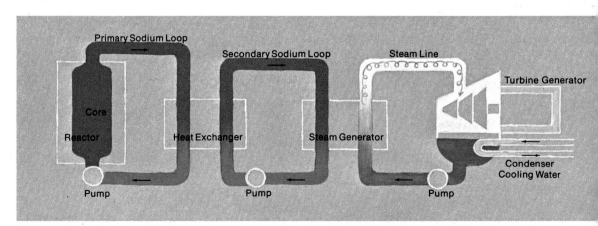

Primary Sodium Loop

Secondary Sodium Loop

Steam Line

Turbine Generator

Core

Reactor

Heat Exchanger

Steam Generator

Condenser
Cooling Water

Pump

Pump

Pump

Liquid sodium transfers 1,060° F. heat from a fast breeder reactor to a steam generator; steam then drives turbines.

ent uranium fuel assembly glows from radioactivity during refueling at the Yankee Atomic Electric Company in Massachusetts.

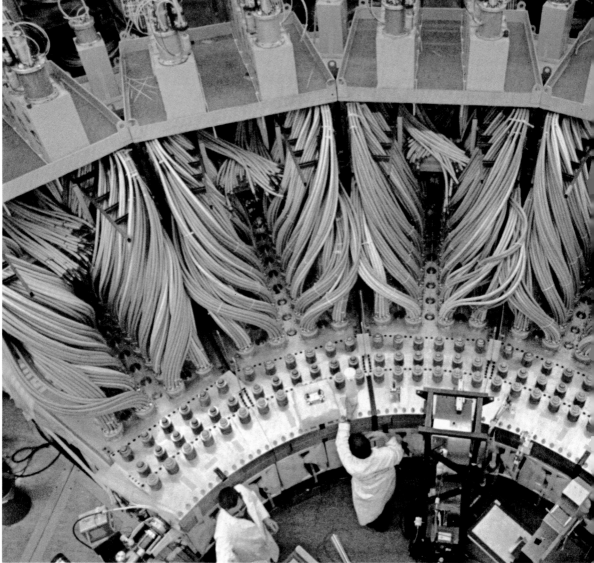

Nuclear fusion research with experimental devices such as the Scyllac at Los Alamos, New Mexico, may provide a key to virtual

Fusion: tomorrow's energy

Fusion, the basic energy process of the stars, can provide a clean, efficient, and low-polluting source of power using a cheap, abundant fuel derived from water. In fusion two atoms combine under tremendous pressure at a temperature of millions of degrees to form a larger atom and release energy. Scientists in several countries, including the United States and the Soviet Union, use a variety of approaches to achieve controlled fusion. Most research now aims at combining two isotopes of hydrogen — deuterium and tritium.

Normal hydrogen, an element abundant in air and water, has a single major atomic particle in its nucleus — a positively charged proton. Deuterium also has a neutron, an atomic-nucleus particle with no electric charge. Tritium has two neutrons. When heated to 50 million degrees Cen-

tigrade under pressure 100 times that of the atmosphere at sea level, these isotopes form a plasma — a gaslike mixture of protons, neutrons, and electrons. The heating and squeezing cause the deuterium and tritium to combine

DEUTERIUM   TRITIUM   HELIUM

forming helium and releasing a neutron and energy (above). Ordinary metals and ceramics cannot withstand the intense heat and pressure, so new types of containers must enclose the fusion ingredients. Some techniques employ invisible magnetic force fields to make "magnetic bottles" to hold the plasma. The arc-shaped Scyllac (top) uses the fields to squeeze the plasma rapidly, and holds for millionths of a second.

After further experiments, scientists will expand the Scyllac to form a complete circle for better control of the plasma at higher pressures, creating a doughnut-shaped

NATIONAL GEOGRAPHIC PHOTOGRAPHER JAMES P. BLAIR; GEOGRAPHIC ART DIVISION (BOTTOM)

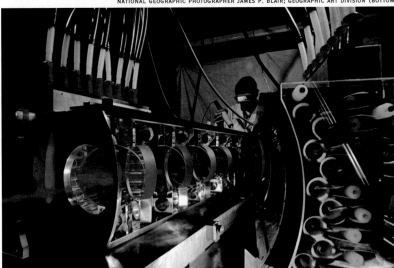

University of Rochester scientists use a laser beam for fusion investigations.

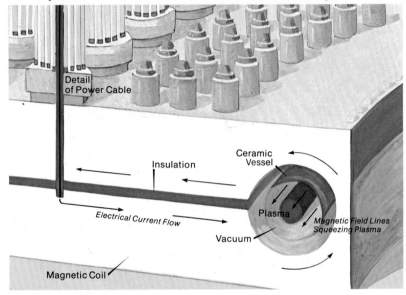

Detail
of Power Cable

Ceramic
Vessel

Insulation

Plasma

Electrical Current Flow

Magnetic Field Lines
Squeezing Plasma

Vacuum

Magnetic Coil

lution-free power production.

Interior detail of Scyllac shows power cables, magnetic coil, and plasma.

ssageway (diagram). In a controlled fusion reaction in e Scyllac, deuterium atoms would enter a ceramic tube, blue, and an electric current, stored in giant capacitors, ddenly would rush into the magnetic coil surrounding e tube. The tremendous magnetic field generated by the w of electricity then would force the hydrogen away om the walls and into a compact mass, creating a tem- rature more than three times higher than at the sun's nter. The sudden jolt of electricity would last only for 0 millionths of a second—but long enough for a large mber of the hydrogen ions to combine.

n reactor operations, magnetic fields would slam the asma again and again, releasing fusion energy. This ergy would produce steam to drive a generator. Since one yet knows the best way to produce fusion, scien- ts continue to test various techniques. Another experi- ntal method (upper right) uses an ultrahigh-energy ser to attempt to heat a pellet of solid deuterium and tium with sufficient energy to fuse the isotopes before

the pellet flies apart. The device has produced plasmas, but practical fusion will require more powerful lasers.

More than ten times as much money now goes into fis- sion development as into fusion research. Limited funds, even less in 1971 than in 1960, plus the need to overcome technological problems indicate that fusion power may not become a reality during this century. Breeder reactors could help meet power needs, but the large number of operating and planned conventional reactors could con- sume much of the readily available uranium fuel before breeder reactors come on line.

Both conventional and breeder reactors produce dan- gerous, difficult-to-store radioactive wastes and emit small amounts of radiation into the air and into discharge water—a practice some scientists consider unsafe. Like DDT, radioactivity accumulates in the food chain.

Fusion would produce only a millionth of the radioactiv- ity of fission, yet just one gallon of seawater would yield energy equal to that obtained from 300 gallons of gasoline.

"When I was a youth, the country was very beautiful.... But now the face of all the land is changed and sad. The living creatures are gone. I see the land desolate and I suffer an unspeakable sadness."

Those words of an old Indian, recalled from Joseph Epes Brown's *The Spiritual Legacy of the American Indian,* came to mind during a late winter twilight as I drove through northern Louisiana on one leg of a long journey to learn what I could of the impact of the Nation's industry upon the environment.

It had been a long, tiring week of hedge-hopping plane rides from one smoky industrial city to another. Now at evening I traveled by car through a strange misty land in the heart of the southern forest.

Miles of loblolly pines closed tight upon the roadside, as regimented as Marines standing at attention. Perhaps it was this man-ordered regularity that caused me to feel a touch of the old Indian's unspeakable sadness.

I was in a forest, but not a wilderness. It was a tree farm planted primarily to feed sawmills, plywood factories, and paper mills. And as I passed through the small city of Bastrop, the stench of sulfides lay heavy in the evening mist, marking the location of a large paper mill.

For nearly two centuries industrial ingenuity has carried America to material greatness, bringing homes and autos, electric toasters and television sets within reach of almost everyone. The tremendous productivity of our economy, which manufactures an average of 385,000 tons of steel, 150,000 tons of paper and paperboard, 11,000 tons of aluminum, and 7,500 tons of rubber for each and every day of the year, has liberated the average American from the chains of grinding poverty and drudgery.

But the vast flood of goods coming off the assembly line has extracted its price in trees felled for lumber and pulp, in lands ripped open for minerals, in rivers and lakes fouled by chemicals and toxic metals, and in air filled with gases and smoke.

Industry has produced steel, copper, aluminum, paper, and nylon, while, like the rest of us, generally ignoring effluents pouring into the water and air. As people awaken to the harmful side effects of technology, they are beginning to insist that industry clean up.

In seeking to understand the extent of damage and what industry can do to repair it, I began by focusing on the pulp and paper industry. It, along with iron and steel, chemicals, and petroleum refining, holds the key to America's industrial might and numbers among the heavy industrial polluters.

"As people awaken to the harmful side effects of technology, they are beginning to insist that industry clean up."

Industry and nature coexist at Baytow

INDUSTRY: PERILS OF PRODUCTION

By Henry Still

exas. Water purification lagoons of a Humble Oil refinery offer sanctuary to roseate spoonbills and other aquatic wildlife.

Nearly three-fourths of the Nation's commercial woodlands — 368,300,000 acres — belong to private owners. Federal, state, and local governments hold the remainder.

Traveling in the Northwest, I saw the forests in a time of bitter controversy. Wood industries and lumbermen pressured for new logging increases in the national forests, where the allowable cut has more than doubled in the past 20 years. Here and in other parts of the country, the practice of clear-cutting — felling all trees in an area as opposed to selective cutting of individual mature trees — had come in for a barrage of criticism in many parts of the United States. A counter-barrage of approbation defended clear-cutting, when properly carried out.

In Montana I saw where the U. S. Forest Service, a branch of the Department of Agriculture charged with managing these federally owned lands, had required lumbermen to clear-cut stands of Douglas fir, ponderosa, and lodgepole pine in the Bitterroot National Forest. Left behind were hillsides bare except for tree stumps and slash — the debris from timber cutting. Professor Arnold W. Bolle, dean of the University of Montana School of Forestry, led a group studying the effects on the land.

They reported an "overriding concern for sawtimber production. . . . compounded by an apparent insensitivity to the related forest uses and to the local public's interest in environmental values." Clear-cutting had altered the brush, wildlife, and drainage patterns of the forest, disrupting the community of living things which flourishes beneath the green canopy of leaves.

Dale A. Burk, state editor of the daily *Missoulian*, told me of his conversation with a rancher near the Bitterroot River, who complained, "Nature previously controlled the runoff. Now more water is coming down in early spring and less in summer. If they keep this up, we might as well forget about farming."

Clear-cutting a forest may expose the denuded land to soil erosion, especially when followed by fire. Silt and humus may wash into streams, and waters may carry away fertility elements. In a carefully controlled study, scientists at the Hubbard Brook Experimental Forest in central New Hampshire clear-cut a patch of forest, applied herbicide, and compared the runoff with that of an intact stand of beech, maple, and birch.

Under these unnatural conditions, runoff increased by 40 percent; "extraordinary losses of soil fertility" were reported by Dr. F. H. Bormann of the Yale School of Forestry, head of the team. Nitrates and other nutrients rapidly leached out of the soil into streams to produce abnormal growth of algae.

In northern California I traveled through some areas where small sawmill operators had bought timber rights from ranchers and farmers, cut the trees, and moved on, leaving the land denuded and torn. But this is not the usual practice. Most large forest owners now replant cut areas immediately after harvest.

Dr. Samuel T. Dana, dean emeritus of the University of Michigan's School of Natural Resources, sympathizes with the proponents of clear-cutting who emphasize its value as a silvicultural tool. "It's the best method of regenerating forests composed of species that don't do well in shade," he says, "trees such as Douglas fir, lodgepole pine, and aspen.

"The dangers of clear-cutting can be minimized by keeping cutover areas small and scattered; by careful logging and slash disposal; and by prompt reforestation."

I talked with Robert O. Lee, vice president of the Georgia-Pacific Corporation, in Portland, Oregon. "Most people accuse lumbermen of destroying the forest, but in stands of 50-year growth-cycle timber, for instance, we harvest only 2 percent a year," he said. "The other 98 percent, ranging from seedlings to full-grown trees, is green and growing. Our policy is to grow more timber than we harvest. Timber, after all, is a crop, not unlike wheat or corn, except that only a fraction of our crop is cut in any one year.

"But if we are to meet product demand," Mr. Lee told me, "we must turn to sources other than our own lands." Before my trip I had read that the lumber industry insisted it would have to increase logging in national forests to supply wood needed for the expected upsurge in housing construction.

Logging practices

Many foresters argue that harvesting the old trees intensifies growth of young oxygen-producing stands and improves forage conditions for wildlife.

"What wildlife are they talking about?" asks Charles H. Wharton, a Georgia State University biologist. "Do they mean a game species such as deer which comes in for a few years to take advantage of the new opening, or the balanced fauna of a mature forest?" Moreover, Dr. Wharton believes that clear-cutting and the planting of uniform stands of trees destroy the diversity of a forest and may herald the decline of the forest ecosystem. He stresses the need for caution and study.

At Crossett, Arkansas, where Georgia-Pacific has large holdings, chief forester Richard A. Williams guided me through stands of loblolly pine, almost entirely young growth, and also one stand of timber preserved as an example of old-growth forest.

Trees in the managed stands were even-size with low undergrowth. The virgin area contained wind-thrown stubs and dense brush and vines among trees ranging up to 150 years of age.

Mr. Williams explained how the southern pines are thinned periodically. The culled young trees, which would be stunted by overcrowding, yield pulp for paper, and the remaining ones, which eventually will be cut for lumber and plywood, can thus mature more rapidly.

From the southern forest I went to see the redwoods, Douglas fir, cedar, and hemlock which rear majestic crowns on the watered west slopes of the Cascades from California through Oregon and Washington into British Columbia. The shaded soil was moist under rotting wood felled by wind and lightning. Birds and small animals nestled in the brush.

In the woods above Springfield, Oregon, Carl Raynor, a resources manager for Georgia-Pacific, escorted me over a muddy, chuck-holed logging road up into the mountains.

With a cold mountain breeze chilling my ears, I clambered over snowbanks and decaying logs to examine an area of slash where the timber had been removed a few years before. The slope appeared to be a wasteland of stumps, cull logs, branches, and low brush. But upon closer examination, I saw evenly spaced young seedlings, already several years along their way to becoming a new forest.

"Some companies keep logging and forestry as two separate operations," explained forester Dale A. Thornburgh of Humboldt State College, located in the redwood country of northern California.

"Logging methods are strongly influenced by costs. After logging, the forester takes over, most often with limited funds."

In the Pacific Northwest ". . . there is far too much evidence of improper, low-cost logging operations," warns the water quality office of the Environmental Protection Agency. Increased sedimentation in debris-clogged streams in some areas smothers spawning beds and buries insect larvae, an important source of food for fish. The turbid waters screen out sunlight vital to the photosynthesis of aquatic plants, and water temperature rises as shade-giving trees are stripped from the banks.

Poor logging is only one facet of pollution

Regimented rows of pond pines cover 10,000 acres on the Weyerhaeuser Company's tree farm near New Bern, North Carolina. Hydraulic feller-bunchers like the one below clear-cut and stack the pines after 20 to 40 years, when seedlings replace them. The timber feeds the company's lumber, plywood, and pulp mills.

Forest management or "timber mining"?

Lumbermen throughout the United States harvest more than 11 billion cubic feet of timber a year—enough to build some six million dwelling units. Wood for such construction comes from private, state, and federal forests totaling 510,200,000 acres. Clear-cutting (far right)—complete, rather than selective, removal of trees—contributes 60 percent of the yield. The pulp and paper industry maintains that the increasing demand for wood products requires large-scale clear-cutting. But one critic, Senator Gale W. McGee of Wyoming, contends that industry finds the practice profitable, because "it is possible to clear-cut an area by upending as many as 1,500 to 1,800 trees a day."

A 1969-70 task force, headed by Dr. Arnold W. Bolle of the University of Montana, called the denuded acreage in the Bitterroot National Forest an example of "timber mining." Such vast operations, investigators said, violate the "sustained yield-multiple use" principle: replacing felled trees with new growth and protecting wildlife, watersheds, and recreation areas as well as timber. Other opponents fear that clear-cutting—especially on mountainsides—may expose the land to erosion, increase water pollution, and disrupt or even destroy the delicate forest ecosystem.

Chief Edward P. Cliff of the U.S. Forest Service says that sound timber management calls for limited clear-cutting: "In some areas it is the only means of making species like Douglas fir grow." Foresters, while admitting mistakes, say that undergrowth prevents severe runoff, and replanting eventually restores the natural environment. They say that America raises more timber than it harvests yearly, and more forested land—nearly 760 million acres—exists today than 50 years ago. "Commercial forests under industrial management are the healthiest and most contributive in the world," the American Forest Institute believes.

Although parks now preserve more than 160,000 acres of old-growth California redwoods, about 200,000 acres remain in private hands. Lumbermen cut and haul away the giants at a rate of 10,000 acres per year.

Truck strains under a 72-ton load.

Logger measures a 700-year-old redwood.

Entire hillsides show the scars of clear

...utting below Washington's Mt. Rainier. Logging and fire roads etch land under reforestation.

stemming from the wood-products industry. Other problems range from sludge and chemicals dumped into lakes and streams to the rotten-egg odor of sulfide gases from belching paper mills. Hydrogen sulfide, a potentially toxic gas, escapes from boiler stacks, and oxygen-demanding wastes leak into waterways.

Although papermaking can be as varied as the thousands of grades of paper produced, the sulfate, or kraft, process—the most common—basically cooks wood chips in a chemical solution. The chemicals dissolve the sugars and the lignins, which hold wood fibers together. The resulting waste, called black liquor, may total as much as 50 percent of the original material. In most plants, water is evaporated from the liquor, and the organic material is burned for fuel. A specially designed recovery furnace reclaims the cooking chemicals. The wood fiber is further refined and bleached with additional chemicals before being made into paper.

In 1970 the Council on Economic Priorities in Washington, D. C., surveyed the largest U. S. paper producers, checking 131 pulp mills. "Pollution of rivers and lakes from pulping seriously endangers the complicated life chain in natural waters from bacteria to plankton to plant to fish life," the council reported. "Yet nearly two-thirds of the effluent discharged still fails to satisfy recommendations for . . . water treatment established by the Federal Government five years ago."

Industry spending

Paper manufacturers report that the industry has spent a billion dollars since 1950 protecting 50 million acres of forest land, 516 million dollars for water pollution abatement, and 130 million dollars to reduce air pollution.

Although the industry concedes that it still has a long way to go, it claims that almost 90 percent of the 800 pulp, paper, and paperboard mills give some treatment to their effluent; a good percentage do the same to their air emissions.

As I visited lumber and plywood mills, I found that they no longer burn the bulk of their waste. Most scrap now goes into hardboard, particle board, pulp, and other products. Operators have learned to use up to 80 percent of a log, compared with perhaps 50 percent some 20 years ago. A number of uses, ranging from mulch to auxiliary fuel, have been found, even for tree bark.

Some mills have installed equipment to absorb chlorine from bleach solutions, to recover chemicals, to reduce odors, and to burn black-liquor residues. Electrostatic precipitators,

similar to those used in some power plants, trap particulates and prevent them from being emitted into the air.

For example, Georgia-Pacific's plant in Crossett, Arkansas, draws 53 million gallons of water per day, most of it from its own man-made lake, but cleans up the resulting effluent before it flows at a controlled rate into the Ouachita River. Chemist Johnny S. Carter said the new controls have reduced water pollution as much as 95 percent.

A firm credited with an excellent record in pollution control is the Weyerhaeuser Company. At the firm's main forest-products manufacturing complex in Longview, Washington, I talked with J. L. "Mac" McClintock, director of environmental resources.

He showed me the laboratory where researchers work toward better use of wood products. One process uses waste fiber mixed with water, grass seed, and fertilizer to spray a paste on earth banks left bare by highway cuts. I also saw pressed-wood panels used in automobile doors and, in another room, a stack of molded female torsos destined to become dressmaking models.

Mr. McClintock introduced me to G. G. De-Haas, a Dutch chemical engineer who now is a trouble-shooter for Weyerhaeuser. In 1949 one of his assignments was to help solve the problem of containing the noxious gases escaping from the paper mill.

Mr. DeHaas bought war-surplus barrage balloons. The huge volume of gas was exhausted into the balloons, then released back gradually to the furnaces where it could be burned at a controlled rate. His scheme worked. The perfected vapor-sphere system, though it no longer employs barrage balloons, has been in large-scale operation for 15 years.

In another office in Longview, I found a man who dreams of the day when men will know enough about water and its varied life forms for entire watersheds to be improved, rather than degraded, by waste.

Eugene P. Haydu has been a naturalist since he was a youngster. "As a youth," he said, "I believed that only in primitive nature could truth, goodness, and beauty be found—that all civilization was sham." Mr. Haydu tried living in the wilderness for a while; then he studied philosophy and biology. In 1952 he joined Weyerhaeuser as the first aquatic biologist in the pulp and paper industry.

Mr. Haydu advises his company on the location of plant operations to ensure maximum compatability with aquatic life. But he looks forward to a time when we will be able to take man-made wastes and use them to enhance the productivity of streams. "Now, this is a dream," he said, "but I believe it can be done."

It was a vision fit for the magnificent beauty of the fragrant evergreens around me, dripping in the rain.

Later, under low, weepy clouds, I drove along the Columbia River. I found the great stream swollen by rain and snowmelt from mountain peaks visible now and then through the clouds. Dozens of filmy, white waterfalls came leaping down the cliffs into the roily exuberance of the big waters.

On the Columbia I finally grasped the significance of the living waters that carried a people across the continent, nourishing their forests and farms, washing away the sweat and dirt of their labor. From there I went to see another river which has carried the burden of traffic and industry since early days.

The once-beautiful Ohio, called "La Belle Rivière" by French explorers, is born full grown at Pittsburgh, at the confluence of the Allegheny and Monongahela Rivers. It then flows west and south 981 miles to the Mississippi. The Ohio and its tributaries drain about a twentieth of the U. S. mainland. One-tenth of the Nation's people live in its basin.

The Ohio Valley, an industrial empire unrivaled in size and variety, has witnessed nearly every manufacturing process known to man. And more than 3,000 industrial plants use the water system as a sewer.

Traveling the river for NATIONAL GEOGRAPHIC, Frederick Simpich wrote in 1950: "Into [the Ohio] many cities dump their sewage; and waste acids and effluents from mines, tanneries, distilleries, and soap, steel, and chemical plants. . . . 'Downstream from factory outlets,' a skipper told me, 'I've seen crawfish crawling out of the water to escape the acid; and I've seen fish piping with their snouts half out of the water trying to get a fresh breath.' "

Two years before Mr. Simpich wrote his article, eight Ohio River-basin states had joined in a compact to curb pollution of the river. The Ohio River Valley Water Sanitation Commission (ORSANCO) binds Illinois, Indiana, Kentucky, New York, Pennsylvania, Virginia, West Virginia, and Ohio in a cooperative venture to protect the river and its tributaries. The commission has but a small budget and no taxing authority; still it is an example of a long-term, basinwide approach using facts— and persuasion—to abate pollution.

Progress has been made in 23 years, yet because of the rapid growth of population and industry, the Ohio still carries a heavy burden of wastes. At ORSANCO's headquarters in

Reeking industrial dump in Devil's Swamp, Louisiana, once received effluents from local factories. Holding ponds contained chemicals that drained into public waterways. In 1971 the state issued an emergency "stop order." The dump now accepts only solid wastes; a levee prevents drainage of liquids still impounded there.

DANGER POISON WASTE

Untreated chlorine and other chemicals pour from a kraft pulp mill in Georgia; stacks belch noxious sulfide gases.

New by-products, purer water

Demanding more water in processing than any other industry, pulp and paper mills use 6.5 billion gallons a day and rank as major manufacturing polluters of our rivers. About half the wood processed for pulp ends up as waste. One common method leaves spent sulfite liquor behind — a mixture of lignins, sugars, resins, and chemicals that defy effective recycling. Released as raw effluent, they discolor and impose high oxygen demands on our waterways. Seeking alternatives to dumping, researchers have developed a variety of sulfite liquor by-products, including binders, emulsifiers, and gels. The St. Regis Paper Company at Rhinelander, Wisconsin, grows torula yeast in sugar residues (below) and converts lignins into adhesives and additives for concrete.

The sulfate, or kraft, process produces waste called black liquor. A plant can recycle it by evaporating excess water, burning concentrated liquids in recovery furnaces, and salvaging chemicals for reuse. Few mills today discharge completely untreated water, but only a handful meet state and federal standards.

Through bacterial action (right), a system of settling, aeration, and retention ponds can reduce a mill's pollution by 60 to 90 percent. Effluent- and color-removing clarifiers can also assist in keeping America from becoming a "water wasteland." When not overburdened by man-made impurities, the rivers once more can purify themselves.

Aerator feeds oxygen to waste-consuming bacteria.

Sulfite liquor supplies sugar to fermenting yeast.

Clarifier removes solids and color from waste water.

Cincinnati I talked with Edward J. Cleary, executive director for more than 20 years before he retired to consultant status in 1968, and with Robert K. Horton, the new director, who has worked with Dr. Cleary through most of those years.

In the Cincinnati offices I also saw the receiving console of an electronic river-monitoring system, most advanced of its kind in the world. Twenty-seven robot monitors along the river and several tributaries continuously transmit information on the quality of water. Whenever a human or electronic monitor detects a surge of pollution, ORSANCO attempts to pinpoint the source.

Tracing pollution

It was such a piece of detective work that provided my opportunity for a flying look at the river. Just before my arrival, the commission had been notified of a mysterious spill of chemicals streaking the river from Cincinnati to Portsmouth, Ohio.

The morning was cold and bright when I took off with Russell A. Brant, ORSANCO geologist, and our pilot, Lloyd W. Porter, in a Cessna-185. As we climbed through the gray haze cloaking the city and part of the surrounding valley, I could see the broad Ohio, brown with silt stirred by winter rains and tributary runoff.

Smoke veiled the distant horizon. With a bird's-eye view of only a fraction of the mighty performance of American industry, I began to comprehend something of the dimensions of the pollution problem.

Along the Ohio, manufacturers add a witch's brew of effluents to the naturally turbid river —ammonia from chemical plants, sulfides from textile mills and tanneries, and such toxic wastes as phenols, cyanides, mercury, zinc, cadmium, and formaldehyde. The vast waters dilute the poisons; bacteria break down some of them; time destroys others, but many wastes persist and may concentrate in the food chain, as DDT has done. Such chemicals pose a threat, not yet fully understood, to the health of Americans generally.

As we flew, I glimpsed a glossy sheen on the water, the widely dispersed trail of what we were seeking. Flood-washed debris matted either bank, and the hills beyond rolled with farms and the gray beauty of hardwood trees waiting for spring.

We approached an industrial complex at Portsmouth, where the sky at 1,500 feet was dirty with brown, yellow, and red smoke from the Detroit Steel Mill. Here also we found the source of the mysterious pollutant—streaks of iron oxide fanning out from the vicinity of the steel company rail yard, covering half the river with a pale blue, iridescent film.

Mr. Brant's job was to identify the problem, then notify Ohio authorities so they could take action. Eventually the offending plant was put under state orders to install pollution controls by 1972.

We flew on to see the Ashland-Ironton industrial complex where iron, steel, oil, coke, and carbon plants filled the sky with a mixture of smoke and fumes. We knifed into the pollutant clouds at 1,500 feet, and within moments the pilot encountered virtually blind, instrument-flying, conditions. He had to climb to 2,500 feet before we topped the pall of smog. By then the acrid taste of sulfur was strong in my mouth.

Now I could better understand the significance of unembellished statistics—figures which show that industry emits 30 million tons of pollutants into the sky each year. But as yet no one has been able to identify every substance that industrial firms discharge into the air and water.

Nor does anyone really know the full cost of air pollution to residents of an industrial city. However, the Council on Environmental Quality has stated that in the United States air pollution costs "many billions of dollars a year," in terms of repainting steel, replacing cracked rubber, laundering fabrics, washing cars, and in the loss of farm crops and livestock.

When my flight was over, I returned to talk with Robert Horton of the river commission. Here on the Ohio men had worked for 23 years on the complicated problem of water pollution. Had they accomplished anything?

"I was on the river 20 years ago," Mr. Horton replied. "In places it was a stinking black mess, septic and anaerobic. I've seen marked changes since then.

"We work by persuasion wherever possible and by compulsion when necessary. Our few experiences with court proceedings show that they average about ten years in litigation."

Frank M. Middleton, research director for EPA's water programs in Cincinnati, questions the effectiveness of persuasion as a tactic in the battle against water pollution. "Only since the introduction of water standards, a permit system, and strong federal enforcement procedures," he says, "has industry begun to clean up in earnest."

Mercury is a case in point.

In 1970 Canadians and Americans learned that thousands of tons of fish had assimilated mercury that reached rivers and lakes from a variety of industrial sources. Everyone assumed that mercury, a heavy metal, sank to the bottom and remained inert. But scientists had discovered that bacterial action converts inorganic mercury into a much more toxic organic form, methyl mercury. From bottom mud this may be carried through the aquatic food chain into the fish we eat.

Mercury poisoning in several forms is no stranger to the medical profession. When mercury in large amounts lodges in the kidneys, brain, and other vital organs, it causes irritability, flushed skin, and loss of hair, teeth, and nails. It can lead to brain damage, blindness, insanity, and death.

In Japan 46 people died between 1953 and 1961 from eating seafood contaminated by methyl mercury. The danger was recognized in Sweden in the mid-1960's but the alarm was not sounded in this country until 1970, when a Norwegian student in Canada found mercury residues in walleye pike taken from Lake St. Clair between Michigan and Ontario.

This led to a frantic wave of fish testing. Within a year elevated amounts of mercury were found in fish and game birds in many states, and tuna and swordfish from the Pacific Ocean. No one has established precisely how much mercury man can accumulate in his body without physical harm, but the Federal Government has set up an action level of 0.5 parts per million in seafood.

The mercury problem exemplifies how fast Government and industry can move once a danger is recognized. By 1971, Government lawsuits and voluntary action reduced mercury discharges directly into waterways to a small fraction of former levels.

Although in this instance industry reacted quickly, several questions remain. Mercury occurs in coal and oil, and it leaches into streams and rivers from cinnabar ore bodies. There is also some evidence that fossil fuel combustion may be a major source of airborne mercury pollution.

No one knows just how many years it may take for the mercury already deposited in rivers, lakes, and oceans to change form and dissipate to harmless levels. Some experts believe it may become even more toxic. And no satisfactory way has been found to neutralize it.

After mercury, what might we expect as the next menacing poison to be found lurking in the air and water? I talked again with Ed Cleary, the former director of ORSANCO.

"Who knows? The question that really bothers me," he said, "is this, how do you establish discharge standards to deal with substances that may be toxic? We know what causes fish

Editorials and comic strips, sports results and classified ads — 568 pages in 21 sections — blanket a suburban driveway. This Sunday edition of the *Los Angeles Times,* with a circulation of about 1.3 million, required 3,100 tons of newsprint. The United States in 1970 consumed 9.5 million tons, compared to 5.8 million for all of Western Europe. Two-thirds of our supply comes from Canadian pulp mills; lumbering waste provides most of the raw material for domestic newsprint production.

kills, but we don't know much about man's response. We cannot use humans to test these potentially dangerous discharges, and we have not begun to fathom the synergistic effects of the 500 new chemical compounds that enter our environment each year."

Dr. Cleary's comments reminded me of the warning by ecologist Barry Commoner that modern science and technology are simply too powerful to permit a trial-and-error approach. "Like the sorcerer's apprentice, we are acting upon dangerously incomplete knowledge. We are, in effect, conducting a huge experiment *on ourselves.*"

"Our greatest frustration," Dr. Cleary added, "is that for five years we've tried to catalog who puts precisely what into the river. We never get very far. Industry is reluctant to reveal such facts, maintaining that the information would tip off competitors.

"They tell us: 'Just measure what's in the stream.' That's like the difference between measuring the needle when it's in a pincushion and waiting until it's hidden in the haystack to find and measure it. Let's put the burden of proof on industry—to prove that their discharges are nontoxic."

In 1970 President Nixon announced that the rivers and harbors section of the 1899 Refuse Act, which prohibits industrial discharges into navigable waterways without a permit from the U. S. Army Corps of Engineers, would be strictly enforced. The law requires industries to disclose what they are dumping into these waters; companies are now beginning to comply.

Toxic substances

Following the mercury emergency, many organizations began surveying other elements to see if any are approaching dangerous concentrations. Possible candidates include lead, gold, silver, copper, thallium, beryllium, cadmium, selenium, and arsenic—all poisonous in small quantities. In 1971 the U. S. Geological Survey reported that water in 12 urban areas contained traces of cadmium and arsenic exceeding public health standards.

Henry A. Schroeder, director of the Dartmouth Medical School's Trace Element Laboratory at Brattleboro, Vermont, sees lead, nickel, and cadmium as the three which may be concentrating in the environment to most dangerous levels. I talked with Dr. Schroeder about his experiments with toxic metals.

"Part of the problem with cadmium and lead," he said, "is that the body has no adequate mechanism to dispose of them; thus they can concentrate to dangerous levels over a long period of time. Lead kills outright in large doses, but in small concentrations shortens the life of experimental animals. Nickel is absorbed into the body, as are most airborne metals. If the nose and lungs are heavily exposed, cancer may result. My experiments with animals have led me to believe that cadmium in the air and water is a factor in the high blood pressure of 23 million Americans."

I found some comfort in knowing that mercury in our waters and in the fish that inhabit them has shocked the Government and industry enough to alert officials to other possible poisons, perhaps in time to avert disaster.

Another pollutant, the phosphate in laundry detergents, though not in the same toxic category as mercury, has also caused a wave of alarm. It has been roundly blamed for encouraging growth of algae in lakes and streams.

Nearly a decade ago the soap and detergent industry was called to task for causing long-lasting foam where home laundry and wash water was flushed into sewage disposal plants and streams. Chemists solved that problem by changing a molecule in the formula.

With the recent uproar, industry attempted to substitute other compounds, including NTA (nitrilotriacetate). Manufacturers halted use of NTA after preliminary research indicated that it caused birth defects when injected into laboratory animals.

As the forces of antipollution close in about them, many industrialists have searched for alternatives to depositing wastes in freshwater streams. One result has been a sharp increase in ocean dumping. According to EPA's solid waste management office, industry dumps nearly five million tons of waste a year into coastal waters—the most productive part of the ocean—brimming with sea life. The industry total of 4.7 million tons includes 2.7 million tons of waste acids. Wastes from refineries, paper mills, and miscellaneous industries make up the remainder.

Another disposal method pumps acids and toxic fluids into rock strata deep in the ground. Ed Cleary at Cincinnati thinks these disposal wells may be risky.

"It's a convenient and economical alternative," he commented, "but what will it do to the groundwater? Will it foreclose future opportunities to extract oil and minerals? Are regulatory agencies staffed to deal with it?" In 1960, he said, there were six such deep-disposal wells in the country. In 1969 there were 150.

Two of these are at the Armco Steel Corporation's Middletown, Ohio, complex, which

once poured spent liquors into the Great Miami River. John E. Barker, Armco's director of environmental engineering, explained the wells to me: "Many people are concerned about this, but if the geology and the wastes meet specific criteria, you can then engineer the well properly."

Waste liquid is pumped under pressure into 300-foot-thick sandstone formations located some 3,000 feet beneath the plant. Mr. Barker believes there is no chance that the waste material will ever reach groundwater or a stratum of rock useful for any other purpose.

Armco, like many companies I contacted, has been slowly cleaning up pollution for many years, principally with new steel-making processes and control devices installed as old furnaces and plants are phased out and new ones built. But many manufacturers have just started along the road of controlling environmental contamination.

"I wouldn't place too much reliance on industry's social conscience," said Dr. Cleary. "I think, however, if I were an industrialist today, I would not wait for regulatory authorities to coerce action to curb obvious pollution.

"Such controls will require money," he added. "But it does not seem that industries would be financially overburdened. It would cost only about 2 to 4 percent of capital investment for them to deal with water- and air-quality standards."

Another point was made by John H. Gibbons, director of a broad environmental study being conducted at Oak Ridge National Laboratory in Tennessee for the National Science Foundation. He said that in many instances cleaning up mercury actually saved some money by recovery of the expensive metal. He visualizes the day when perfection of varied processes will enable industry to reuse much of its wastes, even at a profit.

"We need to look ahead and avoid mistakes," Dr. Gibbons said, "rather than mop up our messes after the fact."

Such a change in national habits seems essential. Somehow we must slow the pace of a technology that rushes headlong into the future with but minimum regard for the environment. If we are to live in a nonpolluted world, consumers as well as manufacturers must be prepared to pay the cost of cleaning up.

It was John Gibbons who reminded me of a statement made by the famed German physicist Max Born, who died in 1970 at age 87: "Intellect distinguishes between the possible and the impossible. Reason distinguishes between the sensible and the senseless. Even the possible can be senseless."

Curbing air pollution, the Bethlehem Steel Corporation installed a wet scrubber system (upper) for its new furnaces at Burns Harbor, Indiana. The furnaces produce steel ten times faster than the older types, but they also generate large amounts of gas containing iron oxides. Scrubbers spray the gas with water to trap the dust and discharge it as sludge for reprocessing (lower). Despite the availability of advanced facilities, industry continues to emit 30 million tons of pollutants into the atmosphere a year.

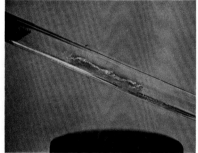

Human hair and mercury microgram

Combustion removes mercury from hair.

Omnipresent poisons

"My vision would blur for just a few seconds.... I got awful nervous. I couldn't hold on to things.... I was so sick that I didn't care," recalls Dorothy Nichols of Rochester, New York (foreground, below). Mrs. Nichols suffers from inorganic mercury poisoning. As a glass-factory worker, she put measuring marks on pipettes. She used a machine to fill the tubes with mercury to specified levels, applied the marks, then let the toxic metal drain out. For more than three years she inhaled mercury vapor; residues contaminated her clothes and hair. In the summer of 1970 doctors at the University of Rochester's Strong Memorial Hospital diagnosed her case and began treatments with an experimental drug derived from penicillin. They describe her condition today as "stable," although she still has constant insomnia and periods of confusion and memory loss.

Mercury in trace amounts occurs throughout the environment. Many industrial and laboratory workers like Mrs. Nichols become exposed inadvertently. Factories and incinerators discharge it into the air and water; burning of fossil fuels provides another source. In 1967 scientists dis-covered that micro-organisms in bottom mud convert inorganic mercury into an even more toxic organic form, methyl mercury, which can accumulate in the aquatic food chain. Inorganic mercury poisoning causes irritability, slurred speech, tremor and withdrawal; medicine, however, can arrest the disease in its early stages. So far, the neurological effects of large doses of methyl mercury usually have proved irreversible and may result in coma and death. Scientists consider 500 micrograms in daily food intake and 0.2 parts per million in human blood dangerous.

University of Rochester researchers seek effective antidotes to toxic compounds and sensitive, selective methods of detecting methyl mercury in the body. At the Eastman Kodak Company industrial laboratory nearby, specialists also concentrate on detection. In a 15-minute test, they can remove mercury residues from hair by combustion and collect them on gold-plated asbestos for analysis (right). "By photoelectronic means," says Director Don H. Anderson, "we can identify a single part of mercury among ten billion other parts. That's the equivalent of finding one crystal of sugar in a truckload of sand." Biologists and chemists also investigate other potentially toxic elements such as cadmium, selenium, and lead.

Dorothy Nichols undergoes computerized test to establish connection between hand tremor and mercury accumulation.

NATIONAL GEOGRAPHIC PHOTOGRAPHER JAMES P. BLAIR; EASTMAN KODAK COMPANY (OPPOSITE TOP)

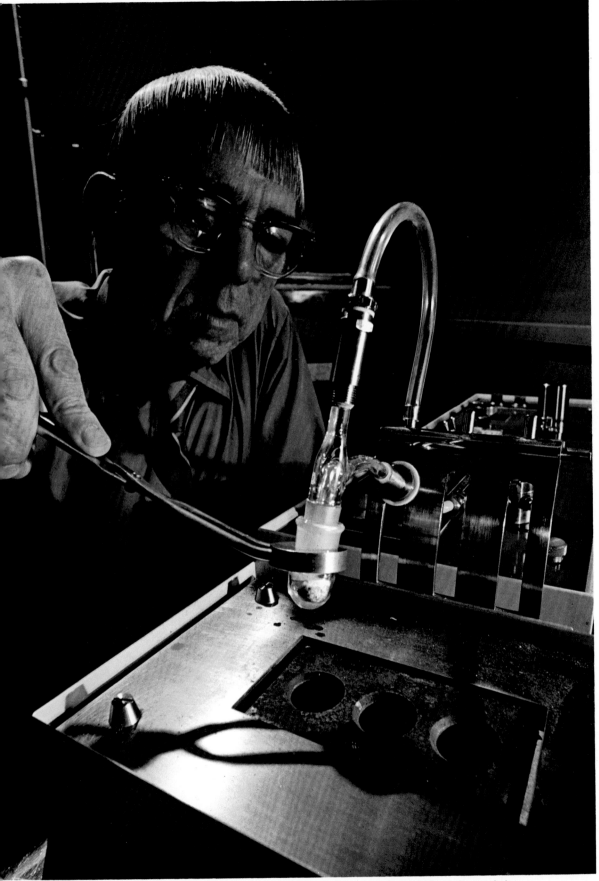

Kodak chemist Jerry Murphy operates a selective mercury analyzer to determine parts per billion in human hair.

"Rush hour should change its name," I grumbled, waiting in the line of traffic. Dull black and dented, the idling sedan just ahead reminded me of the first car I ever drove, a regal wreck bought for $40 by a fellow chore boy on a Wyoming ranch. What the jalopy lacked in luxury it made up in convenience. In those long summer evenings of the early fifties, that old roadster meant freedom, adventure, speed.

Now on another summer evening I sat, temper festering, hemmed in by autos and buses on a street in the Nation's Capital. Impatiently I edged along with the glut of traffic that daily carries Washington, D. C., commuters to their homes in the nearby suburbs of Maryland and Virginia.

Living in the heart of the city, I normally avoid the worst of these traffic jams, but I had accepted an invitation to dinner with my sister and her family in Glen Echo, Maryland. Finally—nine miles and 35 minutes later—I pulled up before their house.

"How do you people do it day after day?" I asked my sister as she greeted me from her oak-shaded veranda. "I could have done nearly as well on a bike."

"That's all right for you. You could get along without a car, living downtown," she replied. "But I'd go mad without mine.

"I'd have to shop at night and give up my teaching in the city if we had only one car. Linda couldn't take music lessons, and Ben and Amanda couldn't have friends outside the immediate neighborhood. Certainly, a second car can be an expensive nuisance, but my station wagon makes it possible for us to do what we want to do."

I remembered another conversation with a newspaper editor over dinner in suburban Virginia, across the Potomac River. "We used to live in the city, on Capitol Hill," he had told me. "When our eldest was a baby, I'd walk home for lunch, but as the kids got older there wasn't much room for them to play. Out here the boys can camp in the woods.

"And the wives have a baby-sitting club. Tomorrow my wife will take her turn—so the Lewises can go to the clean-air meeting."

It's all knotted up in one huge snarl, I thought, worse than any traffic jam. People work in cities. The automobile lets them live in greener places. Then they get together to do something about the pollution that's partly caused by the cars they drive.

PHILIP KOPPER, *a free-lance writer based in the Nation's Capital, has worked on the news staffs of the* Washington Post *and the* Baltimore Sun.

"Today the car is king—and not a very benevolent one. A single automobile may dump up to a ton of pollutants into our atmosphere each year."

San Francisco's nearly finished Bay Are

TRA.'CPORTATIO.':.'ATIO.' O.' THE GO

By Philip Kopper

...apid Transit (BART) will offer fast electric-train service as an alternative to the automobile, a major source of air pollution.

From the Long Island Expressway in New York to the Bayshore Freeway in San Francisco, America's automobile drivers create an environment of tense, noisy tangles of traffic. To many motorists, it must sometimes seem that all of the Nation's 87 million automobiles are on the road at once.

In 1969, the latest year for which figures are available, transportation—chiefly automobiles—accounted for 60 percent of the country's air pollutants by weight, according to the Environmental Protection Agency's Office of Air Programs. "Remember, that's only a national average," John T. Middleton, deputy assistant administrator for OAP, told me. "In urban areas the average zooms to 80 percent or more, for not only is the concentration of motor vehicles higher, but also the internal-combustion engine performs at its worst in stop-and-go traffic."

The Washington, D. C., area, for example, blames motor vehicle emissions for 80 percent of its air-pollution problem. And that's no small problem: In 1967 the Department of Health, Education, and Welfare ranked the Nation's Capital as the 18th dirtiest city in the country. Nearly a million people commute to work, park all day, and compete for road space driving home.

Obviously, if more people used public transportation, pollution as well as congestion could be cut significantly. But the trend has been in the opposite direction. As recently as 1960 some 27 percent of Washington-area commuters traveled to and from work by bus. Eight years later the ratio had dropped to 19 percent. Throughout the country, the number of passenger trips made on public transit declined almost 15 percent during the same period, even though the metropolitan population increased by some 50 million. Two hundred fifty-eight public transit companies have collapsed since 1954, and many others are in dire financial straits.

By what process has the Nation become so dependent upon the automobile? Economics, convenience, and legislation all have played a part, I found. Mass-produced cars are inexpensive enough for most American families to own at least one. And with a car, they can go almost anywhere they want—to the other side of the subdivision or the continent—any time they choose.

The automobile has liberated Americans by making us mobile, but the new freedom has forged its own chains: air pollution, noise, auto graveyards, highways that slice through cities and encroach upon the countryside.

At first a prestige toy for the affluent, the motor car ultimately became the country's chief form of transportation. From 4,192 in 1900, yearly sales of automobiles climbed to more than 1.9 million two decades later. Increased demand for cars soon prompted better roads, which attracted more cars. Concern for national defense in two world wars accelerated road building. The post-World War II years brought new highs in automobile sales— a record 9,305,561 in 1965—coupled with more and better roads.

Interstate highway system

In 1956 Congress passed a Federal-Aid Highway Act. That law funneled federal taxes on gasoline, cars, and accessories into the Highway Trust Fund, which has financed road building all over the Nation ever since. As a result, an interstate system of roads, called "the largest public works project in history," now stretches across some 31,900 miles. Its cost so far has reached 43.3 billion dollars.

The fund pays 90 percent of major interstate highway construction costs, and states provide only 10 percent. By comparison, states must pay a minimum of one-third to one-half the cost of mass transit systems.

Ironically, many segments of this intended cross-country network serve commuters who drive only a few bumper-to-bumper miles to work in the morning and home at night.

Gradually such a highway system has led to ever larger rings of suburbs around our central cities—cities that often seem empty after business hours. Some 55 percent of the workers in Newark, New Jersey, for example, live in other towns and cities.

As the suburbs have grown, the number of cars has increased. This, in turn, has increased traffic, which has strengthened the hand of those who argue for more roads, which attract more commuters who use cars. Voicing his concern, Secretary of Transportation John A. Volpe has pointed out that "a road can create more problems than it solves, if it simply causes massive congestion by pouring automobiles into a downtown bottleneck."

This self-defeating cycle was described by Helen Leavitt, a neighbor of mine who began investigating matters when a highway designed for suburban commuters' convenience threatened her Washington home. The result was a book, *Superhighway—Superhoax*. In it she observes that a third of the land "in 53 central cities in the United States has already been converted to street use." More than half the land in Minneapolis is devoted to roads and parking; that's like giving half your home over to hallways and shoe racks. And of course, new roads aren't restricted to cities only. Surveyors plotted a four-lane highway through the corral of that ranch where I worked in Jackson Hole, Wyoming.

While road building remains a 12-billion-dollar-a-year industry, metropolitan freeway construction proposals in recent years have sparked the opposition of highly vocal citizens' groups in a number of cities, Washington, Memphis, San Antonio, and New Orleans among them. One reporter viewed federal plans for an expressway near the famed French Quarter as "the biggest threat to New Orleans since Admiral David Farragut came up the river in 1862 with his warships bristling with guns."

Planners had designed a route to carry an elevated six-lane road along the Mississippi River within a short distance of the French Quarter with its historic Jackson Square and Bourbon Street, the birthplace of jazz. Walking is the best way to get around that colorful neighborhood. Cars seem out of place on narrow streets where lacelike wrought iron embellishes balconies. Even snail-pace traffic intrudes on the district's charm, but an overhead freeway would have destroyed it.

Convinced that "public benefits from the proposed highway would not be enough to warrant damaging the treasured French Quarter," Secretary Volpe, in a precedent-setting move, halted the project. But the problem of intense traffic congestion in the adjacent downtown business district remains unresolved. "We need some way to bring people downtown," architect Edward C. Mathes said. "Eventually, the answer for New Orleans has to be some form of mass transit."

San Francisco, facing a similar problem, looks to its Bay Area Rapid Transit system (BART) as a partial solution. Scheduled to open in 1972, the 75-mile-long, high-speed rail system is being built at a cost of 1.38 billion dollars, little of it in federal funds.

"BART will be the most modern commuter rail network in the world," said its general manager B. R. Stokes. "A central computer will monitor traffic and dispatch 80-mile-an-hour trains to coincide with passenger demand.

"Instead of fumbling for coins or tokens at the turnstiles, riders will be able to purchase magnetically-coded passes to activate the entrance gates. At the exit gates, machines will 'read' the length of the ride, compute the fare, and subtract it from the balance of the ticket—or, if a passenger has used up his balance, order him to pay the difference."

Lowell Georgia, who photographed BART

Underwater tunnel section for BART's San Francisco-Oakland line slides off steel-yard ways (top). Trains using the tunnel beneath San Francisco Bay will reduce rush-hour commuting time between the two cities from 30 to 9 minutes. Along its elevated tracks in suburban areas, BART has created park areas.

LOWELL GEORGIA; NATIONAL GEOGRAPHIC PHOTOGRAPHER DEAN CONGER (OPPOSITE BOTTOM)

Watchful attendant in train cab will overrule distant computer in case of an emergency.

Monitoring board lights pinpoint the exact location of each train.

Computers dispatch BART trains

Tracks blur (opposite) as an automated BART train accelerates smoothly to 80 miles per hour in a test run. At BART's central headquarters in Oakland, sophisticated equipment will start and space all trains on the 75-mile network, set their speeds, and guide them to precision stops to pick up and let off passengers. If trouble should occur, the computerized system will warn a dispatcher (top) to assume control and will print out a corrective strategy for him to follow in holding or rerouting trains.

Color-coded bars identify train for electronic sensors.

Design of lightweight fiberglass cabs and aluminum coaches reduces air resistance at high speeds.

for this book, rode with engineers as they tested a new streamlined train on a 15-mile segment of track. "My fellow 'passengers' were lead weights," he said. "The train hit 93 miles an hour without a jolt, a lurch, or even the sensation of acceleration. The smoothness and the quiet are unbelievable. It's just like riding into the year 2000."

That initial stretch of track passes through rolling suburbs. In downtown Berkeley, San Francisco, and Oakland, the trains will run underground. To cross San Francisco Bay, BART trains will move under water through a four-mile-long tube sunk into a trench carved into the bay floor. The San Francisco-Oakland run will take nine minutes—about one-third the time an automobile requires in peak traffic.

Los Angeles, too, plans to build a high-speed rail transit system. And in my hometown of Washington, D. C., tunneling has begun for Metro, a 98-mile-long subway network designed to improve inner-city transportation and to link the business districts and Government complexes with suburban communities.

Commuter trains are economically feasible only in areas which have corridors of dense population like New York, Boston, Philadelphia, and Chicago. Elsewhere, mass transit planners expect their systems to create such corridors. Where population spreads out more evenly, buses may prove to be a better alternative, if people can be coaxed into riding them.

Reserved bus lanes appear to hold some promise. When the Department of Transportation experimented with this concept on a heavily traveled highway linking the Nation's Capital with suburban Virginia, bus passengers increased by 79 percent in the first 18 months. And riders from the farthest point cut their commuting time by as much as 30 minutes per trip. Encouraged by the initial success, the Northern Virginia Transportation Commission used federal funds to buy 30 new buses to expand the service. All will be equipped with special emission-control devices. And, as added passenger inducements, they will offer carpeting and wider, more comfortable seats. New York, Seattle, and San Francisco also have special bus lanes; Milwaukee, Los Angeles, Boston, and Kansas City are likely candidates for them.

Designers are at work on more sophisticated vehicles that would revolutionize intercity ground transportation in the decades ahead. One of these, the Tracked Air Cushion Vehicle, would employ compressed-air streams to support it on concrete guideways at 300 miles an hour. Such a vehicle may utilize a linear induction motor, an electromagnetic propulsion system that would ride a single aluminum guide rail. Looking further ahead, some engineers envision trains that will travel in a vacuum through special tubes which pose no air resistance. With these systems ground speeds of 500 miles an hour might become feasible.

But these are vehicles of the future. Today the car is king—and not a very benevolent one. A single automobile may dump up to a ton of pollutants into our atmosphere each year. The source of these pollutants is the much maligned internal-combustion engine, which explodes a mixture of gasoline and air and in the process creates a series of complicated chemical reactions.

Gasoline and its leftovers

Gasoline is a complex mixture composed of various-size hydrocarbon compounds: small ones to get the fire started, medium-size ones to keep it going during warm-up, and larger ones for cruising speeds. Uneven burning of these compounds during combustion produces noxious carbon monoxide and hydrocarbon leftovers. Meanwhile, high combustion temperatures create unwanted nitrogen oxides.

Colorless, odorless, and poisonous, carbon monoxide (CO) accounts for 47 percent of our air pollution by weight. Although CO results from the incomplete burning of almost any substance, including tobacco, the lion's share comes from the automobile. CO dilutes rapidly in the atmosphere, but it signals the presence of other noxious emissions; thus it is used as an approximate gauge of air pollution.

In the bloodstream, CO behaves like a determined hitchhiker, attaching itself to red blood cells and pre-empting the place of vital oxygen. Large doses can cause suffocation by preventing the hemoglobin in the blood from absorbing oxygen, but doctors disagree about the effects of small doses.

From the standpoint of physiology, the average CO level in the air over an extended period is more significant than a brief peak reading. Some doctors believe that heart patients are endangered even by relatively low levels of CO, if exposure continues for as long as eight hours, because the heart must work harder to pump oxygen-depleted blood back to the lungs.

Drivers and pedestrians on busy streets often are exposed to from 10 to 100 parts per million of CO. Some studies indicate that 10 parts per million over a period of eight hours may dull mental performance. Researchers at Stanford University have found that CO levels of 50 parts per million for 79 minutes can affect judgment and hearing.

Hydrocarbons—compounds of hydrogen and carbon—undergo a transformation in the combustion process which makes them "capable, no doubt about it, of producing cancer," says Dr. Paul Kotin, vice president for health sciences and dean of the medical school at Temple University. Dr. Kotin painted laboratory mice with a concentrated mixture of these hydrocarbons, and skin cancer resulted.

Little is known about health effects of nitrogen oxides, which result from any intense burning, though a recent study in Tennessee suggests that children become more susceptible to respiratory ailments if exposed even to low levels of these oxides. Moreover, like hydrocarbons, they play a key role in the formation of photochemical smog.

The chemical reactions inside the engine are simple compared with what happens to the end products when they reach the air. In the presence of sunlight, hydrocarbons and nitrogen oxide compounds break up, releasing free oxygen atoms. Some of these oxygen atoms drift off to seek photochemical mischief, joining pairs of oxygen atoms already in the atmosphere to form ozone, a lethal, unstable gas. In high concentrations ozone kills, or explodes; in small amounts it irritates our noses and throats and withers beans, melons, grapes, citrus fruits, and tomatoes.

Elsewhere in the air, other free oxygen molecules combine with hydrocarbons to form peroxyacyl nitrates (PAN's), which cause eye irritation and also damage plants. PAN's and ozone combine and then join with still other auto emissions in a frenzied, noxious carnival of interaction.

By 1940 residents of Los Angeles were sniffing bleachlike odors and rubbing their eyes whenever a brownish haze appeared over their city. This problem continued to increase in frequency and severity. In 1948 the newly established Los Angeles County Air Pollution Control District promptly took steps to limit smoke and fumes emitted by factories and refineries. This brought some improvement, but residents still complained of eye irritation, and noticed that their trees and plants still suffered mysterious damage.

Then Arie Jan Haagen-Smit of the California Institute of Technology in Pasadena identified sunlight as a partner in crime with tailpipe emissions in the production of smog. The problem intensifies in Los Angeles because the pollutants are imprisoned by mountains and trapped by temperature inversions which lie over the area most of the year. Dr. Haagen-Smit rightly predicted that any city with a combination of heavy automobile traffic and copious sunlight could have smog.

Not only does smog cause physical discomfort and damage to plants, but it also decreases visibility, creating hazards for pilots and drivers and clouding once-scenic vistas.

J. B. McCarter, a lifelong resident of Ontario, California, 35 miles east of Los Angeles, cited an incident from his childhood. "About 50 years ago," he recalled, "my great-uncle came to visit us. One morning I discovered that he was starting out for a pre-breakfast mountain hike. I tried to persuade him that the nearest mountain was at least ten miles away, but in the clear air of those days the San Gabriel Mountains seemed to be looming up right out of our own backyard."

"Now," Mrs. McCarter added sadly, "our magnificent mountains are shrouded in smog more than half of the time. Visitors may not even realize they're there. It is a crime to lose a view like that."

More than that has been lost. Dr. Harris M. Benedict, a plant physiologist at the Stanford Research Institute in Irvine, California, has estimated that the damage to plants from air pollution may cost the United States as much as 280 million dollars a year.

At Riverside, some 50 miles downwind from Los Angeles, the University of California maintains an air pollution research center. In a cluster of greenhouses there, scientists and graduate students keep vigil over samples of many types of California vegetation. Transparent plastic cubes contain simulated atmospheres in which damage to plants by pollutants can be observed and measured.

Plants thrive in some cubes containing filtered air; in others, the leaves of tomato and cabbage plants wither and are discolored by smog pulled into the greenhouses from the outside.

California became the first state to pass a law to control automotive emissions. It required new vehicles, beginning with 1963 models, to have a positive crankcase ventilation system to trap unburned gases and recirculate them through the engine. Since 1968 these devices, which eliminate 25 to 30 percent of automotive pollutants, have been required on all new cars sold throughout the United States.

But much remains to be done. Detroit had failed to give priority to the problem of automotive air pollutants for years, and the Justice Department eventually sued the four major car manufacturers for delaying the application of emission-control technology. As a result the companies have stepped up corrective research efforts.

By 1970 the automotive industry achieved an 80-percent reduction in hydrocarbons and a 70-percent cut in carbon monoxide emissions in new cars coming off the assembly line. However, the added controls, chiefly modifications in the carburetor and the ignition system, do not reduce nitrogen oxides, and tend to lose their effectiveness altogether if engines are not properly maintained.

Curbing automobile emissions

Even more important, in 1970 Congress amended the Clean Air Act, establishing stricter standards on automotive air pollution. By 1975, under the act, Detroit must cut remaining carbon monoxide and hydrocarbon emissions by 90 percent, and reduce nitrogen oxide emissions to only 10 percent of present levels by the following year.

Whether these deadlines can be met remains to be seen. S. William Gouse, Jr., associate dean of Carnegie Institute of Technology in Pittsburgh, Pennsylvania, predicts that "the automotive industry will come very close to meeting the requirements. . . . Whether they meet them, or how close they come, depends to a large extent upon just how the test requirements are interpreted."

Cleaning up the internal-combustion engine has already raised the cost of the automobile. Cars with control devices meeting 1974 standards will cost the American driving public an additional $48 per unit or a total of 2.6 billion dollars. The controls to meet the stricter standards in 1975 will add about $200 to the price of the automobile.

The Clean Air Act amendments have forced a much more comprehensive examination of the ills of the internal-combustion engine, as well as more substantive research into possible alternate power systems.

Even as the new amendments were being considered, automotive engineers had begun to experiment with more sophisticated emission control devices.

A car specially developed by Wayne University students won the Clean Air Car Race, a cross-country marathon in which prizes went not to the swiftest but to the least polluting cars. The winner—a Mercury Capri body fitted with a Mustang engine—used lead-free gasoline. Its emission controls included an exhaust-gas recirculation system, a temperature-sensing carburetor, and four platinum catalytic reactors.

Catalytic reactors convert hydrocarbons and carbon monoxide into carbon dioxide and water. Many engineers favor such reactors—made from materials cheaper than platinum, of course—over other control devices even though they do not reduce nitrogen oxide emissions. The reactor's over-all promise has prompted recent moves to make gasoline free of lead, the additive that can ruin most catalysts in a few hours of running time.

Nearly all lead in the air comes from gasoline exhaust. Its long-range, low-level effects upon health, like those of carbon monoxide, hydrocarbons, and nitrogen oxides, are difficult to assess, even though we know that heavy doses are lethal.

Still, some scientists feel we should not subject our bodies to any more lead buildup than they now carry. "Today's city dweller has accumulated 50 to 100 times the amount of lead that primitive man carried," warns Dr. Clair C. Patterson, a geochemist at California Institute of Technology.

"We must move toward conversion to unleaded gasoline," says Dr. Charles F. Jones, vice chairman of the board of Humble Oil & Refining Company. "In the long term a catalytic reactor and unleaded gas will emerge as the optimum system."

If such reactors should prove too costly to produce, the industry may turn to the thermal reactor, now in the experimental stage of development. Unlike the catalytic reactor, which transforms dangerous emissions into harmless substances by a chemical process, the thermal reactor uses extremely high heat to incinerate combustion residues. It works on a principle similar to that of the modern self-cleaning oven.

In the minds of some experts, such proposed modifications fail to get at the real culprit—the high-horsepower, internal-combustion engine. The Government, the automotive industry, and independent designers are involved in efforts to develop efficient and economical power sources to replace internal-combustion engines or to clean up their emissions by using other fuels.

In some respects current trends in automotive design seem to be returning to the no-nonsense approach of an earlier day—to a time when a customer of Henry Ford could have any color car he wanted, just so long as it was black.

At the Ford Motor Company, I found that engineers had wired monitoring equipment to a truck to study the performance of its gas-turbine engine. They reminded me of doctors hovering over a patient in an operating room. (Continued on page 138)

A LOVE AFFAIR WITH THE AUTOMOBILE

Where rutted wagon trails once wound through rolling hills, heavily traveled superhighways—tangible evidence of a national reliance on automotive transportation—cut gently curving courses. America's first automobiles, custom crafted and finely appointed, drew buyers chiefly from among the wealthy class. But in the early 1900's Ransom Olds and Henry Ford turned their backs on the handcrafted horseless carriage and began producing low-cost, uncomplicated, sturdy cars. In doing so, they tapped a seemingly limitless mass market.

With industry-wide application of assembly-line techniques, the advent of paved roads, and the eventual launching of a cross-country highway network, automobile sales boomed. By 1970 U. S. private-car ownership had skyrocketed to 87 million. The automobile's speed, power, comfort, and convenience surpassed mass transportation systems and, in many places, contributed to their demise.

In exchange for its unrivaled gifts of independence and mobility, the car reduced Americans to almost total dependence on it. Today air pollution, congestion, and proliferating expressways present new concerns that call for far-reaching solutions.

n Bernardino Freeway sweeps toward the heart of Los Angeles.

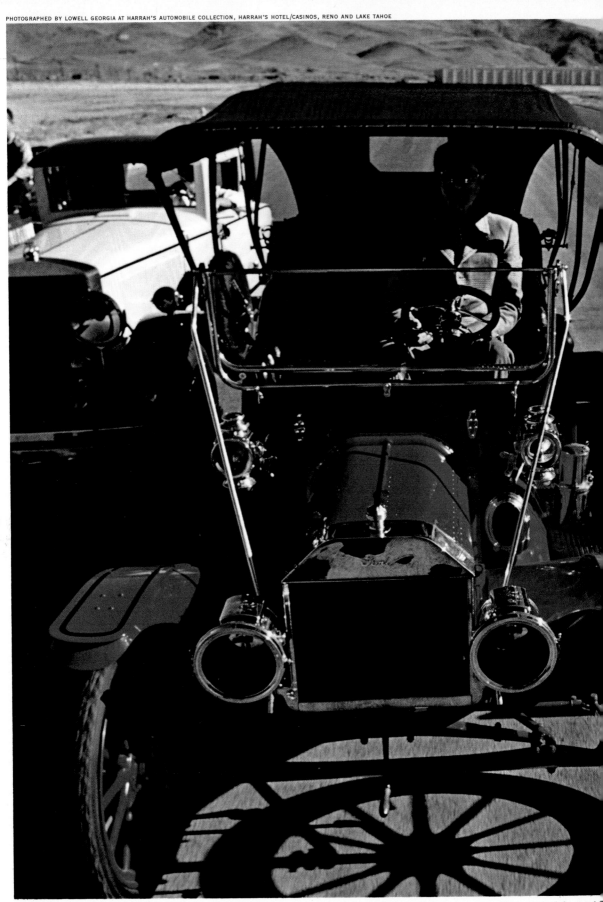

Driving a restored 1909 Model T, William F. Harrah of Reno, Nevada, leads a contingent of vintage automobiles, part of the world

gest collection. The red Ford edges past two steam-powered vehicles, a 1925 Doble coupé and a 1909 White touring car.

1931 Pierce-Arrow radiator mascot

The Auto Age: changing ideas of elegance

1938 Rolls-Royce Phantom III grille

1909 Thomas Flyer side lamp, bulb horn

1910 Oldsmobile Limited purloined its name from a train it outran.

Racing greyhound rides a 1932 Lincoln.

Advertisement for 1970 Ford Thunderbird

LOWELL GEORGIA; MICKEY MCGUIRE, COURTESY FORD MOTOR COMPANY (BOTTOM)

Nickel-plated eagle graces 1913 Coey Flyer.

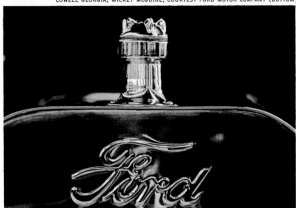

Unadorned fittings of 1909 Model-T Ford stress economy.

Radiator mascots and polished accessories of the restored automobiles in Harrah's Automobile Collection at Reno, Nevada, reflect their manufacturers' pride of craftsmanship. Hallmarks of early 20th-century elegance —morocco upholstery, satin trim, mahogany-rimmed steering wheels, and beveled plate-glass windows—once affirmed the status of automobile owners. But with the introduction of the Model-T Ford and other low-priced cars, the emphasis of the auto industry shifted to unadorned economy. Beginning in the 1950's as car makers competed for the attention of increasingly affluent buyers, assembly-line styling came into its own.

projects an image of prestige and luxury.

Ready to race, the driver of a custom-designed dragster zips up his asbestos suit. Such machines, often called funny cars, may

Death curve at Santa Monica, California, claims Sunbeam-6 entry in 1914 Grand Prix.

The lure of speed

The automobile's power and speed – in part responsible for more than 56,000 fatalities and 2 million injuries on the Nation's highways each year – reach their peak in competitive racing. Some 3,000 drag strips and raceways around the country attracted 42 million fans in 1970 — more than professional or college football or major league baseball. Frank Duryea won America's first car race in 1895, averaging 6.66 mph over a muddy 52.4-mile course. In winning the 1971 Indianapolis 500, Al Unser averaged 157.7 mph

Funny car's lightweight body of fiberglass improves speed.

Rolled car bursts into flames during an Atlanta race.

ost up to $20,000. The body tilts back to permit access.

Contestant waves a checkered flag over his winning stock car at a Maryland speedway.

Plethora of arrows confronts users of a much-traveled street in Wichita Falls, Texas, where computers control traffic lights.

Moving the masses

Harried New York motorist

Stop-and-go driving, myriad directional signs, and monstrous traffic snarls all contribute to the frustrations that plague today's urban motorist. For the architect, the city planner, and the auto owner, parking presents its own set of pressing problems. Some office-complex designs follow a rule of thumb of allowing 100 square feet of floor space for each employee and 300 square feet of space for each automobile. Warns Secretary of Transportation John A. Volpe, "Our obsession with the private car is destroying the quality of life in our urban areas. More cars... require more roads... bringing increased pollution and congestion."

Commuters inundate the Harbor Freeway in Los Angeles; bumper-to-bumper congestion creates severe air pollution.

LOWELL GEORGIA (BELOW); NATIONAL GEOGRAPHIC PHOTOGRAPHERS BRUCE DALE (OPPOSITE TOP) AND JAMES P. BLAIR

provised parking-lot car locator

Automobiles pack a multistory garage in downtown Oakland, California.

Alternatives to congestion:
Cities seek relief from the aut

Some urban residents remember — and others have nev
discovered — the exhilarating atmosphere of city life fre
of the domination of the automobile. In the late 193C
San Antonio, Texas, created the Palacia del Rio, a tre
shaded river park in its downtown area. Somewhat n
glected after its development but later restored, the pa
drew high praise from visitors to San Antonio's 19
HemisFair. Today tour boats ply the waterway, cruisi
past sidewalk cafes.

Beginning on Earth Day of 1970, New York City launch
a series of experiments banning motor vehicles from c
tain mid-Manhattan thoroughfares in an effort to redu
air pollution and relieve congestion; delighted pedestria
abandoned sidewalks for streets emptied of their us
traffic jams. Over the intersection of two busy streets
Hartford, Connecticut, the willow-shaded mall of an offi
building complex isolates pedestrians from the ca
below. In Davis, California, a college town with mc
bicycles than automobiles, officials have set aside spec
lanes for cyclists. Other cities — New York, Washingt
Chicago, Milwaukee, and Miami among them — ha
begun to follow suit.

More dramatic innovations to relieve municipal tra
congestion have not always met with such acclaim. In t
mid-1960's city planner Victor Gruen proposed to restr
automobile traffic in downtown Fort Worth, Texas,
building an inner-loop freeway lined with garages a
constructing moving sidewalks to carry pedestrians t
rest of the way to their destinations. The plan never n
terialized. But in Fresno, California, a Gruen design fo
six-block-long traffic-free downtown shopping mall prov
a near instant success, an alternative to what Mr. Gru
calls "Autopia" — a city surrendered to the automob
Enthusiastic responses also greeted pedestrian malls
Urbana, Illinois, Kalamazoo, Michigan, and Nashville, Te
nessee, leading still other cities to consider similar pla

Riverboats glide through the center of San Antonio, Texas.

Pedestrians stroll New York City's Lexington Avenue.

Hartford, Connecticut, plaza welcomes sun seekers.

Cyclist pedals along a reserved lane on a tree-lined street in Davis, California.

"Vibration-detecting devices attached to the engine register almost nothing," said Ivan Swatman, chief engineer. "That's a good sign —shows the engine isn't shaking."

Powered by either kerosene or diesel fuel, the motor produces a substantially cleaner exhaust than other types of internal-combustion engines, but its emissions of oxides of nitrogen exceed the levels required by the 1970 Clean Air Act amendments.

Already on the road in a number of places are hybrid engines that run on gasoline in open country but switch to bottled gas at the flip of a dashboard switch for city driving. Utility companies in Philadelphia and California have equipped their fleets of trucks to use propane fuel. They have found it to be more economical and cleaner-burning than gasoline.

Rankine-cycle engines

Among alternatives to internal combustion are Rankine-cycle and battery-powered engines. In the Rankine-cycle engine, which appears to hold the most promise, external burners heat a working fluid, converting it to a vapor that is harnessed for power. The vapor then condenses and goes to work again within the closed system. This engine does not pollute because the fuel burns completely at an even rate at atmospheric pressure, creating only harmless carbon dioxide and water.

Working with Ford and the Federal Government, engineers at the Thermo Electron Corporation are designing a Rankine-cycle engine to run on almost any fuel. Robert Howard, the company's vice president for research and development, said, "We expect to have a 100-horsepower demonstration vehicle by 1973 which could be mass-produced by 1978. We could put a car together any time, but we want a practical device: competitive, efficient, high performing." Two other firms, the Steam Engine Systems Corporation and the Aerojet Nuclear System Company, also are working to develop a pollution-free Rankine-cycle engine for automobiles under EPA contracts. Three California cities plan to begin testing steam-powered diesel buses designed to emit almost no pollutants.

William P. Lear, who designed the small jet plane that carries his name, is independently developing a Rankine-cycle engine using a secret working fluid called Learium. Built on the turbine principle, his motor has few moving parts, which would reduce maintenance problems. Lear thinks his Reno, Nevada, company might be able to build these turbine motors for $30 apiece. More important than economy, "the emissions are hardly enough to measure," he boasts.

Another effort to produce a low-pollution car is underway at Kinetics, Incorporated, a Sarasota, Florida, company headed by a lightly graying former New Yorker, Wallace L. Minto. The company has been trying to develop a 70-horsepower Rankine-cycle engine designed to operate on Freon, a common refrigerant which neither burns nor freezes and vaporizes at 117° F.

Airplanes also pollute the air. Although their contribution amounts to a scant 1 percent of the Nation's total air-pollution problem, airports and their surrounding neighborhoods suffer relatively high concentrations. Over Los Angeles International Airport, for example, planes daily dump nearly seven tons of particulates—dust, soot, smoke, and unburned carbon—and 115 tons of nitrogen oxides, carbon monoxide, sulfur dioxide, and hydrocarbons. Some improvement has been made, however. Today's planes are being designed to produce less pollution than earlier jets, and the airlines are modifying older engines to reduce emissions.

The mounting concern over environmental problems partly influenced the decision by Congress to halt development of the supersonic transport, or SST, in 1971. Some scientists posed major environmental questions, saying the planes would fly so high that radiation levels might be dangerous to passengers and crews. Others expressed concern for the integrity of the stratosphere, that rarefied envelope of gases which starts six to ten miles above the earth's surface. Fleets of SST's flying regular commercial routes would leave vast trails of carbon dioxide, water vapor, and other exhaust gases. Since vertical mixing takes place very slowly, pollutants would remain in the stratosphere probably more than a year. Some meteorologists speculate that this could increase cloud formation or even reduce natural ozone concentrations which shield us from ultraviolet rays of the sun.

The SST controversy also raised questions about the sonic boom, the result of the shock wave caused by a plane flying faster than sound. This wave follows a plane like a ship's wake, striking the earth below in a path up to 50 miles wide, depending on the plane's design, on its altitude, and on weather conditions.

The Federal Aviation Administration studied reaction to sonic booms in Oklahoma City, where military aircraft broke the sound barrier more than 1,200 times over a six-month period. Twenty percent of those interviewed found the boom "unacceptable," and half termed it "annoying"—though the planes were smaller than the proposed SST's and created less intense booms than anticipated.

Noise from airplanes already disturbs people living under a flight path as far as 15 miles from an airport, and by 1975, some 15 million people in this country may be affected. The new John F. Kennedy Center for the Performing Arts in Washington, D. C., required five million dollars' worth of extra sound-proofing to muffle noise from jets using National Airport nearby.

Periods of quiet seem almost to have disappeared for the urban dweller. His ears are battered by both sudden, startling sounds and by continuous background noise. Dr. Samuel Rosen of the Mount Sinai School of Medicine in New York City, has described the physiological response to startling sounds: The blood pressure increases, the pupils dilate, the eyes close, the mouth and tongue get dry, skin color pales, certain muscles contract, and the heart beats faster. "Noise pollution is a health hazard," Dr. Rosen warns.

What of prolonged exposure to noise? The Council on Environmental Quality has estimated that "16 million American workers today are threatened with hearing damage" from excess noise on the job. And, one study showed that steelworkers exposed to loud noise for long periods had an unusually large number of cardiac disorders.

Heavy city traffic frequently reaches 90 on the decibel scale, a measure of sound. A steady exposure to noise at that level, many experts agree, can cause permanent hearing loss.

According to Dr. Leo L. Beranek, a Boston acoustical engineer, "Transportation is the biggest source of rising noise levels." In his mind, much of the problem could be overcome without great outlays of funds. He estimates it would cost manufacturers about $25 a car, on a mass-production basis, to equip automobiles with more effective mufflers, better-enclosed engines, and quieter tires.

We pay our money and take our choice, to paraphrase an old saying. We bombard our ears in the name of progress. We assault our lungs for the sake of convenience. But sometimes the choices run exceedingly thin and narrow.

In the broad field of transportation, we increasingly find ourselves headed down a maze of one-way streets, squeezed by congestion, cloaked by smog, and deafened by the racket. Yet we have alternatives; we can turn around and find new ways to go—ways toward a better environment.

Advocates of a return to the external-combustion principle used by early steam-car builders, William P. Lear (top right) and Wallace L. Minto (above) check out working models of their Rankine-cycle automobile engines. In contrast to internal-combustion engines, such systems emit few pollutants, burning fuel at atmospheric pressure to turn a driving fluid into a power-producing vapor.

Engineering mockup of the proposed U. S. supersonic transport, halted by Congress in 1971, dominates a virtually deserted buildi

Transportation priorities: a looming national issue

Faced with overcrowded airports and dwindling railrc passenger service, the Nation begins to re-evaluate past transportation investments. Calling for a balanc system, citizen groups have argued that while Congre

Popular Metroliner travels the 240 miles between Washington, D. C., and New York City in three hours.

Boeing Company Developmental Center in Seattle, Washington.

...ropriated 864 million dollars for the development of a ...ersonic transport (above), only 10.5 million dollars ...t toward research and development to improve pas...ger trains in the densely populated Northeast corri-dor. After lengthy debate, Congress in 1971 withheld funds for further work on the SST. Metroliners and the experimental TurboTrain (below) continue to attract riders seeking less dependence on the airplane and the automobile.

...en track bed slows experimental New York-Boston TurboTrain to half its potential 170-mph speed.

"**L**ike many other United States cities, mine is in danger of going broke," says Mayor Terry Schrunk of Portland, Oregon. "Thousands of middle-class families have moved out to the suburbs, taking their tax dollars with them. In their place have come the aged, the handicapped, and the minorities. These people desperately need expanded city services, but instead, we've been forced to cut back."

The deputy to the Mayor of Philadelphia told me his city faces similar problems:

"In some areas of Philadelphia, overcrowding causes problems," said Anthony P. Zecca. "Three, four, even five families sometimes live in homes that formerly held only one. That means trash and garbage have to be picked up more often, and more firemen and policemen are needed. We used to have more money and need fewer services; now it's just the opposite."

San Diego, California, has problems, too. Citizens' Assistance Officer George Story told me: "The population of the northern part of our city may increase by a million within the foreseeable future. That's a lot for a city that today numbers about 700,000. Our planners are fighting for more time so they can plan for orderly growth."

The flight to the suburbs ... increasing needs and costs of city services ... businesses leaving downtown ... rising crime and unemployment ... lack of adequate planning—I heard these phrases time and again in cities across the United States.

Many cities recognize their problems and face immense tasks in overcoming them: They must rebuild themselves and revitalize their environment. The decline of downtown business districts—dying as shops, theaters, and services flee to the suburbs—is one of the city's major problems, and shows clearly the crisis faced by urban areas today.

When I visited Sacramento, California, I found a concerned community making its downtown attractive enough to lure back customers, and renovating its slums.

One Saturday morning I sat on a bench in the downtown business district of California's capital city. The springtime sun, risen hours earlier over the blue Sierra Nevada to the east, glinted off the golden dome of the capitol. All about me shoppers bustled from store to store. A sidewalk would have been crowded with jostling throngs, but here there was room —room for walking, room for benches, room

---

H. ROBERT MORRISON, *of the Society's Special Publications staff, writes of urban problems with an insight gained in visits to cities from coast to coast.*

"The 1970 United States census revealed that three times as many people live in urban areas as in rural ones."

Smog shrouds Los Angeles. Commu

URBANIZATION: THE GREAT MIGRATION

By H. Robert Morrison

...ving cars from the city to the suburbs aggravate the problem of air pollution as they attempt to escape it.

for shade trees and fountains—for the automobile is banned from nine blocks of K Street in the heart of Sacramento's shopping district.

Making shopping malls out of downtown streets is not unique to Sacramento. It has happened in Kalamazoo, Michigan, Miami Beach, Florida, and a number of other cities. In Sacramento, as elsewhere, the merchants helped to design and build the new mall.

Once K Street was a very ordinary thoroughfare, like that of the average main shopping district in a city of about a quarter of a million people. Most of its buildings still rise only three or four stories; many show a distinct demarcation where the second floor begins, between the modernized façade and the original architecture.

The new downtown

What distinguishes the area today is the open space where the street used to be. Grass, shrubs, and trees cover parts of it, but fountains and sculptures dominate it. Constructed of concrete slabs, they rise in hard-edged triangles and rectangles as high as 15 feet. One sculpture spreads a shady canopy of taut red-orange nylon, like a section cut from the crown of a giant sorcerer's hat.

"I like the mall, but not the fountains," Mrs. Harold Johnson commented. "I live in Sacramento, and I shop here just about every week. Maybe I don't understand modern art, but I don't see anything attractive about all that concrete. I'd like to see more grass and flowers and trees."

Other residents defended the sculptures. I noticed that children enjoyed climbing the slanting concrete and jumping the man-made streams—as many youngsters romped there as in the playground on the mall.

"The mall is so much nicer than a shopping center," said Mrs. Patrick Modar. "You can get out into the fresh air and sunshine here, and there's no traffic to worry about. I live in Dixon, 24 miles to the west, but I come to Sacramento as often as I can."

A plan drawn up some years ago recommended renewing the city's shopping district. A few businessmen did try to rehabilitate small parts of it, but their piecemeal efforts met with little success.

As the area declined, merchants began to move away. The Redevelopment Agency of the City of Sacramento, formed in 1950, began constructing the first three blocks of the pedestrian mall.

After the project got under way, the city and the merchants formed an assessment district

to finish the mall from 7th to 13th Streets.

The mall will connect with a new shopping plaza. Built on top of a parking garage with space for 1,600 cars, it will house more than 200 shops and several restaurants.

But shopping areas are not the only signs of Sacramento's renewal.

Lining the western approach to the capitol, sleek office buildings rise near luxury apartments. Other areas contain some federally subsidized units for low-income families.

"Once this area was the worst slum in the West," says Sacramento's Planning Director Joseph Avena. "Although it contained only 8 percent of Sacramento's land and a fifth of the city's population, this section was responsible for 26 percent of the fires, 36 percent of the juvenile delinquency, 42 percent of adult crime, and 76 percent of tuberculosis cases. It was a blighted urban core.

"So when we tackled downtown, we began on the perimeter and worked inward to contain blight. Extensive clearing was the key factor in the early renewal program."

In its concern for the new, the city has not forgotten the old. Officials plan to revive "Old Sacramento," a section that sprang up along the Sacramento River during gold rush days. There, more than 30 developers are revamping a variety of historic buildings.

The ring of hammering and the whine of an electric saw echoed through the streets as I strolled past cleared lots and buildings in all stages of disrepair and renovation.

Projects to rebuild cities and to recapture their charm are underway in many urban areas throughout the United States—even in San Francisco, the city many consider the Nation's most beautiful.

Keeping San Francisco beautiful is of deep concern to M. Justin Herman, executive director of the San Francisco Redevelopment Agency. He has spearheaded renewal efforts for that city since 1959.

An energetic, enthusiastic man, he has strong ideas about what a city should have to make it livable. "Above all, the city environment should offer variety," he told me. "Where else can an individual find so many choices—places to live and work, to shop and be entertained, and to meet other people?"

Mr. Herman said that planners should emphasize, not obscure, the geographic features which give character to a city. For example, he believes the views of the bay from San Francisco's hills have great impact on the attitudes of the city dwellers.

I mentioned the downtown Golden Gateway renewal area on the waterfront. The agency, he said, insisted that architects for the area's two large-scale developments orient tall buildings to preserve and enhance view corridors from San Francisco's hills to the bay.

Preserving a view of the bay points up the critical issue of land use facing other cities today: what to conserve as open space and what to develop. In the next decade urban expansion will cover some five million acres, an area equal to that of New Jersey. If poorly planned, this growth could damage irreplaceable land resources and much of the beauty of America's landscape.

Mr. Herman's assistant, Mrs. Margaret Tillman Brown, escorted me on a tour through the Golden Gateway Center. "This used to be San Francisco's wholesale produce market," she told me. "But as the city grew, the market became crowded and obsolete. Loading platforms on the clogged streets discouraged trucks and even fire engines from moving through the congestion.

"The city and agency moved the market from the area to the edge of the city, into new facilities with ample trucking areas," she continued. "Then the agency cleared the land. Before we go up into the center, take a look across the street and you'll see how the change has inspired owners of nearby buildings to renovate. That handsome office complex was once a rundown warehouse."

I had wondered at her expression, "go up into the center." I soon discovered what she meant. Crossing a neatly manicured park, where low, grassy mounds invited lounging, we climbed a broad stairway rising to a pedestrian bridge across Jackson Street. Below us, arcades shaded sidewalks, a bank, a supermarket, a drugstore, and other shops catering to the needs of residents.

Reaching the plaza two stories above the street, we entered another world—a world of bright, sunny promenades, fountains, and sculpture gardens. Rows of townhouses hid behind tiny green-filled private courts. High above us stood a 25-story apartment house, and beyond rose the Alcoa office building. Occasionally, sounds of impatient automobile traffic drifted up, faint intrusions on the plaza's serenity.

"Roughly one-third of the Golden Gateway renewal area is devoted to residential use, almost a fourth to commercial and office use, and the remainder is left open," remarked Mrs. Brown. "The sculptures you see throughout the area result from the agency's requirement that 1 percent of the developers' construction cost be used to purchase exterior works of art."

Flag-raising ceremony (upper) marks the dedication on August 1, 1956, of Pruitt-Igoe Apartments, a public-housing project in the heart of St. Louis, Missouri. Plagued by complex problems, among them overcrowding and poor design, the same building 13 years later (lower) stood vacant, a vandalized shell.

When the neighboring Embarcadero Center is complete and joined to the Golden Gateway Center, pedestrians will be able to stroll many blocks, two stories above street traffic.

San Franciscans should love the developments—or should they? Plans for the Embarcadero Center include a 60-story office tower, which would be the tallest in the city, and the question of skyscrapers downtown creates controversy in San Francisco today.

"High-rise office buildings concentrate thousands of people who need expensive city services—water supply, police protection, sewer systems, and so on," says Alvin Duskin, a dress manufacturer who campaigns to keep his city livable. "I'm concerned with saving the good quality of life San Francisco is famous for, as well as preserving the views of the bay."

The views may be saved, but the bay itself has been the victim of urban expansion. For a city's effect on the environment does not stop at the city limits; it can alter a much greater area. In San Francisco, surrounded on three sides by water, a major conflict concerns the extension of land into water, the filling of San Francisco Bay.

"If California ever becomes a prosperous country," wrote Richard Henry Dana in *Two Years Before the Mast*, "this bay will be the center of its prosperity." When he saw the bay in 1835, water covered almost 700 square miles at high tide. At low tide, vast marsh areas and mud flats lay exposed.

Within 20 years filling and diking began; today the bay's area at high tide has been reduced to about 400 square miles.

During the 1849 gold rush, ships that had carried hordes of prospectors were transformed into hotels and offices when their crews, infected with gold fever, abandoned them at the wharves. To make more room, entrepreneurs packed earth between the ships, thus extending the bay front.

Today, much of downtown San Francisco stands on reclaimed land. Some pilings supporting the Golden Gateway Center pierce wood of the old ships' hulls.

In the 1920's citizens diked and drained marshlands around the bay to eliminate insect breeding grounds. "Was that shrinking the bay or reclaiming the marshes?" asks Frank M. Stead, former head of the environmental division of the State Health Department.

"Of course, in those days just about everyone assumed the tidal flats and marshes were worthless, especially compared with the potential value of dry land at the edge of the bay. Only a handful of scientists realized the importance of wetlands to the ecosystems of the bay. Flooded at high tide and exposed at low, they concentrate nutrients from both land and water. For example, clams, mussels, and worms, living in the mud, eat microscopic plankton and algae and in turn are eaten by fish or birds. And the shallow waters near shore provide breeding grounds for nearly a hundred species of fish.

"We know now that mud flats and marshes in an estuary, where fresh water mixes with water from the sea, are some of the world's most valuable food-producing areas. Their destruction would knock out a vital link in the bay's ecology, endangering marine life there and in the ocean beyond.

"So trading a square mile of marsh or mud flats for a square mile of dry land," he concluded, "was a very poor bargain indeed."

During the same period, housing construction indirectly helped fill the bay. Residents of the crowded region moved up into the hills nearby; they dug basements for their new homes, and authorities permitted dumping of the excavated dirt on the tidelands. Berkeley, San Francisco, and other bayside communities then began dumping refuse on the tidelands, using sanitary landfill—layers of waste covered with earth—to extend the shore.

The filling of San Francisco Bay is only one of many examples of how cities abuse coastal waters. On the East Coast, during the last 15 years, drainage, landfill, and highway construction have ravaged almost 10 percent of the wetlands in the Chesapeake Bay area. Residents of major urban centers such as Baltimore, Richmond, and Washington create an ever-increasing demand for commercial and sport fishing on the bay. Today its wildlife must live on 50,000 fewer acres of these wetlands than in the mid-1950's.

Throughout the United States, wetlands dwindled from 74.4 million acres in 1956 to 60 million today. Dredging, draining, and filling have destroyed more than half the wetlands that existed here when Columbus made his first voyage to the New World.

If San Francisco Bay and Chesapeake Bay represent urban growth encroaching on wetlands and water, then the Everglades represent a disregard for nature in general.

Before man's incursions, the southern tip of Florida comprised a uniquely balanced ecosystem. A vast sawgrass swamp collected rainfall from thousands of square miles and filtered most of it slowly to the sea. The area supported a great variety of plants and animals, notably the Everglades kite and the wood stork, both of which are now threatened with extinction. *(Continued on page 166)*

THE AMERICAN VILLAGE

Seemingly set apart from the crucial concerns facing American cities, the village of Newfane, Vermont (left), recalls a pattern of living typical of half a century ago. Today, however, the pressures of urban expansion have visibly affected life here. Many residents depend on visitors for their livelihoods. Newfane lies in the southeastern corner of Vermont, about a three-hour drive from New York City. Tourists support the Newfane Village Traders' country store, the Four Columns Inn, and the Newfane Inn.

This village and others like it also have an effect, though less obvious, on city dwellers. For many urbanites, villages represent an ideal—an escape. But few people can live in such communities, so they learn to adapt to different environments. Other communities besides Newfane show how Americans shape their dream of the good life into the varied molds of local neighborhoods.

Along 18th Street, N.W., in Washington, D. C., an active, diverse community in the midst of change struggles to prevent the neighborhood from turning into a slum. In the new town of Reston, Virginia, planners translated the very idea of neighborhood into their design. Such a technique costs more but adds another dimension to the traditional method of suburban development followed by builders of nearby Sterling Park, Virginia.

iumned Windham County Courthouse fronts the Newfane, Vermont, common.

Free for the day, schoolchildren escape homeward through fallen leaves on Newfane's common, past the spires of the Union Ha

Mirror reflects flea-market browser.

Haven in Vermont

Established atop nearby Newfane Hill in 1787 and moved to its present location in 1825, Newfane, Vermont, wears its age with visible pride and grace. Its roots remain in an era in which villages sprouted in response to the needs of nearby farmers. Newfane then provided a focus for a rural county. Its inn lodged litigants, lawyers, and judges come to circuit court, along with traveling merchants and other wayfarers. Its community hall sheltered temporal celebrations, and its Congregational Church spiritual ones. In the village lived the special-ist, such as the blacksmith, who ga nered his livelihood from large nu bers of customers living in the s rounding area. Newfane existed the working adults who built it; the two-room schoolhouse stands not the common but at the edge of tov as if built as an afterthought.

Today—one reflection of change schools and the taxes supporti them form a major topic of convers tion in Newfane, although one re dent recalled that "at the last tov meeting we spent more time d cussing snowplows than school To increasing numbers of touris Newfane offers a measure of nost gia, at a price. A small billboard i field just north of the village pr

r left), the Congregational Church, the Windham County Courthouse (center), and the Newfane Inn (far right).

aims "The Original Newfane Flea arket." Here the past turns a profit, d age becomes a salable asset. But for elderly people, small villges like Newfane offer few special dvantages. The towns were built for d by settlers in life's prime, so the ied, as well as the young, find few cilities here for their special needs, though neighborliness and the miliar beauty of the changing seaons provide a sense of unity. Mrs. arold Cobb, who served nearby ownshend as postmistress until her tirement, finds shopping difficult, it such problems do not dampen r spirits. "It's such a lovely time of ar," she said one bright spring day, when everything's coming to life."

Mrs. Harold Cobb, a 50-year resident of nearby Townshend, smiles from her window.

149

Putting down roots

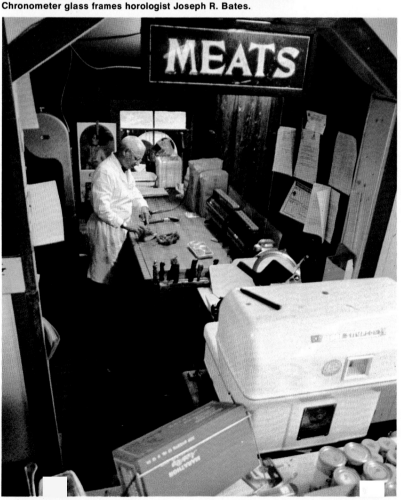

Newfaners adapt in a number of ways to the chang[e] about them. Farms, once the backbone of village trade, [no] longer support it—the last working farm in Newfane Tow[n]ship closed down in 1970. "If I had to rely on this area [for] my business, I'd go broke," said Joseph R. Bates (left)[. In] his shop, called The British Clockmaker, he rebuilds, [re]pairs, and hand-duplicates fine antique clocks for cus[to]mers throughout the United States.

Bill Schommer (opposite), a graphic designer who on[ce] lived in New York City, vacationed nearby and liked [the] area so much he looked for a way to stay. "At firs[t I] planned to drive into New York once a week and work h[alf] at home. Then my wife Shirley and I found this old st[ore] for sale. It takes up most of our time now," he said.

Albert Marcott (below left), meat cutter in the Newfa[ne] Store, moved to Townshend—five miles distant—in 19[ ] because he had grown tired of city living. "The day aft[er I] arrived, Earl Morse, the owner of this store, called a[nd] asked me if I wanted a job," he recalled. "It was t[hat] simple." Don Williams, 19 (below right), has lived in Ne[w]fane all his life. "I don't have anything holding me her[e,"] he declared, "but nothing's pulling me away, eithe[r."]

Chronometer glass frames horologist Joseph R. Bates.

Albert Marcott trims pork chops behind the meat counter at the Newfane Store.

Afternoon feeding time: Don Williams ha[

Schommer, a village trader of Newfane, takes a break from raking leaves in front of his store.

oad of silage for the cows at Courtney Nau's farm in Brookline Township, across the West River from Newfane.

Apartment houses, rowhouses, and streetside shops crowd an 18th Street neighborhood in northwest Washington, D. C.

Neighbors stop to chat on Belmont Road near 18th Street.

During a Saturday morning football game at a neighborho

A metropolitan neighborhood

ancy brickwork, carved lintels, brownstone steps, turrets, and cornices—the embellishments once flaunted by the well-to-do of the city—survive alongside the tenements and rowhouses on 18th Street in northwest Washington, . C. But the backs of these mansions contrast sharply ith their still-proud fronts: Ladders and landings of fire scapes zigzag from one apartment to another.

Years ago the broad thoroughfare formed a backdrop r the leisure of Washington's prosperous. Gentlemen silk hats escorted bejeweled ladies into a glittering eater, where today only a brick-strewn vacant lot re-ains. The street has become a crossroads for different lasses of people, with far different concerns. In some locks, flowers brighten gardens, the pride of homeowners. he low rent charged for many of the apartments attracts those who have but little to pay: the poor and near poor, the out-of-work, and the underemployed. The busboy, the dishwasher, and the yet unrecognized artist can afford to live here. City buses bound in various directions stop nearby, a necessity for those who cannot bear the expense of an automobile.

These people cope daily with the problems of the inner city. "Drug pushers are all over the place," a teen-ager observed. Said a merchant: "I keep the door to my store locked most of the time. People living around here are very nice, but I don't let in suspicious-looking strangers." With the recognition of the area's many problems has come a determination to do something about them, and the future would seem to hold hope.

Even a short walk along 18th Street reveals a strong sense of neighborhood—a feeling of community identity. "A few years ago, you never saw anything like now," one resident remarked in wonder. "Look at those youngsters. They've got pride and spirit. Things sure have changed."

layground, a young ball carrier twists toward a diminishing gap in the defensive line.

153

Teen-agers spruce up the RAP Shop.

His shop window gives Tung Foo Lee a streetside vantage.

Customer inspects produce at a sidewalk stand.

Street-oriented living

Store-front establishments along a half-dozen blocks of 18th Street offer residents a variety of goods and services. Latin Americans have bought familiar foods and spices at La Sevillana, Inc., for 17 years. "I cannot move from here," said proprietor T. A. Mateos (opposite). "I'm 74 years old, and I don't have the energy or the spirit to start somewhere else." Tung Foo Lee (above) has operated a carry-out restaurant in the neighborhood for the past 16 of his 85 years. Regional Addiction Prevention (RAP), a private self-help, nonprofit corporation, fights drug abuse by re-educating addicts. Area youngsters can borrow toys from a library (below), thus enriching their preschool learning. A curbside vendor (left) sells fresh fruit and vegetables; his stand bears a sign welcoming food stamps.

Susanna Gray, her infant son Joshua, and Elizabeth Enwright rest on the steps of the Toy Lending Library.

Variety of imported wares surrounds T. A. Mateos and his granddaughter Katrina Lawson, 4, in his Spanish grocery.

Artist Arthur Beatty demonstrates clay-sculpture technique during a class at The New Thing, an 18th Street community organization

Reformed addicts Peggy Romaine (left) and Barbara Farr sing at a RAP residence.

City melting pot

"So many different kinds of people live here," says artist Arthur Beatty. "that it's almost like all of New York City crammed into a few blocks. And it's close to a lot of galleries and theaters. That's why I like living in the neighborhood." Here onetime drug addicts begin new lives; a Legionnaire walks down the sidewalk in uniform; youths in bell bottoms argue politics and morality; and carpenters work through the autumn afternoon too busy to take much notice of others.

at also sponsors a jazz workshop.

Carpenters work atop a truck bed.

Ernest Graves: World War I veteran

Two young people pause before an 18th Street doorway.

Heron House, a 15-story apartment building, towers over Lake Anne Village Center in the new town of Reston, Virginia.

new town
ises in Virginia

eston, Virginia, a totally planned
ew town 18 miles west of Washing-
n, D. C., represents one attempt to
mprove urban environment. In 1971
ore than 14,000 people lived here
apartments, townhouses, and de-
ched houses. Planners contemplate
opulation of 75,000 by 1980. Shops,
restaurant, a library, and other com-
unity services line Washington Plaza
ght) in Lake Anne Center, focal point
r the first of five villages.

Nearly half of Reston's residential
ea will remain open space; light
dustries will occupy some 1,300 of
e total 7,400 acres. "Many of us
el we're participating in an experi-
ent just by living here," said one resi-
nt, "and we want it to succeed." One
sult: a willingness to try new ideas.
"I doubt that most parishes would
cept me as readily as this one does,"
ated the Reverend Embry C. Rucker
elow), Vicar of the Episcopal Congre-
tion of the Church of Reston for the
st two years. "For example, I don't
nt a church building. I can devote
ore time to community service if I
n't have to worry about furniture."

Grocery shoppers share Washington Plaza with patrons of many community services.

e Reverend Embry C. Rucker strides toward the coffeehouse where he conducts Episcopal services each Sunday.

Outstretched hands reach toward the audience as The Inner Voices, a group of prisoners from the Lorton Correctional Facilit

Bus riders drink coffee, read, and chat on the way to work.

"Bringing people together"

The Common Ground (above), a nonprofit community co
feehouse staffed by about 80 volunteers, also serves
the Sunday meeting place for the Episcopal congreg
tion and as the headquarters for the Reverend Embry
Rucker. "I see myself as an 'enabler,'" he says, "som
one who brings together people who want to solve pro
lems. For example, many young people and housewiv
who wanted to work part-time couldn't find jobs, so
helped set up an employment agency here for them."

In their spare time, Restonians participate in ma
group activities. One of the largest and most active orga
zations, the Reston Community Association, sponsors c
zen committees concerned with Reston's architectu
health, safety, and recreation. The group also offers cha
ter bus transportation (left) between Reston and ma
employment centers, a profit-making operation. Ride
publish a newsletter and celebrate at an annual "Bus Ba

JONATHAN S. BLAIR

amatize the dangers of drug abuse at The Common Ground. Mr. Rucker stands against the counter.

mming team practices in the indoor pool of the Reston Golf and Country Club.

Morning wind whips strollers beside sun-dappled Lake Anne.

Autumn leaves veil Mrs. Elizabeth Espino as she carries her son Peter along one of Reston's walks.

JONATHAN S. BLAIR

Thirteen-year-old Alicia Maguire: "I like living in Reston."

Reston's magnetism

"It took my husband and me a while to get used to living here," recalled Mrs. Elizabeth Espino (opposite lower). "We had moved here from a home in the country, and at first, Reston seemed too crowded. At one point, we even decided to move away. But suddenly we found we couldn't. We knew we'd miss Reston too much."

Residents of the new community feel it offers them a lot: quiet moments beside the lake, bustling activity around Washington Plaza, leisurely walks along tree-shaded paths, and the chance to participate in sports ranging from polo to Little League baseball. When asked how she liked living in a new town, 13-year-old Alicia Maguire (above) replied, "New? Reston's already seven years old. But I guess you could call it new— lots of towns are older than that."

rk Diane Brooks watches from a shop overlooking the Lake Anne Village Center.

Set on green lawns, houses in Sterling Park, Virginia, 28 miles west of Washington, D. C., line streets in a pattern familiar to resident

A converted barn houses the Sterling Park Volunteer Fire Department and other community activities.

On the urban fringe: promise of a self-contained community

Row upon row, new houses stand among neatly kept lawns of Sterling Park, Virginia, not far from Reston. Begun in 1962, the community will eventually house more than 20,000 residents. Most will live in detached houses, others in townhouses and apartments.

Among the features of this community, planners included underground utilities and thoroughfares separated from residential streets. Growing numbers of prospective home buyers find many attractions: a shopping center with more than 25 stores and a movie theater, a golf course, a community center (opposite lower), a swimming pool, a baseball field, tennis courts, and elementary schools within walking distance. A three-bedroom house here sells for as low as $26,900; at Reston, prices for detached houses begin at about $32,500.

Tom Quinn, president of the U. S. Steel Corporation subsidiary developing Sterling Park, does not want the community to become a densely populated urban area, preferring to continue its predominant pattern of individual houses. He hopes a 547-acre industrial park will attract enough companies to enable many residents to work near home, and he believes this will happen as nearby Dulles International Airport becomes busier.

The financial difficulties of Sterling Park's original development corporation—and the resulting takeover by an industrial giant—reflect one of the greatest problems plaguing builders of new communities. To develop effectively, they must have available huge sums of money.

f many suburbs across the Nation.

embers of the Sterling Park Volunteer Rescue Squad arrive for a weekly meeting.

Frank C. Craighead, Sr., has studied the ecology of southern Florida since 1951; for the past five years, the National Geographic Society has helped support his research there.

"In his greed, man could see only rich farmland under the clear waters of the Everglades," he said. "His first efforts centered on draining. Water which had formerly filtered slowly seaward rushed through canals, carrying tons of organic ooze which filled coastal bays and threatened the fishing industry. Then, builders divided much of the reclaimed farmland into lots and constructed thousands of houses."

The U. S. Army Corps of Engineers built levees and canals, created reservoirs, diverted water from the developed areas, and regulated its flow to the Everglades. Levees form a large water storage area and block the normal drainage course to the Everglades National Park. During the heavy rainfall years of 1968-70 the engineers periodically released water through openings in the levee in amounts far exceeding the park's needs, according to some biologists. This surplus often raised the water level of the marsh, causing destruction of vegetation and wildlife.

A year later, severe drought, aggravated by flood-control measures, killed much of the wildlife and threatened south Florida's supply of drinking water. Fires swept more than half a million acres, burning the rich, peaty earth over wide areas.

"Such destruction will happen again and again," Dr. Craighead declared, "unless we can restore the marvelously balanced ecosystem of 70 years ago. We must learn to view each project not as just an engineering problem, but as a matter of ecology as well."

The abuse of land

As people fled the congested cities, their great migration to the suburbs resulted in haphazard, careless development that exploited the land around ever-expanding metropolitan areas. Between 1960 and 1970, suburbs were responsible for 84 percent of the growth of metropolitan areas. The 1970 United States census revealed that three times as many people live in urban areas as in rural ones. For the first time, more Americans live in suburbs than in cities.

The suburbs of Atlanta, Georgia, illustrate the penalties of this expansion. Five counties around Atlanta—Cobb, Fulton, Clayton, De-Kalb, and Gwinnett—bear the brunt of the growth. A tour through them quickly reveals that much of the problem here stems from

land abuse. Acres of earth lie denuded—raw, red clay furrowed by erosion.

I spoke with three men who have spent their lives in the Soil Conservation Service fighting man's ignorance in the use of land: Assistant State Conservationist Robert W. Oertel, Area Engineer Earl Jenkins, and Area Conservationist Robert Peeples.

"The things we learned in rural areas," Bob Oertel emphasized, "have application for cities. If you cut down trees and scrape away grass and topsoil, the land can't hold as much water. So it runs off quickly, carrying topsoil. The silt chokes streams, increasing the danger of floods, not to mention the immediate results of erosion and ugliness."

As we talked, they gave me an example of how one man's use of the land created problems for others. The developer of a Fulton County subdivision created a two-acre lake, and nestled attractive homes in the woods around it. Then another developer began clearing land beside a stream that ran into the lake, sawing down trees, and cutting streets in the area. Erosion soon started.

"The stream has silted in and is killing the lake," said Mr. Oertel. "Once it was an attractive asset to the community. Now mud bars and murky water are making it a liability."

Robert Peeples pointed out another potentially troublesome spot. "One new apartment complex," he told me, "is partially built on what was once a ten-acre lake, a natural storage area for floodwaters. About 80 percent has been filled in, though; only about two acres of brown, silt-laden water remains." The fountain jetting water at one end of the pond seems a mere token compared to the natural beauty that has been demolished here.

"The way they've graded and built on the floodplain," added Mr. Jenkins, "may be setting residents up for a surprise. Some night after a heavy rain, people in the lower apartments may step out of bed into water from the nearby stream overflowing its banks."

"That certainly won't happen now in neighboring Gwinnett County," Mr. Oertel told me. "Its citizens adopted a strong ordinance restricting the development of floodplains to recreational and other uses that don't interfere with the land's natural functions."

"The most intense soil loss I've ever observed," he declared at another point, "comes from construction sites." Pointing to land gullied by erosion, he said that seeding it to prevent soil runoff should have cost no more than $500 an acre. Now it will cost much more just to replace the lost earth, and the damage downstream may never be repaired. "Each year they are losing about six inches—a thousand tons—of soil per acre," he estimated.

One state, Maryland, recently adopted regulations requiring builders to prevent erosion during construction. The move came partly in response to the rampant land development around our Nation's Capital. Though all Washington suburbs in Virginia and Maryland have been subjected to the great land rush, it has been especially apparent in Prince Georges County, Maryland.

Prince Georges County's population zoomed from almost 200,000 in 1950 to more than 650,000 in 1970. Personal income soared to more than two billion dollars a year. "Notwithstanding this economic growth, services haven't kept up with the needs of residents," says Harry E. Taylor, Jr., an attorney who lives in the county. He has been active in its government for years and presently heads the Total Environmental Action Committee there. "The schools and roads are heavily overcrowded," he added, "and there has been a severe problem of overflowing sewers."

During the late 1950's and early 1960's, builders were granted scores of permits to rezone rural land for apartments, often without regard for the county's general plan for development. In 1963 one developer promised a zoning-board hearing that he would protect the natural beauty of a heavily wooded site. Today apartments stand on the land, which is nearly bare of trees. When it rains, silt-laden rivulets running down erosion-scarred banks carry soil into drainage ditches. To prevent these practices from recurring, the county has now set restrictions on future development of land.

"Prince Georges County demonstrates the fallacy of mistaking short-run economic gains for long-term progress. When we despoil nature while building our urban environment, we will some day have to spend a lot of money to make it livable," says Norman G. Kurland, vice president of Agenda 2000, an innovative city and regional planning group with offices in Washington, San Francisco, and Guatemala City, Guatemala.

"So it is in our interest to plan now for the restoration and preservation of a healthy urban environment," Mr. Kurland added. "We must implement these plans even if we must radically overhaul outdated tax laws, costly and restrictive labor practices, and obsolete corporate financing policies."

Tomorrow's planners undoubtedly will benefit from lessons learned in new towns like those springing up near Washington: Reston, Virginia, and Columbia, Maryland. Both will become complete cities with industries, schools, parks, and recreational facilities. Residents can choose from among detached houses, townhouses, high-rise apartments, and garden apartments.

I walked along one of the paths used by strollers and bicyclists in Columbia. Completely separate from streets, this network of trails links neighborhoods with each other and with shopping malls and recreational centers.

Everywhere a pleasing landscape met my eye—trees, grass, sparkling streams. Mallards gabbled at the shore of Wilde Lake. Townhouses cast reflections in the water. Two kites tugged at their strings without danger of tangling in power lines—in Columbia's residential areas all utility lines are underground. Nonetheless, among the town's thousands of trees at least a few must surely be kite-eaters.

Walking in Columbia was fun, and it showed; when I passed strangers, we smiled.

James W. Rouse, president of The Rouse Company, also smiled when asked about his new town. Rouse's firm and the Connecticut General Life Insurance Company began developing Columbia in 1966.

"We had two objectives," he recalled: "to build a city and to respect the land. We wanted to dignify, not degrade, the environment. We wanted to ennoble the landscape."

He walked to a window in his office and looked across Kittamaqundi, first of the city's four man-made lakes to be completed, and named for an American Indian word meaning "settlement" or "village."

"This hasn't been a noble sacrifice," he added. "Nor has it been a gigantic financial investment. We've created values greater than the costs. We believe we've earned a greater return on our investment by respecting the land."

That respect includes maintaining stream valleys and forest lines. It means spending a million dollars to plant 70,000 trees and bushes along the streets and plazas, and moving 5,000 others to parks and open spaces. Planners began by identifying land conditions to be honored. They started with a topographic outline map and added overlays to identify streams, slopes, and tree lines.

"We wanted the land to speak out to us, to tell us what should be developed and what should be left alone," he said. "Thus, we set aside 3,200 of the 13,700 acres as permanent open space."

Nevertheless, soil erosion remains a problem, though controlled somewhat by a number of preventive measures, among them scheduling construction to prevent bulldozed land from standing idle.

"If you read the local press, you'd sometimes think we are villains in soil erosion," Mr. Rouse remarked. "But soil conservationists use us as an example in showing how to carry out good control procedures. We are doing better than most — much better — but not well enough yet to satisfy ourselves or the public." In fact, perhaps the most severe criticism comes from the residents themselves.

"I believe Rouse really has good intentions, but he is caught squarely between conflicting forces," said Dr. James Olsson, who has lived in Columbia since 1968. "He has to contend with builders, who are primarily concerned with making a profit, and also with residents who want to preserve a good environment."

I asked Dr. Olsson why he decided to move to Columbia.

"First of all," he replied, "it is located conveniently near my work in Baltimore. Second, we liked the styling and cost of the home we bought here. And last, we enjoy the conveniences and the attractiveness of Columbia. The recreational facilities are close by, and Columbia is a beautiful place in which to live.

"We formerly lived in an apartment in Prince Georges County, and before that on Capitol Hill in Washington, D. C., so we had already tried conventional city and suburban living.

"When we arrived, Columbia's development was still in the early stages. Woods surrounded us on three sides, and I could exercise Hildy, our German short-haired pointer, nearby. Now the area is more built-up, and I have to take her by car to a place where she can run."

He thought for a moment, then continued. "I've talked with a lot of my neighbors, and we agree that Columbia offers much more than an unplanned community — more open space, more recreational facilities. After you visit a typical suburb, it's good to come back here.

"My wife June says that shopping for food and some other items is convenient; for clothes we still have to drive to Baltimore or Washington. That may change when our downtown shopping mall opens this summer."

Although it may not yet be a prototype of the "new American city," as some persons call it, Columbia has one advantage over most other cities: It was planned before construction started. Less fortunate than Mr. Rouse are municipal officials throughout the country, who must start with existing urban conditions in dealing with environmental goals.

"Building a new town like Columbia, which started from scratch, does not answer the problems of the older cities, but it does offer some lessons in how to construct a good community," said Leo A. Molinaro, president of the American City Corporation. Business leaders of Hartford, Connecticut, have retained the corporation, a subsidiary of The Rouse Company, to plan and implement a program that would relate the inner city to the communities surrounding it.

The immense difficulties cities encounter in carrying out their redevelopment programs lead them to look for federal help in solving many of their problems. Responding to the increasing needs of urban areas, the Government has created a number of programs, among them public housing.

Federally funded housing began in 1933 with the Public Works Administration, which built and operated public housing projects. Federal spending on construction aimed at boosting both the national economy and the sagging housing industry. Just four years later, Congress passed legislation providing federal funds to local housing authorities to build new homes for low income families.

Buildings like fortresses

Charles Agle, now an architect and planner in Princeton, New Jersey, worked as a planning executive with the Federal Public Housing Agency from 1935 to 1944.

"We wanted to replace slums with decent housing," he recalls, "but we ended up with fortress-like projects because officials insisted that the buildings be designed to last at least 60 years and to crowd in at least as many people as were already living in the area."

After World War II, Congress passed the Housing Act of 1949, which proclaimed the goal of a decent home and a suitable living environment for every American family. It created an urban renewal program, provided some assistance in housing people displaced by slum clearance, and authorized construction of 810,000 new units.

Although Congress intended the act to be administered locally, the Federal Government established overly rigid restrictions which weakened chances of the program's success. By 1967 — eighteen years after the passage of the act — only a little more than half the authorized number of units had been built — and most of them were in areas where high concentrations of poor people already lived.

One of those projects was Pruitt-Igoe, built in the heart of St. Louis, Missouri, at a cost of 36 million dollars. Its 11-story buildings contained nearly 3,000 apartments — a density of more than 50 dwelling units per acre.

At least one architectural magazine hailed Pruitt-Igoe as the modern solution to public housing. An innovation in the buildings was the "skip-stop" elevator. It stopped only at the first, fourth, seventh, and tenth floors. Architects hoped this arrangement would help neighbors to meet when walking between floors and thus promote a sense of community. To discourage loitering, the buildings contained no public rest rooms: A child playing outside had to return to his apartment to use the bathroom, even if it was 11 floors up.

Caught between soaring costs and little money, architects cut corners: no balconies, few playgrounds with adequate equipment, exposed steam pipes inside apartments—a hazard to young children.

"Pruitt-Igoe is a product of the times," a local civic leader told me. "At first segregated, with blacks living in Pruitt and whites living in Igoe, it was soon desegregated and rapidly became 99 percent black. It's difficult enough to find reasonably priced housing for a large family if you're a middle-class white; if you're black and poor, it's nearly impossible."

Within two years 2,640 families lived in Pruitt-Igoe, a 92-percent occupancy. It has never been that full since. When I visited the project in 1971, about 800 families lived there.

"As near as I can remember, it wasn't too bad at first," recalled Benny Burnett, as the elevator groaned its way up to the tenth floor. He has lived 16 of his 21 years in Pruitt-Igoe. "I spent a lot of my time on the basketball court; there wasn't much else to do."

The elevator stopped, and we stepped out into a lobby resounding to the shouts of children at play. A dozen preschoolers, who had taken it over for a lively game of kickball, made way for us as we walked to the stairway at the end. It took a moment for my eyes to adjust, for grimy window screens filtered out most of the afternoon sun.

When I looked around, I realized that I hadn't seen a building resembling this since my military training days. Concrete surrounded me; concrete-block walls, concrete ceiling, concrete floor. I couldn't imagine having to live there.

The stairways were worse: narrow, cramped, lit only by an occasional bare bulb. It was a long walk down.

I began to comprehend what Leroy Graham, manager of the project, had told me. "The eleventh floor is no place to raise nine kids. They don't have anywhere to play but the halls. You can't keep an eye on them in the playground when you're that far away."

I asked Mr. Graham what could be done to improve Pruitt-Igoe. "Tear it down," he replied without a moment's hesitation. "Don't

get me wrong," he added. "We need more public housing, not less. But not like this."

Pruitt-Igoe became a home of last resort within a few years of its opening. Some fortunate tenants moved to better public housing; others crowded into slums that were not Government-built, and not so dreary or dangerous.

I asked architect Charles Fleming of St. Louis what lies ahead for Pruitt-Igoe, and he spread a thick sheaf of blueprints across his drawing table to show me his vision. "A study revealed that it would cost 38 million dollars to make Pruitt-Igoe a decent, safe, sanitary place to live. Here's what we can do for a little more than half that much.

"We'll begin by tearing down the unoccupied buildings and putting up 600 garden-style apartments clustered around open courtyards —no high-rises this time. After we fill them with families now living in Pruitt-Igoe, we'll demolish the last of the dilapidated structures and add 300 more living units and a commercial center with stores, offices, and a community center. The stores are important; residents now can't buy even an aspirin within walking distance after 5 o'clock.

"We're trying to capture an architectural feeling of something warm and alive," he continued as he leafed through the drawings. "When we finish, we'll have lowered the density to about 17 families per acre. And we've included seven acres of parkland."

I asked him when he expected construction to begin.

"Well, we hope to avoid past mistakes. We consulted with families there and incorporated their ideas. They live there, and they know the problems better than anyone else.

"We finished our preliminary planning in May of 1971, and we hope to begin in the fall if we can get federal approval."

By mid-year, St. Louis had not yet received that approval. "We haven't made a decision either way," said George Creel, director of public affairs for the Department of Housing and Urban Development. "We have a number of possible solutions to the problems of Pruitt-Igoe under review, but we haven't settled on any particular one yet."

The project must have the sanction of the Federal Government, the source of money for public housing. Rent money pays only for operating expenses and maintenance.

"We found ourselves in the position of operating a hundred million dollars' worth of property, and not having a penny for repairs," says Thomas P. Costello, acting director of the St. Louis Housing Authority. "The problems of Pruitt-Igoe demanded so much of our budget that we had no money left for even the most basic preventive maintenance in our other projects."

Only recently has Congress slowly begun to recognize how desperate are the needs of many public housing tenants—the chronically poor. To aid the harried housing authorities, Congress allocated additional money in 1969 to provide some social services, help with maintenance, and reduce rents to 25 percent of the tenant's income. Previously, some tenants on fixed pensions paid as much as 75 percent of their income for housing.

Not all public housing looks like Pruitt-Igoe. Experts across the country recommended that I visit Akron, Ohio, if I wanted to observe a successful public housing program.

"You can see for yourself," said Jack Saferstein, the tough, efficient executive director of the Akron Metropolitan Housing Authority. "Here's one of our *developments*," he said, as we pulled into a small parking lot. "I don't call them projects once they're completed."

Pleasant townhouses clustered around a neat court; the playground was visible from every house. Underground utility lines kept the sky clear of wires, and a community TV antenna eliminated the need for a forest of bristling masts.

"How old are these houses?" I asked.

"Just about a year," he replied. "They replaced nine derelict buildings, seven of which were condemned."

Not a scrap of loose paper fluttered among the shrubbery. Shining windows and scrubbed steps gave unmistakable evidence of the tenants' pride in their homes.

"I keep my developments small and scattered," Mr. Saferstein told me as we drove across town. "That way we don't create instantly identifiable colonies of public housing. And I hold down density to a maximum of 12 units per acre. Two-bedroom apartments account for half the units in each development—that automatically limits the number of children in it.

"Children create a terrific amount of wear and tear on housing—all housing, not just ours. So we try to place large families in single homes here and there throughout the city, rather than lumping them all together in one overcrowded spot."

He turned down a gravel road toward row upon row of plastic-wrapped cubes, each cube about 12 feet square. "Here's what makes it all possible," he said. "Factory-built housing. There's a finished section of a house inside each cube, complete with copper plumbing, electrical wiring, carpeting or vinyl flooring

(depending on the room), heating and air-conditioning ducts, and even light bulbs already in the sockets.

"I maintain an inventory of about 2,000 modules, the equivalent of some 500 houses. Once I have a location prepared, I can erect a house on it and be ready to move in a family in less than a week.

"We're trying to operate just like private enterprise, but our profit is people—people living in decent, safe, sanitary homes," he stated. "And I can build 2,000 more units by the end of 1972, if I can just get the money."

There it was again, the same refrain I had heard from coast to coast.

"Solutions to the problems that threaten to make ghost towns of our cities within this decade will have federal dollars as the chief variable of effectiveness," Mayor Wesley C. Uhlman of Seattle, Washington, declared. "Soon we must take seriously the advice of John Kenneth Galbraith, noted economist: 'Having contemplated all other remedies for urban decay, we must now try using money.'

"There are precedents," Mayor Uhlman continued. "Look at international affairs. Through federal policy in a war effort, we defeated and laid waste much of Germany and Japan. But when the war was over we committed our Nation to a total renewal effort for our former enemies to put them on a firm basis with other self-sufficient countries.

"If we can do this for Japan or Germany, why can't we do it for Seattle, Newark, Cleveland, New York, or any other city on the brink of catastrophe?

"Again through federal policy, our Nation has financed and encouraged the abandonment of central cities. As FHA and VA loans became available, builders naturally went to the suburbs, which offered a greater supply of land for new homes. We built highways and the basic economic and service infrastructure to support them. Central city taxes went up, living quality went down. Meanwhile, people, capital, and growth went to the suburbs. Over the last two decades in most large cities, this has added up to something similar to a bombed-out Germany and Japan. And, the Federal Government has responded only with half measures and piecemeal programs."

Is there hope for America's cities? In the words of Mayor John Lindsay of New York: "As we look to the year 2000, the cities are all that we can see. With all our problems and frustrations, cities are the future.

"The cities can be governed. They can be livable. And if the world can save its cities, it can save itself."

SAN FRANCISCO AND ITS BAY

The bay makes San Francisco. It helps temper the climate. It offers recreation—swimming, fishing, sailing. It shelters ocean vessels in an incomparable harbor. From innumerable points within the city, the bay gives urbanites a chance to enjoy refreshing vistas of sparkling water.

This resource must have seemed inexhaustible to Forty-Niners arriving during the gold rush. Then the bay covered nearly 700 square miles at high tide. Soon thereafter, San Francisco and nearby cities found their landward growth limited by ridges of the Coast Range. So they began expanding into the bay by dumping refuse and earth into shallow shore areas—one example of the ways many cities affect their environment.

Today, the bay's high tides cover only about 400 square miles. Filled land has replaced water to provide sites for houses, drive-in-theaters, freeways, salt evaporating ponds, oil refineries, airports, and dumps.

Lone ship crossing sun-spangled San Francisco Bay heads south toward Angel Island.

To drivers inching across the San Francisco-Oakland Bay Bridge, the bay becomes more obstacle than asset.

Commuting by ferry

Most commuters who cross San Francisco Bay en route to and from their jobs depend on the landmark Golden Gate Bridge and the newer, longer San Francisco-Oakland Bay Bridge (above). Their automobiles regularly jam the spans and clog San Francisco's streets. The city has more automobiles per square mile than any other in the U. S. To ease Golden Gate Bridge traffic, transit officials in 1970 began operating a passenger ferry (below) between San Francisco and Sausalito, in Marin County to the north. It proved an immediate success.

Many regular riders claim the same spot every day for reading (opposite upper), watching the lights of the city (opposite lower). A concession sells coffee and pastries in the morning; in the evening, homebound workers can buy a cocktail. Although the modest 50-cent, one-way fare does not cover the ferry's operating expenses, transit officials make up the difference from bridge-toll profits.

Ferry M. V. *Golden Gate* provides a popular alternative to automobile commuting.

Glowing lights of San Francisco silhouett

rning commuter finds time to read as the ferry passes Angel Island on its half-hour run to San Francisco.

meward-bound workers riding the ferry to Sausalito.

JONATHAN S. BLAIR; NATIONAL GEOGRAPHIC PHOTOGRAPHER JAMES L. STANFIELD (OPPOSITE MIDDLE AND BOTTOM)

Garbage and trash hauled from San Francisco pile up beside the bay at Candlestick Cove. Until 1971 about half a million tons

Jet takes off from a runway built on bay fill.

Junked cars foul the bay at Butchertown.

Gas storage tank dwarfs Potrero Hill residences.

use a year ended up here.

bay despoiled

en acting in ignorance, man has
ned vast portions of San Francisco
y. In 1970, 38 percent of the area's
use accumulated in dump sites in
d beside the bay. Industrial com-
xes crowd close to residences,
d towering refineries and shallow
aporating ponds of salt works re-
ce marshes and mud flats.

uch wetlands form a vital link in
e ecosystem of the bay, for they
cumulate nutrients for crustaceans,
n, and birds. Their destruction
eatens wildlife throughout the bay.
nkyards clutter shallow water with
to hulks. Fill land extending from
e shore has become an airport,
minating breeding grounds for
re than a hundred species of fish.
hough construction of treatment
nts has lessened pollution from
wage, periodic overflows of storm
ter pour tons of waste into the bay.

Sign warns of danger at Bolinas Bay, where herons and other rare birds nest.

Richmond plant of Standard Oil of California reaches onto bay landfill.

Newark salt harvester gathers crystals from 54 square miles of former marshland.

Embattled skyline

Controversy rages over the question of skyscrapers in San Francisco. The skyline, increasingly embellished with towering structures, has undergone more dramatic change within the past five years than at any other time since the city rebuilt from the ruins of the 1906 earthquake and fire. Boosters refer to this growth as

Viewed from Telegraph Hill, skyscrapers dominate the San Francisco skyline.

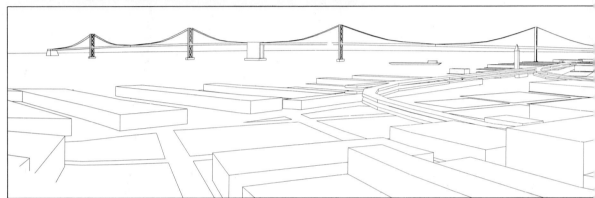

The view southeastward from San Francisco's Telegraph Hill appears in outline above much as it looked in 1960; structures built since then do not appear. A computer plotted the drawings above and below from numbers representing the dimensions, shape, and location of each building. Arthur Paradis, founder of Computer Graphics in Berkeley, conceived the program, and with financial assistance from the architectural firm of Skidmore, Owings & Merrill, directed the electronic

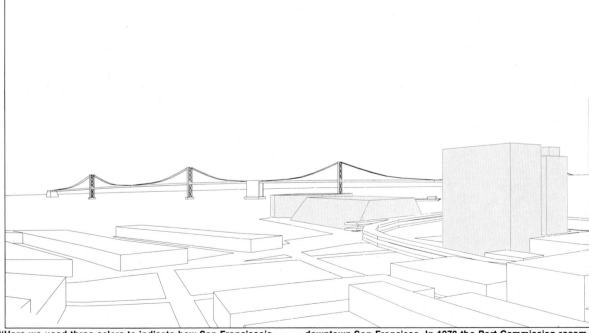

"Here we used three colors to indicate how San Francisco's skyline may look in 1980," said Mr. Paradis. "Black outlines represent structures standing in 1970, blue identifies buildings under construction, and red shows other buildings proposed by mid-1970." Whether it will actually look like this depends on the outcome of the current struggle over skyscrapers in downtown San Francisco. In 1970 the Port Commission recommended approval of a proposal by the United States Steel Corporation to replace five obsolete piers with a passenger terminal (in red, extreme left) and a 550-foot-high office building (mostly hidden by two red buildings in foreground) on a platform extending a thousand feet into the bay. Instead, the naissance. Critics, claiming it will ~~br~~ing problems similar to those New ~~Yo~~rk City experiences, call it the "~~M~~anhattanization" of San Fran~~ci~~sco. Until recently, no one could ~~pr~~edict exactly how a planned build~~in~~g would relate to the rest of the city ~~wh~~en completed. Today, with the ~~he~~lp of the computer, architects can ~~co~~mpare the view from Telegraph Hill ~~in~~ 1970 (left) with that of 1960 (imme~~di~~ately below), or even with a pro~~je~~ction for ten years ahead (bottom).

Skidmore, Owings & Merrill architect works 18 stories up in the Alcoa Building.

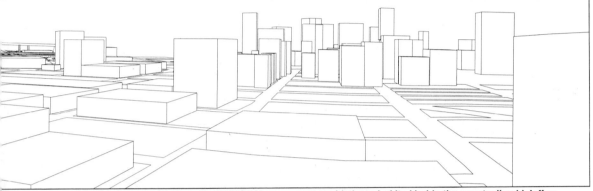

~~g~~ain to transform this data into graphic form for NATIONAL ~~GE~~OGRAPHIC. Making pictures of the skyline, photographer ~~Jo~~nathan Blair assisted Mr. Paradis in reproducing the ~~pa~~norama. "To my knowledge, this graphics program is the most sophisticated of its kind in the country," said Jeffrey Heller of Skidmore, Owings & Merrill. "It can reproduce views of highly complex subjects, yet its calculations take less time to run on a computer than those of similar programs."

~~Bo~~ard of Supervisors accepted the recommendation of its ~~pl~~anners and imposed a height limitation of 84 feet on most of ~~th~~e city's northern waterfront. Alvin Duskin, a local manufac~~tu~~rer, advocates a height limit of six stories on all new con~~st~~ruction throughout San Francisco. His supporters collected ~~en~~ough voters' signatures to petition the issue to referendum in November 1971. Mr. Duskin cites statistics showing that although high-rise office buildings generate millions of dollars in taxes, the thousands of commuters who work in them may require services that cost the city even more. "If skyscrapers really bring so much extra money to the city government," he said, "New Yorkers' taxes should be down to zero by now."

Trans-America Company's headquarters in 1970.

Steel skeleton of San Francisco's new Trans-America Buildi*

Shadows of tall buildings darken Montgomery Street.

A sense of scale

"One of the nicest things about San Francisco is its huma*
scale," said a longtime resident. "It seems like you ca*
almost take the entire city and hold it in the palm of yo*
hand." Today sheer growth threatens to overpower th*
rare quality. In the financial district, towering office buil*
ings (lower left) turn once-bright streets into gloomy ca*
yons. Companies construct monumental edifices for the*
headquarters (above), leaving unique older building*
(upper left) to less affluent tenants or to the wrecking ba*
Alert to these threats to their envied quality of life, Sa*
Franciscans struggle to preserve their unique urban e*
vironment. They gain encouragement from a local prece*
dent. In the late 1950's, citizens forced a halt to furthe*
construction of the Embarcadero Freeway (right), savi*
both an area of quaint buildings and views of the ba*

ts skyward. When completed in 1972, it will thrust a needle-like pyramid a thousand feet into the air.

nfinished ramps of the Embarcadero Freeway end in mid-air. Angry San Franciscans forced a halt to construction.

The big trucks muttered past in solid procession, winding along a temporary dirt road down into a man-made crater a quarter of a mile wide in the earth of California's Palos Verdes Peninsula. Twenty feet below the rim they backed one by one to the lip of an embankment and spewed their contents over the edge—paper and glass, beer cans, plastic bottles, cereal boxes, splintered lumber, and leaky water heaters—part of the mountain of solid waste generated by the seven million people of Los Angeles County.

From a hilltop nearby, I watched this sanitary landfill process at work. A mild breeze stirred the branches of the eucalyptus trees around the $75,000 homes behind me. Except for smog, the wind carried no unpleasant odor and surprisingly little dust.

Tractor-crawlers, busy as dung beetles, crushed the refuse, crunching metal, fragmenting wood, compacting paper and plastic.

"By the time it gets here the stuff already has been compressed in packer trucks to about 400 pounds per cubic yard," said Art Bonnell, assistant field superintendent for the Los Angeles County Sanitation Districts.

"Then we compact the refuse to a third of this volume. Later we cover the day's layer with dirt—one part earth to four parts refuse."

That combination, he explained, is the formula for good landfill. Despite its disadvantages—possible settling and seepage and a tendency to create methane gas—sanitary landfill offers a substantial improvement over a foul-smelling open dump that breeds rats and disease.

Were there other ways to rid our towns and cities of their growing glut of refuse? What about the great flood of sewage, treated and untreated, that daily pours into our rivers, lakes, and coastal waters? This was my first stop on a trip crisscrossing the country to learn more of our Nation's waste-disposal problem and what can be done about it.

I learned of three basic ways to combat the garbage explosion. One is to reduce the bulk of what we throw away. Another is to produce less, which automatically would cut down what we discard. The third solution—and most promising in the long run—is to turn our discards into something useful, to recycle.

I talked with scientists and engineers, officials and businessmen, housewives and husbands about short-run solutions and about the exciting technology of recycling. I visited Government-sponsored pilot plants and observed company projects which are testing new ways to reuse wastes.

Clearly, in coming years we will move to

"Traditionally, from the time man first tossed a bone outside his cave, we have dumped, buried, or burned our trash."

Children seek salvage amid acrid fume

WASTE: THE BURDEN OF AFFLUENCE

By Henry Still

...om burning refuse in Florida. Nationwide, more than 82 percent of municipal solid waste amasses in 14,500 open dumps.

more and more recycling as shortages of timber, metal, and water teach us to stop wasting our resources. But until that time we have to do a better job of waste disposal.

As I traveled, I found that most American communities still simply haul their refuse to an open dump where it rots in a pit or is partially destroyed by smoldering fires. Across the Nation about 82 percent of all collected rubbish goes into some 14,500 ugly, unsanitary, open dumps.

"A major first step toward improvement of the country's solid-waste disposal situation would be the conversion of those 14,500 dumps to sanitary landfill," says Hugh H. Connolly, a solid-waste management specialist at the Environmental Protection Agency.

Many metropolitan areas, I learned, are encountering problems in finding places to hide their waste. New York City and Philadelphia expect to run out of fill space in a few years. San Francisco, which had filled in part of its beautiful bay with refuse, found a temporary solution when the nearby community of Mountain View agreed to take the city's solid waste for fill material to create a park.

Said Houston's Mayor Louie Welch, expressing the plight of many municipalities: "Everyone wants us to pick up his garbage, but no one wants us to put it down."

The dimensions of the dilemma seem to grow with each passing week. In 1920 the average person generated about three pounds of refuse a day. By 1970 the figure was twice that much. In the same 50-year span the population of the United States nearly doubled.

Looking toward 1980, some experts see our ever-burgeoning Nation creating solid waste at the rate of eight pounds per person per day.

Already Americans annually jettison 30 million tons of paper, 26 billion bottles, 48 billion tin and aluminum cans, and more than 7 million automobiles.

Of this tremendous volume of solid waste, litter accounts for perhaps 3 percent, but the beer cans on our beaches and candy wrappers on our streets rank among the most unpleasant marks of man's careless passage, and are one of the most expensive, proportionately, to clean up.

"You can talk about polluted air and water, but refuse must be put somewhere, now," said Patrick Bradley, director of the Solid Waste Division of American Hoist & Derrick Company of St. Paul, Minnesota.

Mr. Bradley's company is working on a way to reduce bulk that could make sanitary landfill more efficient. At a central baling plant a massive press applies a force of more than five million pounds to crush waste matter so that it occupies a mere 1/20 of its original space. Bales weighing 2,500 pounds but compressed to the size of an office desk are trucked 17 miles and bound and stacked like firewood to fill a 55-acre excavation.

When it is filled and covered, the site—on what was once low-value land—may become an industrial park.

Another garbage compactor on a small scale, a trim appliance that fits under the kitchen counter, squashes a week's trash in a plastic bag. "It still means trash thrown away," complains the biweekly *Environmental Action*. "You would have to pull the material apart to recycle the crunched paper and glass."

Meanwhile, the mountain of trash grows larger. "The trend toward packaged goods in disposable containers has put more paper, plastics, glass, and metals . . . into refuse," said the President's Council on Environmental Quality in its first report to Congress. "And the technology of solid-waste collection and disposal has not kept pace with this change."

Disposable cups, disposable bottles, disposable towels, disposable clothing. But how do we dispose of the disposables? We spend 3.5 billion dollars annually to pick up and dispose of refuse. About 80 percent of this goes for collecting and hauling.

"Superfluous" packaging

In the fall of 1970 two New Yorkers tried a week-long experiment to learn what a housewife could do to cut down on the burden that ever-mounting piles of garbage present. "Most of us don't realize how many of the things we buy are overwrapped," said Adele Auchincloss, wife of novelist Louis Auchincloss. "Why, for example, do we need to put bacon wrapped in cellophane into a cardboard box?"

Mrs. Auchincloss carried home her fruits and vegetables in a reusable mesh shopping bag, bought returnable bottles, and politely refused to accept "superfluous" packaging. Her friend Martha Sutphen, representing the average consumer, did her marketing as usual. At the end of the week the Auchincloss garbage weighed 57 pounds, and the Sutphens', 107 pounds.

Traditionally, from the time man first tossed a bone outside his cave, we have dumped, buried, or burned our trash. At present about 10 percent of the Nation's solid waste goes into incinerators used by some 300 communities. But incineration, like sanitary landfill, has its drawbacks. Without particulate control devices, smoke will pollute the air.

Plastics pose a special problem. These man-made materials do not degrade rapidly or decompose naturally. Some melt rather than burn, and the residue may clog or corrode incinerator grates. Several plastics, such as polyvinyl chloride (PVC) used in many unbreakable bottles, can produce acid fumes when burned. In Europe, Canada, and the United States a number of researchers are experimenting with the chemistry of plastics, trying to develop an inexpensive product that will disintegrate naturally with time or exposure to sunlight.

Although burning, like compacting, reduces the volume of solid waste, the leftover ashes, glass, and metal create their own disposal dilemmas. A small percentage of the fly ash and cinders from incinerators is used to make bricks and as filler in asphalt paving; fly ash from power plants also can be used as a substitute for cement in concrete. The U. S. Bureau of Mines is developing ways to sort and separate the incinerator residue and to use the metals, minerals, and glass left after burning. These projects are part of a new and promising campaign aimed at transforming solid waste into useful products. Under the landmark Resource Recovery Act of 1970, the Government authorized spending 450 million dollars in a three-year period to finance a bigger war on garbage in an effort to find ways to recover the resources buried in solid waste.

Throwaway bottles can create "glasphalt," a pavement sparkling with fragments of green, brown, and clear glass. Rubber from scrap tires can produce carbon black, a key ingredient for new tires. Corn stalks, wood chips, and sugarmill waste, rich in cellulose, can yield a product containing protein. Investigators at Louisiana State University have isolated micro-organisms that will convert 100 pounds of these wastes to 25 pounds of light brown protein flour.

"We still have to reduce the cost, currently about 10 cents a pound, if we are going to compete in the animal-food market with soy flour," said Dr. Clayton D. Callihan, the chemical engineer coordinating the research efforts. "But municipal solid waste is 50 to 60 percent cellulose, and we propose to convert part of that into protein for feed."

Whether it's protein from cellulose or fuel from refuse, recycling promises to rescue us from the garbage explosion.

For a boy who grew up on an Iowa farm, recycling is not a new or strange idea. Mother canned much of our food in reusable mason jars, so we did not accumulate many tin cans. The junk that did pile up helped to stop

Madison, Wisconsin, fights its waste problems. Dan Lalley (top) loads bundled newspapers destined for recycling, part of the city's daily collection of 12 to 14 tons. In another project, John Reinhardt (center) holds a sample of the 60 tons of waste shredded each day—the first use of pulverized material for landfill. Although this milled refuse contains food for rodents, the small particles force rats to work so hard for sustenance that they starve or turn to cannibalism. At the U. S. Forest Products Laboratory in Madison (bottom), Richard J. Auchter checks the quality of experimental paper incorporating from 5 to 70 percent waste fiber, also from the city's shredding program.

Polluted waters:
a national blight

Clean water, once taken for granted now flows polluted with domestic and industrial wastes. Raw sewage pours into rivers, lakes, and oceans from 1,400 U. S. communities; 2,400 plants remove only heavier solids by primary treatment. Secondary treatment, used in nearly 10,000 plants, employs bacteria to break down sewage, yet 10 to 40 percent of polluting material remains. To compound the problem, industry adds three times the waste of all municipal sewage.

Following a 21-month survey, a task force headed by investigator Ralph Nader reported that wastes render many of our waterways almost unfit for anything but navigation and continued dumping. Damage occurs in many ways. Bacteria transmit disease; chemicals poison aquatic life. Algae flourish on the organic and chemical nutrients, creating foul-smelling slime. Biochemical oxygen demand (BOD) soars as decomposition removes oxygen from the water.

Advanced sewage treatment can remove up to 99 percent of the BOD, but only ten municipal facilities offer this. Just to provide secondary treatment for the entire United States would cost more than 12 billion dollars during the next five years, says the Environmental Protection Agency.

Untreated municipal sewage flows into the Hudson River near Watervliet, New York.

Barge dumps sewage sludge outside New York Harbor. Some scientists say such practices imperil ocean-floor marine life.

LAKE CLOSED

THIS WATER HAS BEEN TESTED

FOUND HAZARDOUS
NO FISHING, SWIMMING, WADING,

BOATING OR OTHER BODY CONTACT
PERMITTED UNTIL FURTHER NOTICE

ign in Fairfax County, Virginia, warns against the use of a lake contaminated by pollutants carried by storm runoff.

erosion in the ditch on the "back forty." Food scraps went into the swill bucket for the hogs. Animal manures were returned to the fields.

Nearly everything was used until it was worn out, stored for reuse, or recycled directly back to the earth. Of course, not everyone lived on a farm in the 1930's, but in those depression years people had a different attitude toward goods. Thrift was more than just a word. "Waste not, want not" was a way of life.

The years of World War II taught every housewife how to save metal cans, collect kitchen grease, and bale old newspapers. But when the war ended, we gave up those economies with a sigh of relief. For a few more years, garbage, metals, glass, and trash were segregated into separate barrels for salvage. Then the burden of trash became so large and raw materials so readily available that we virtually stopped this practice. Almost everything ended up in the big compactor trucks, which squeezed it all together.

Recycling efforts

Today many Americans once again are becoming increasingly concerned about the items which move from the kitchen to the trash barrel. Such a person is Mrs. Rae Forte, one of the founders of the Conejo Environmental League of Thousand Oaks, California, a rapidly growing city near Los Angeles.

"We're all looking for some way to do something about pollution," Mrs. Forte told me. "For a start our league is financing itself through collection and resale of waste paper, glass bottles, and aluminum cans."

Mrs. Forte and others like her have learned that such financing sometimes is hard to come by. During 1970, for example, as more and more groups began to collect newspapers, the price of used newsprint plummeted in places to about 1/10 of what it had been. Supplies had far exceeded current demands.

Waste-paper reclamation poses its own problems. "When you recycle pulp fibers, you get a weaker product the second time around," said J. L. McClintock, director of environmental resources for the Weyerhaeuser Company of Tacoma, Washington, a major U. S. wood-products firm. "Eventually, although you may have chased the paper around the cycle a bit, you still have to dispose of it." Mr. McClintock believes we will one day burn the bulk of waste paper to create energy, thus conserving other resources.

Many people, scientists and citizens alike, have begun to call for Government incentives or subsidies to support recycling experiments.

Industry now finds it profitable to reclaim as much as 19 percent of our waste paper, and about half of our copper comes from scrap. But recycling runs into trouble when the price is not right, as the example of waste-paper collection demonstrates.

The automobile makes another case in point: In the days before 1958 the salvage industry took care of old cars and made money doing it. Then came the new steel furnaces that required substantially less scrap. Soon auto wreckers could afford to pay so little for old cars that it often became cheaper to abandon them than to tow them to a junkyard.

I have heard auto wreckers around the country sing a chorus of complaints. Said one: "I make my living on spare parts. Sure, there's good steel in that hulk, but it's tough to get rid of it and break even."

New monster shredders that can chew a car into small fragments in minutes may prove a boon to the auto-scrap dealers, but it is doubtful that these giant machines will offer anything but a partial solution to the widely dispersed number of junked cars that exists today. To transport these cars to the shredder still is not economical.

Present salvage operations eventually could form the nucleus of a national industry to recycle all our trash, but recycling firms must be able to sell the material they reclaim at a reasonable profit.

Unfortunately, this has not always worked out. Four cities, for example, turned over their trash to composting operations that convert organic materials—paper and garbage—into a humus product sold as a soil conditioner. Of the four, three have run into crippling marketing problems.

Ingenuity and necessity may yet produce positive results in other recycling ventures, however. In tiny Delaware, where land for trash disposal is scarce, the governor chose Robert J. Berndt, a member of the state legislature and a research chemist, to head a committee to seek new solutions to the state's looming solid-waste problem.

"My home produces garbage and trash like every other, so like you, I was already an expert," Representative Berndt recalled with a smile. "A compactor truck comes to my house about twice a week, picks up my refuse, drives on down the street, turns the corner, and the problem is solved—for me.

"But seriously, our committee studied all the possibilities. After considering shredding, baling, incineration, and barge disposal, we decided to go in the direction of total recycling. Eventually we contracted with Hercules, Incorporated, of Wilmington, to build an experimental waste-reclamation plant."

Hercules engineers are working on ways to incorporate a variety of techniques into one package. Their plans, still on the drawing board, will include such operations as magnetic separation, composting, and pyrolysis, a process pioneered by U. S. Bureau of Mines researchers that burns organic material in an oxygen-free chamber to produce oil, gas, and carbon. Dr. Robert W. Cairns, Hercules vice president for research, believes that "a Nation struggling to create goods that end up in the trash can is a wasteful dissipation of our essential resources."

Most people would agree that Hercules, along with many other companies, still faces thorny problems. Such operations must find economical ways to sort the metals, glass, plastics, paper, textiles, and garbage from the total mass of refuse which arrives on a trash truck. And they must be able to sell their recycled products at competitive prices.

Refuse also can be used to produce electric power. "About 15 cities in Europe burn waste to generate steam for power plants," said Dr. Hartmut Bossel at the University of California in Santa Barbara. "We could meet about 12 percent of our current demand for electricity just by burning the garbage we throw away."

The Combustion Power Company of Menlo Park, California, supported by a contract from the Environmental Protection Agency, is attempting to develop a system which would incinerate waste in a combustor, producing high-pressure gas to power an electricity-generating turbine.

"At full capacity our system is expected to consume 400 tons of refuse a day, the amount produced by a city of about 200,000 people," explained Richard G. Reese, general manager of the CPC's commercial division. "The plant should be able to supply about 1/10 of the electrical power such a city requires."

By now I had come to realize that there is no magic push-button way to combat pollution. It will take years to teach ourselves to use and reuse our precious resources.

The Adolph Coors Company of Golden, Colorado, has made a significant start, I found. Like most of the major can producers, Coors has gone into recycling aluminum cans. By the end of 1970 it had paid 10 cents a pound for some 140 million of them.

"One reason for spending so much effort on aluminum," said Everett L. Barnhardt, Coors vice president, "is that it can be recycled so conveniently, and the end product is worth $200 a ton." *(Continued on page 192)*

Worker at the Adolph Coors Company of Golden, Colorado, unloads used aluminum cans slated for recycling. Coors and other manufacturers pay 10 cents a pound for such cans, then salvage the valuable metal. Across the Nation in 1970, companies reclaimed 200 million of the containers, out of 4 billion produced. Below, new cans speed past inspectors at the Coors plant.

Workman hoists unsorted refuse onto a conveyer for shredding.

Project Engineer Bert Hildebrand chec

Upward air flow isolates combustible materials.

Putting trash to work

Trash may yield electrical energy for U. S. cities if a fe
erally funded experimental program at Menlo Park, Ca
fornia, succeeds. Engineers of the Combustion Pow
Company test a process designed to shred refuse, scre
out metals, glass, and nonburnable material for recyclir
then use the residue to fuel gas-turbine generators. B
of glass, iron, and steel (above right), awaiting reclamati
and recycling by industries, include two pieces of twist
red metal, the remains of the toy fire truck (upper left)

After a jet of air (left) separates the combustible tra
a pneumatic feeder injects it into a chamber containing
bed of sand heated to 1,600° F. High-pressure air flowi

edded refuse. Burnable material (left) will fuel the Combustion Power Unit; glass and metals will go to recycling plants.

ough the sand causes the bed to act like boiling water,
ubbing each particle of the waste. The trash burns
tantly, even as the feeder shoves in more refuse. The
d material, temperature, and oxygen-rich environment
inerate the trash without creating air-polluting carbon
noxide or hydrocarbon emissions.

Company engineers hope to use the heated gases pro-
ced by burning trash to generate electricity. They
ject that a full-scale Combustion Power Unit could
ndle the refuse from a city of 200,000 people, using
 combustible portion of the trash to provide about
 percent of the city's electrical demand. With added
uipment the gas-turbine stage may also provide energy
desalt ocean water or to operate a centralized refuse-
lection system, using a network of vacuum pipes linked
h waste-disposal points in the surrounding urban area.

Engineer's face reflects glow from the combustion chamber.

Recycling plant in Puerto Rico converts organic refuse into humus. The huge digester tank holds decomposing waste.

eam rises around augers as aerobic, heat-producing bacteria digest shredded garbage.

ompost from recycled garbage

tating augers speed bacterial decomposition of organic
ste, one step of a process that turns garbage and refuse
:o soil conditioner in San Juan, Puerto Rico. Three giant
gester tanks like the uncovered one, opposite, form the
art of the Fairfield Engineering Company recycling system. Here the refuse aerates for three to five days while
the bacteria generate heat and do their work. Air-cured
and pressed into pellets, the end product dries in a kiln
(below left); no unpleasant odor remains. In operation
since 1969, the plant produces 75 tons of pellets a day
from 300 tons of waste. Delaware plans to complete a
similar plant by 1972; it also will include a separate process
to convert tires, plastics, and rags into carbon, fuel oils,
and hydrocarbon gases — all without polluting air or water.

-drying prepares compost for bagging.

Earthy smell characterizes the finished product.

Coors hopes eventually to be able to recycle every scrap of material used in its beer manufacturing process. The 135 tons of spent malt, hops, barley, and rice left each day go into cattle and dog feed as a protein supplement. All paper and defective cartons are baled and sold for scrap. Broken glass bottles become cullet—the 10 to 30 percent of old glass used in making new. Polyethylene is ground up and remelted to make bungs for barrels. Lumber is reused and scraps go for firewood.

"Our biggest loss used to be 20,000 gallons per day of unavoidable waste from our packaging operations," said Mr. Barnhardt. "Now 90 percent goes into cattle feed after alcohol has been extracted. Eventually even the alcohol will be marketed.

"We are about 30 percent along toward our goal of 100 percent recycling of all materials. Four months ago we were hauling 25 truckloads of trash to the dump each day. Now we're down to four. But we don't want anything to go to the dump."

That, I thought, could be a good slogan for all of us to follow.

Nature, of course, has been in the recycling business for a long time. The water you drank this morning may have swirled around the feet of a dinosaur or rinsed Cleopatra's hands. It may have rained onto the Pacific Ocean or trickled from the edge of a glacier to feed a cold Canadian river.

And part of the same water, long cleansed of prehistoric mud and Cleopatra's perfume, may be flowing out of Lake Itasca into the Mississippi or down New England's Merrimack River to the sea.

Born fresh from high New Hampshire lakes, the Merrimack winds through Concord and Manchester and turns eastward to the Atlantic through the Massachusetts cities of Lowell and Lawrence. Once it was a clear-flowing stream that gave pleasure to those who lived along its banks. But no longer.

Franz Scholz, a reporter for the *Lowell Sun*, traveled the Merrimack Valley during the summer of 1970, retracing a journey made 131 years earlier by Henry David Thoreau, the 19th-century naturalist.

"The river that Thoreau called a silver cascade, man has turned into a dump for raw sewage and waste," Franz said.

He told me what he found at Manchester during his trip. "A pipe about 12 feet in diameter poured raw sewage over a man-made waterfall into the river. A city engineer estimated that there were about 40 other outfalls."

In an earlier day when waste quantities were small, natural biological processes purified the river water before it reached the next town. But now the Merrimack—like many other waterways—is taxed with an ever-greater flow of sewage from growing cities and suburbs. Pollution forced the closing of most of the clam beds in the river's estuary back in 1926, Franz reported. "Today commercial fishing is completely ruined."

At Lowell, downstream from Manchester, swimming was permitted in the sand-bottomed Merrimack until 1963. Now a "Bathing Prohibited" sign stands beside the bathhouse.

"The river's white-sand banks shaded by willows and pines could make lovely beaches and picnic areas," said Franz, shaking his head.

Slowly, cities along the Merrimack are taking action. Lowell has committed funds for a sewage treatment plant to curtail the burden it has been placing on the river. Manchester is following suit.

"All of us recognize what a mess the Merrimack is," affirmed James R. Bucknam, executive editor of the *Manchester Union Leader*. "I wouldn't eat fish from the river, even upstream. But there is just so much money to go around. The city has to share the wealth with schools, highways, and demands from every direction."

Winning the race?

Some 1,400 municipalities still channel raw sewage into the nearest river or stream, but this practice is decreasing. Today nearly 64 percent of the people of the Nation are served by sewage plants operated by about 12,000 cities. Almost 10,000 of the plants provide both primary and secondary treatment.

Primary treatment, which EPA water quality officials consider "entirely inadequate for most needs," simply settles and removes larger solids from the water. Then the water is chlorinated to kill disease-causing bacteria and discharged. Conventional second-stage sewage treatment depends on accelerating the natural action of bacteria to decompose organic matter.

A high waste load supports more bacteria, and the bacteria require oxygen to do their job. From this action sanitary engineers derive their basic yardstick of water pollution—biochemical oxygen demand, or BOD.

As the oxygen supply decreases, the water grows murky, and many forms of aquatic life are affected. If *all* the oxygen is consumed, anaerobic bacteria, which do not need oxygen, take over. The water turns dark and repulsive, and the smell is foul. Thus, one major objective of conventional treatment is to lower biochemical oxygen demand.

I watched both primary and secondary treatment at work at the Whittier Narrows Water Reclamation Plant near Los Angeles. My guide, Joe Haworth, a young environmental engineer who was graduated from Stanford in 1968, helped me understand the basic mechanics of the two-stage process that removes about 95 percent of the suspended solids.

Whittier Narrows draws 15 million gallons of sewage per day through its plant. The water first flows into two long concrete basins for primary treatment. Sand, grit, and other solid fragments settle to the bottom, and mechanical scrapers remove the mass of solids, called raw sludge. Then the sewage drains into another set of tanks for secondary treatment. Jets of high-pressure air churn the water into a brown, oily mass, and a sharp earthy odor—not entirely unpleasant, I found—rises from the tanks.

"This is activated sludge," Joe explained. "We bring bacteria-rich sludge, the concentrated matter left at the end of the treatment cycle, and mix it with the sewage. We aerate the mixture by bubbling air through the tanks to give the bacteria the oxygen they need. The addition of bacteria and air to the sewage speeds up the work of decomposition."

From here the sewage flows to another sedimentation tank where the fattened bacteria clump together in a process known as flocculation. The clumps of floc material settle to the bottom and are removed. Much of the remaining sludge then returns to enrich the aeration stage.

From the top of the last tank, water—now a clear, light green—trickles away through surface channels and moves to the next station where chlorine is added to kill most of the harmful organisms.

"If you can visualize a wide, deep-flowing stream," Joe said, "what we're doing here on maybe an acre of ground is what happens naturally in many, many miles of river."

Joe dipped a beaker into the channel of chlorinated effluent and held it up to the sunlight. The water was as clear and sparkling as that which comes from my tap at home.

"Could I drink it?"

"I wouldn't advise doing so," Joe replied. "It still contains some viruses and bacteria."

Cities like Atlanta, Detroit, and Cleveland, which have expanded far beyond the capacity of their sewage plants, have as their minimum goal adequate secondary treatment. But Whittier Narrows provides more than secondary processing. The treated effluent goes into dryland percolation basins, and slowly trickles underground. By the time the water is pumped

Trees flourish in formerly sterile soil from strip-mined areas after irrigation with treated sewage. Those in the upper box died in similar but untreated soil. Not only does sewage stimulate crop and forest growth, a related experiment showed, but the soil also purifies waste filtering through it. The Pennsylvania State University experiments provide a way to reclaim two million acres of denuded land, offering a constructive use for the effluent from sewage treatment plants now polluting many of the Nation's waterways.

up, the soil has filtered it and removed most of the harmful impurities, including the viruses.

In the Nittany Valley in Pennsylvania, Spring Creek once ran sparkling and clear on its way toward the Susquehanna River. But then the borough of State College—home of Pennsylvania State University—began to mushroom. Gradually, the BOD and the nitrogen and phosphorus content of the water increased, and Spring Creek grew turbid and choked with algae.

A team of Penn State scientists set to work solving the problem in the early 1960's, and gained an added benefit in the process. The researchers tapped into the borough's two-stage sewage-treatment plant and drew off part of the nearly clear but nutrient-rich effluent. This they sprayed onto experimental plots of cropland.

Trees doubled their growth; corn yields increased from 40 to 100 percent; alfalfa, 300 percent—without any degradation of ground-water quality. And Spring Creek grew less murky. With expansion of the project to use all the plant's effluent to irrigate some 500 acres of cropland and forest, officials hope to see the stream run clear again.

Advanced treatment

The Whittier Narrows and Penn State operations employ natural processes to reduce the nitrogen, phosphorus, and minerals that still remain after secondary treatment. In Cincinnati, the Robert A. Taft Water Research Center, part of the EPA's water quality program, is exploring more advanced methods of removing these impurities from the effluent.

Frank M. Middleton, the director, is a quiet, thoughtful chemist who has devoted 30 patient years to the cause of clean water. The bulletin board in his outer office carries such slogans as "Live in the Past: It's Cheaper" and "Save Water—Bathe with a Friend." But these touches of humor offer only brief respite from the notably serious business of providing research and guidance to improve water quality throughout the land.

Mr. Middleton talked first about upgrading conventional biological treatment. Pure oxygen, which supports more bacteria in a smaller space and thus speeds up biological action, can be used instead of air in the activated sludge process, he explained. As a result aeration takes two hours instead of six, and the aeration tanks need not be so large.

Chemical methods can supplement biological treatment, he added. The introduction of lime, alum, or iron salts spurs flocculation,

forcing organic material to clump together and settle to the bottom.

"To make waste water usable over and over again," he continued, "we need three more stages: excellent filtering through sand or sand and coal, polishing by sending the water through a tank of carbon granules to remove final traces of organic materials, and finally, disinfecting with chlorine.

"If a city were threatened with a dry-up of its water supply, we could turn out drinking-quality water tomorrow by applying even more advanced treatment to remove the dissolved minerals," he said.

The Taft Center operates a number of pilot plants, including one at Pomona, California, which provide this treatment. There John N. English, the resident director, showed me a carbon tank similar to the ones I had seen in Cincinnati. Columns of carbon granules cleanse the treated waste water of trace organics. "Then we go on to remove salts or dissolved minerals," my host explained. "We are evaluating three different methods—electrodialysis, reverse osmosis, and ion exchange."

In electrodialysis, electricity causes ions to move through selective membranes which separate the salts from the water. In reverse osmosis, pressure forces water through cellulose acetate membranes, leaving salts behind. In ion exchange, mineral ions such as calcium and sodium are removed in resin beds. Of the three, the last currently appears to be the most feasible method of demineralization.

"With broad-scale application of the processes tested at Pomona," Mr. English told me, "we could renovate a substantial portion of the 700 million gallons of waste water that Los Angeles County generates daily."

High in the Sierra Nevada along the California-Nevada border, another pioneer advanced-treatment plant helps to protect the pristine waters of Lake Tahoe. A pipeline carries waste water, purified of nitrogen and phosphorus, 27 miles to Indian Creek Reservoir for water sports, trout fishing, and irrigation. At Santee, a town of 22,000 in southern California, recycled effluent feeds five recreational lakes and a swimming pool, and is used to irrigate a golf course, a tree farm, and a Little League baseball field.

Sludge, the mass of solid matter that settles out of sewage, creates a disposal problem for all treatment plants. The South Lake Tahoe plant burns its settlings, and the sterile ash that remains goes for landfill. Santee has been using sterilized sludge as a soil conditioner; in most places, however, sludge just keeps piling up.

Cooking under pressure and vacuum or

pressure filtering can be used to dewater the residue, but many plants simply set their sludge out to dry. They may try to give it away for landfill or fertilizer, but the supply far exceeds the demand.

John R. Sheaffer of the University of Chicago Center for Urban Studies has a plan to dispose of both sludge and sewage. He proposes that we stop dumping waste into the water—entirely—and start to return treated wastes to the land, "where they belong."

For more than 60 years, in his view, "we have been adding to a basic system of sewage disposal that won't work."

The Federal Government is supporting an operation in Muskegon County, Michigan, that will apply Mr. Sheaffer's concepts. The project will channel raw sewage from 12 cities and townships into one large outlet, carrying the waste to an area of poor, sandy land 15 miles away. Once treated, it will be sprayed onto the unproductive soil.

Scheduled to go into operation in 1972, the plan is expected to quadruple the agricultural value of some 6,000 acres, and to reduce the pollution of Lake Michigan, where most of the effluent currently winds up.

William A. Cawley, head of water-quality research for EPA, believes that "in another 20 years, nothing will be dumped into our waters —if the present desire to protect the environment persists.

"The technology is there," he said. "Concerned citizens are needed."

One community, Windhoek in arid South-West Africa, gets about 27 percent of its drinking water from treated sewage, but common use of waste water for this purpose is still down the road—even though techniques exist to make it possible. Researchers currently are more intent on demonstrating how recycled water can be used in industry and agriculture, and for recreation.

"There are many parts to the over-all problem of water pollution, and many solutions will be required," Frank Middleton had told me when we visited in Cincinnati. "At the outset, I feel we need to learn to pollute less; where possible we can treat the polluted water, and then recycle it.

"And we haven't even begun to get people to save water. We don't have to send so much water to the sewage plant, but in most areas water is still so cheap that people feel they can afford to waste it."

So here again, I learned the key lesson of all: Once we come to regard our resources as the precious commodities they truly are, we will have a cleaner environment.

Water reclaimed by advanced sewage treatment in Santee, California, fills recreation lakes such as the one below. Water district employees bulldozed land for the lakes in their spare time; residents contributed trees and shrubs. Percolation ponds (above) polish the treated water prior to its release to the lakes for fishing, swimming, irrigation, and industrial use.

Nation's most advanced municipal water-recovery system provides purified water from sewage at South Lake Tahoe, California.

Tanks—each containing 22 tons of granulated carbon—remove taste, odor, color, and detergent and DDT molecules.

eration speeds bacterial action on sewage.

Jets of reclaimed water cascade from treatment-plant fountains.

Protecting a pristine lake

ompleted in 1968, the water-recovery plant at South Lake ahoe, California, pioneers in advanced sewage treat-ent. Like other systems, its primary and secondary tages include a settling pond and adjacent trench-like eration basins to speed biological breakdown of the

waste (aerial photograph, opposite); three settling tanks further clear the sewage. Advanced treatment begins in the tank at right with addition of lime to remove algae-nourishing phosphates. Water then goes through the near-by ammonia-stripping tower to remove nitrogen. White, sausage-like containers and carbon columns filter the water a final time. Eliminating a major source of pollution in one of the world's clearest lakes, the plant demonstrates that, with proper treatment, waste water becomes reusable.

ludge burns to sterile ash.

Sanitarian Al Kruse studies samples from three of the principal processing stages.

POPULATION: A LOOK TO THE FUTURE

By Charlton Ogburn

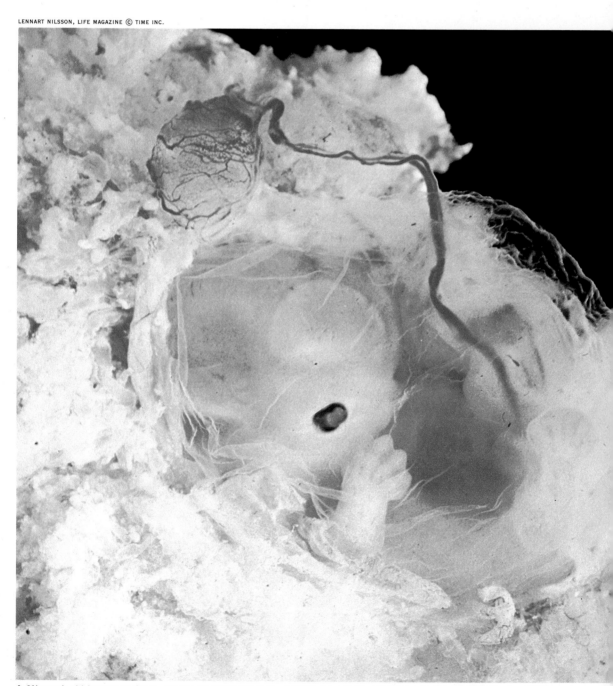

A 6½-week-old human embryo—shown 10 times life-size—already has distinct features. In the world today four births occur every

"Slowly we are beginning to realize that a rapidly growing population is placing a greater and greater burden on the earth."

...econd, a 25 percent rise in 20 years.

"**I**f you had to predict what the population of the United States would be in the year 2000, knowing that a bolt of lightning would strike you if you missed by more than five million, what would you say?"

The slightly built, gray-haired man sitting across the cafeteria table from me smiled at my question. "I believe I would just go ahead and drop dead," he replied.

A topflight demographer, Conrad Taeuber was reflecting the caution of his profession. He is associate director of an institution so proficient at amassing and digesting information about population that countries all over the world send specialists to study its methods. For I was visiting the United States Bureau of the Census.

My question had been prompted by four varying projections Dr. Taeuber had given me showing the probable population growth in the United States for the years ahead. Each estimate assumed a different number of children born per female.

"You'll notice," he said, "that the most conservative projection shows a population of somewhat over 266 million by the year 2000. I think that's low. The second indicates more than 280 million—and that, I think, may be fairly close. The next one projects a population of more than 300 million, and the highest, more than 320 million."

The famous clock in the Department of Commerce illustrates how our population is growing. A light below the clock flashes once every 8.5 seconds, signaling a birth. Another registers a death every 16.5 seconds. Two others indicate an immigrant every 71 seconds and an emigrant every 23 minutes.

A meter resembling the odometer of an automobile balances these figures and records the current population estimate. By August 1971, the total had reached 207.8 million—just about twice that at the end of World War I.

Although the figure is increasing all the time, this does not mean that American women are having more children; in fact, they are having fewer. But the number of births continues to grow because there are more American women than ever to bear children.

The Census Bureau seemed a logical place to begin to find out what our expanding population may have in store for us. I also would have to look beyond our borders—for mankind as a whole, now numbering 3.7 billion, is multiplying at a rate twice our own.

CHARLTON OGBURN, *writer for a decade on many environmental subjects, is the author of* The Winter Beach *and* The Continent in Our Hands.

High-voltage forest—nurtured by an ever-increasing demand for consumer goods—looms behind a row of look-alike houses in an

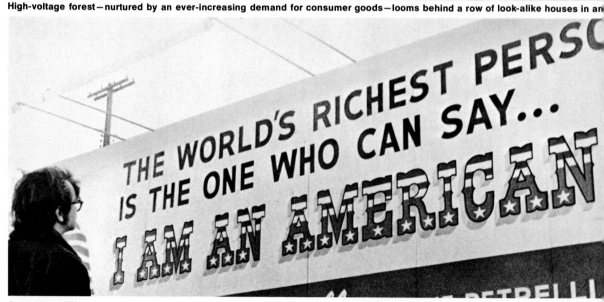

Campaign billboard salutes an American birthright. More tangible riches have brought a rapid increase in consumer spending.

Rising U.S. consumption taxes world resources

Networks of power lines crisscross America—a graphic indication of the burgeoning demands an affluent Nation places on the earth's finite resources. Between 1950 and 1970 the population of the United States increased by about a third, passing the 200-million mark. In the same period, U.S. electrical consumption quadrupled, and the demand for natural gas more than tripled. Sales of consumer goods continue to spiral upward, and so does the use of raw materials to produce them.

Though Americans represent only 6 percent of the world's population, they account for 35 percent of the annual consumption of nonrenewable resources, including more than half of the silver, over a third of the lead, and a quarter of the iron, tin, and copper. An American, who eats more food and uses more water than his counterpart in any other country, requires 30 times more raw materials than a citizen of India. To power their 87 million cars, Americans burn 61 billion gallons of gasoline a year —then must endure the resulting smog and traffic jams.

Such unbridled consumption ultimately may lead to disaster, warns John P. Milton, director of the Conservation Foundation's office of international affairs: "If we impose no conscious restraints on our power to 'conquer' nature, our material and population growth will . . . stabilize at the point where shortages of food, water, breathable air, raw materials, energy resources, and space exert their own tyranny. . . ." The likely answer, suggests Hans H. Landsberg of Resources for the Future: a reduction in the variety and volume of goods. "Technology," he believes, "will continue to find new sources of raw materials or devise substitutes. Letting things slide certainly will get us into deep trouble, but I see no reason why this society cannot make an orderly transition to an acceptable way of life that encompasses respect for the demands of nature."

nois suburban community.

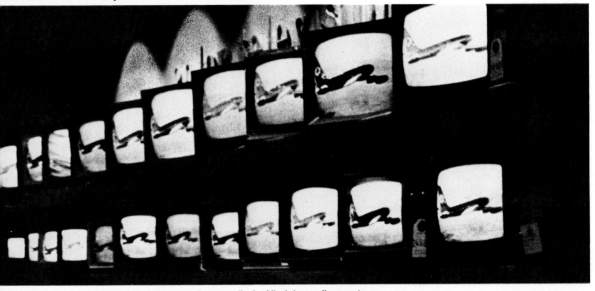

oduced for a mass market, television sets line a wall of a Virginia appliance store.

Like most parents, I wonder anxiously about what kind of world my children will live in when they are adults. They are in high school and at the turn of the century will still be younger than I am now. What has the future in store for them? Three-dimensional television, commercial rocket ships, immunity to cancer, mechanical hearts? But will they find clean air and water? Will they enjoy livable surroundings? And will they have those intangible rewards that have made life worth living for most of my generation?

If I took my daughters to the Long Island shore or the New Jersey marsh, once happy hiking grounds for my boyhood bird club, we'd find the first occupied by apartment houses, the other by a smoldering dump. The ospreys I used to see sailing northward with the spring thaw, the bald eagles riding the ice cakes on the Hudson—they are going, or are all but gone, from the whole country.

From other regions of the globe come more grievous calls of distress—reports of ill-fed, unemployed, or underemployed millions in festering slums. If my daughters ignore or isolate themselves from the hunger and poverty elsewhere, they will be guilty of the logic described by Paul R. Ehrlich, professor of biology at Stanford University: To consider the population explosion and the attendant threat of starvation solely as a problem of the underdeveloped world is like saying to a fellow passenger, "Your end of the boat is sinking."

I once studied a zoology textbook published in 1943 that predicted the world population would stabilize around A.D. 2100 with some 2,645,000,000 people. We reached that number 17 years ago.

What on earth has happened?

Robert C. Cook, former president of the Population Reference Bureau, told me that question had been posed to him many times. "To understand," he said, "you have to go back to shortly before 1800, when an English physician, Edward Jenner, discovered a vaccine for smallpox. Deaths from smallpox in London fell almost overnight from more than 2,000 a year to about 600.

"Until that time a fourth of the babies usually died within a year of their birth. Half or fewer reached maturity. Disease and famine sometimes wiped out a quarter of a country's inhabitants in a single year. But after Jenner, a wave of discoveries in medicine, sanitation, and agriculture gradually helped to bring major diseases under control and to extend the average life span. Women once had to bear six to eight children just to maintain the population. When the same high birth rate continued as the death rate declined, the population swiftly increased."

Mr. Cook, a wiry, youthful septuagenarian, turned to statistics to emphasize what happened. "It took nearly 700 years—from 1086 to 1750—for the population of England and Wales to increase from 1 million to 7.5 million, but between 1750 and 1901 it jumped from 7.5 to 30.5 million.

"Still, that quadrupling took some 150 years. As more of their children survived, the Europeans began to realize that they did not need so many offspring to replace themselves. They responded spontaneously, and had fewer children. By 1925 much of the Western World was approaching a near balance between births and deaths. Moreover, Europe had a safety valve during this adjustment period in the vast unsettled lands in the Americas and elsewhere, and more than 60 million people emigrated to these regions from crowded cities and impoverished farms.

"In Latin America, Asia, and Africa, especially after World War II, the campaigns against malaria and other dread diseases caused the death rate to plummet. In Ceylon, for instance, it decreased by 50 percent in less than a decade—a feat that had taken the United States the first half of this century to accomplish. But in most of the developing nations, women have kept on bearing just as many children as before."

Geometric progression

What this means in population growth is illustrated by a Middle Eastern legend. A minister of the king's court invented the game of chess for his monarch's pleasure, so the story goes, and the king sought to reward him. The clever minister appeared to want but little. "Just give me one grain of wheat for the first square," he said, "two for the next, four for the next, eight for the next, and so on, doubling with each of the 64 squares of the board."

The king quickly assented, for it seemed such a modest proposal. But he soon found that he could not fulfill his pledge—even with all the wheat in his realm.

In many countries human beings today are multiplying by that same geometric progression, doubling every generation.

For millenniums the birth rate and death rate maintained a near equilibrium, and the population grew, but slowly. It took centuries—from the early years of the Christian Era to the founding of Jamestown—for the world population of some 250,000,000 to double.

TED SPIEGEL, COURTESY ROCKEFELLER FOUNDATION (TOP AND BOTTOM);
NATIONAL GEOGRAPHIC PHOTOGRAPHER JAMES P. BLAIR

But by 1850 the population again had doubled, to more than a billion. And by 1930 it had doubled once more, to two billion. On a global scale the doubling period will be down to an estimated 35 years by 1975.

But won't birth rates in developing nations drop as they did in countries like ours?

I carried this question to New York and to the Rockefeller Foundation, which has sponsored programs of public health in needy countries for half a century.

Said Dr. John Maier, associate director of the foundation's program that supports family planning in more than 20 countries:

"In places with populations of hundreds of millions, increasing by 2 to 3 percent a year, we haven't got a hundred years to slow the birth rate. In most of Asia, Africa, and Latin America a spiraling population largely cancels out the increases in food production. These countries find themselves running to stay in the same place.

"But this doesn't mean that the industrialized nations stand in the clear. A growth rate of about 1 percent a year, like that of the United States, doubles the population in 70 years. Even if couples began *right now* having only enough children to replace themselves, our population wouldn't level off until the 2030's."

"And what would happen if it went on increasing?" I asked.

"Look around you," Dr. Maier replied.

I already had. Rockefeller Center had been an inspiring sight when the grouping of tall buildings took form back in the days of the Great Depression. But now, huge dark slabs of other structures towered all around, blocking out the sky. I said that they made me think of bar graphs of ominous statistics.

"Maybe they are—if they show the way cities are going," Dr. Maier replied. "In any case, we are already witnessing a deterioration of the quality of urban life—declining public services, crowds when offices let out, more noise, more dirt, more insecurity, less access to cultural opportunities.

"This is congestion. In the United States the number of people alone has something to do with the effect on the environment; but how they are distributed has even more. Seventy percent of us are jammed onto 2 percent of the land, with the imbalance steadily growing."

Forty-two floors below Dr. Maier's office, I jostled with lunch-hour crowds. Where work sheds and machines—harbingers of yet another behemoth building—crowded the sidewalk, the pedestrian overflow spilled out into the traffic-filled streets. On a crowded Manhattan bus, which was taking twice as long to

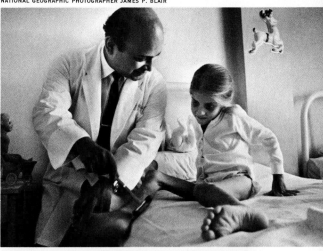

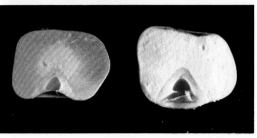

Seriously deficient in protein, a 9-year-old youngster undergoes tests at Candelaria, Colombia (top). To treat her, doctors used a diet of a new strain of corn containing a protein-enriching gene, opaque-2; the mutant (above right) packs twice the nutrition of ordinary corn. Recovered (below), the child chats two years later with Dr. Alberto Pradilla, who pioneered medical application of the corn. New grains may help curb malnutrition while man seeks to slow population growth.

get me where I was going as it did when I was a boy, I thought back to when I was 12 or 13. My friends and I had marched up and down a stretch of Long Beach on Long Island yanking out stakes that marked the boundary lines for future subdivisions. Futilely we hoped to rescue the beach we loved from the developers, from the rash of houses that today spread over the area.

Anthony Storr, a British psychiatrist, wrote in his book, *Human Aggression:* "The closer we are packed, the more easily resentful of each other we become. It is probably on this account that many people find life in cities irritating and exhausting, since they are compelled to control aggressive impulses which arise solely as a result of overcrowding."

Studies of animals suggest that crowding can be damaging in unsuspected ways. In experiments conducted by John B. Calhoun of the National Institute of Mental Health in Bethesda, Maryland, crowded rats showed highly abnormal forms of behavior. Some became aggressive, some apathetic. Even when given more space, they huddled together compulsively in a "pathological togetherness." And eventually they stopped reproducing.

Dr. Calhoun of course recognizes that we should not leap to conclusions about human beings based on observations of the behavior of rats. However, he believes that the effects of overcrowding in his experiments are so disturbing that the world cannot wait for proof that they apply to man.

Population explosions among deer and rabbits in confined areas have sent death rates up as a result of stress and other psychological problems. While on the staff of the U. S. Naval Medical Research Institute in Bethesda, Dr. John J. Christian performed autopsies on deer that had died mysteriously in great numbers for no apparent reason. He concluded that stress associated with high population density caused physiological changes that weakened and killed the animals.

If the herding of people into spreading cities compounds the problem of population growth, modern man's capability and zeal as a producer and consumer pose major threats to the environment.

"More and fancier" has been the slogan of our civilization. We wrest what we want from the earth, caring little what damage we leave in our wake. Then we dump what we create when we no longer want it.

For Americans, more people traditionally have meant more business, greater prosperity. Specialists I talked with as I traveled agree that the population problem in affluent America differs from that created by the hungry poor in developing countries. Slowly we are beginning to realize that a rapidly growing population in the United States, as well as in the rest of the world, is placing a greater and greater burden on the earth.

Technology and ingenuity could stretch the limits of the earth's resources; but authorities disagree on just what those limits are. They argue about the optimum population. They argue even more about controlling population growth. Deeply concerned, some ecologists contend the problem is infinitely more serious than most of us realize, and they ask: Is there *anything* we can do at this eleventh hour with the world's population of billions to stave off a colossal disaster?

In the opinion of Philip M. Hauser, director of the University of Chicago Population Research Center: "Given the present outlook, only the faithful who believe in miracles, the optimistic who anticipate scientific wonders, the fortunate who think they can continue to exist on islands of affluence in a sea of world poverty, and the naive who anticipate nothing can look to the future with equanimity."

"We're adding some 40 million to our population in 15 years, and that creates problems," said George H. Brown, director of the Bureau of the Census. "But while our population is going up by about 1 percent a year, our incomes have been increasing by as much as 4 percent. Convert the expanding population and incomes into the resources it takes to make the things people buy and the wastes left over, and you have an idea of the magnitude of the problem we are going to face.

"Don't mistake me," he quickly added. "I'm not against affluence. Apart from everything else, it offers people options in life. And I trust people. I believe they'll decide to devote some of their affluence to saving the environment."

Is there a choice?

But will we? In the opinion of Professor Ehrlich, outspoken apostle of population control, we have but little choice. The United States must "move from an enormously wasteful and ecologically dangerous economy," he said, "to a safe, resource-conserving economy.

"Americans must begin to question their fundamental assumptions," he added. "Is property really more valuable than human life? Does a person automatically have a high standard of living if he makes $50,000 a year and has two expensive cars, while his children are having their lives shortened by air pollution? Can a person have a high quality of life while people are going hungry in his city? In his country? On his planet?"

I have discussed this issue many times with Richard M. Scammon, a colleague from my post-World War II days in the Department of State, who later served as director of the Census Bureau. We have debated whether the United States can continue to thrive with a rapidly expanding population.

Dick takes the optimistic view that "our 400 million Americans of the next century will be better off than we are today." He adds, "I don't worry about an increasing population so long as technology is advancing too. Population itself is no problem."

Not many demographers would agree with Dr. Scammon on this last point, but George Brown expressed a similar confidence in technology: "The engineering capabilities exist to accomplish almost anything we want," he said. "You might even get a pollution-free car, for example, if you were willing to pay the price."

Meanwhile, we are living far more extravagantly than most other peoples.

In his lifetime an American born today will consume 9 tons of milk and cream, 5½ tons of meat, another 5½ tons of wheat, and 56 million gallons of water, including the amount used for his needs by agriculture and industry. And he will buy 37,000 gallons of gasoline.

By conservative estimates he will use at least 30 times more natural resources than a resident of India, assuming the present gap in income continues—and in fact that gap is growing wider.

"Obviously, what counts is not so much the number of us but our growing productivity and appetites," said Hans H. Landsberg, director of the appraisal program at Resources for the Future, Inc., a private, nonprofit research organization in Washington, D. C.

"Let's take a look at a few figures," he said, turning instinctively to one of the shelves of bound reports that line his office.

"Today we generate eight times more electricity than we did 30 years ago. But expanding consumption, not population growth, accounts for 90 percent of that increase.

"Population growth alone would have raised the demand for beef by 35 percent in 20 years. In fact, we devour 120 percent more beef than we did in 1950. Substantially greater numbers of us are eating better and using more power and natural resources."

"But will resources continue to be available to support us in such a style?" I asked.

Mr. Landsberg replied with a qualified yes. "For the foreseeable future, they will. But there will have to be substitutions—such as

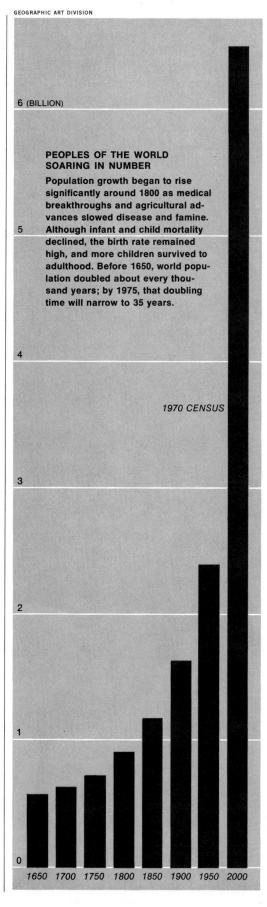

PEOPLES OF THE WORLD SOARING IN NUMBER

Population growth began to rise significantly around 1800 as medical breakthroughs and agricultural advances slowed disease and famine. Although infant and child mortality declined, the birth rate remained high, and more children survived to adulthood. Before 1650, world population doubled about every thousand years; by 1975, that doubling time will narrow to 35 years.

1970 CENSUS

6 (BILLION)

5

4

3

2

1

0

1650 1700 1750 1800 1850 1900 1950 2000

Famine: warning to a crowded world

Crops wither, animals die, farmers give up their parched fields to an unrelenting sun — and the specter of famine haunts parts of India. Food shortages, caused by failure of the monsoons in 1966-67, affected more than 70 million people, mostly in Bihar State. Some areas recorded almost total crop failures. Although natural calamity brought widespread starvation to India's Bihar State, the expanding world population — if it continues to increase at the present rate — could result in suffering and deaths among billions instead of millions during future famines. Sheer numbers of people might outstrip the earth's productive capacity.

Responding to India's plight, the United States shipped 8 million tons of grain in 600 ships — the largest such relief operation in history. But American and international surpluses cannot long fill the gap. Already, many millions of people may starve to death each year, and at least half of the world's 3.7 billion inhabitants suffer either from undernourishment (lack of food) or malnutrition (serious dietary imbalances).

Some population and food experts foresee cataclysmic famines within the next decade. The crisis began after World War II when population growth began to outrun food production in a number of countries. By 1958 serious shortages occurred. In 1966 the earth's population expanded by 70 million, but food production showed no compensatory gain. Fortunately, improved varieties of corn, rice, and wheat came into large-scale use about this time, and the so-called Green Revolution began.

First from experimental plots and then from vast fields, new grains sprouted — hybrids of older varieties that contained the most desirable characteristics of each strain: increased yield, higher quality protein, greater disease resistance, and better milling and baking properties. The Philippines, after 65 years of importing rice, became self-sufficient. In India and Pakistan wheat production jumped 50 percent, and Pakistan even began exporting rice.

Despite new grains and greater yields, some authorities still fear that world population will outrun food supply. "We have only delayed the world food crisis for another 30 years," warns Norman E. Borlaug, winner of the 1970 Nobel Peace Prize for his development of wheat. By 1980 India's population will jump 150 million; even the United States, with its efficient agricultural system, would have to struggle to keep up with such a surge. Some experts think the distant years look even bleaker. Predicts Dr. Borlaug: "If the world population continues to increase at the same rate, we will destroy the species."

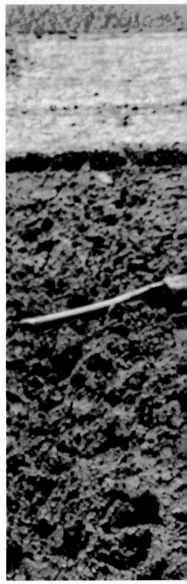

His bullock dead, an Indian farmer qu

Open hands await a ration of free grain after drought and crop failures swept India's Bihar State.

barren field. The 1966-67 drought brought widespread hunger.

haris divide U. S. wheat, part of a shipment that reduced America's surplus by one-fifth.

aluminum for copper, which already has gone quite a way, and plastics for timber. Altogether, we probably have only begun to explore substitution possibilities, and the same is true of recycling. Thus the outlook for nonrenewable resources is not nearly so gloomy as a look at any one of them in isolation would lead many of us to believe.

"Take water—we are terribly wasteful of this resource. If we made the consumer pay the true cost of what he uses or pollutes, he would use less water. We need to employ economic incentives to preserve the environment.

"I know there are distinguished scientists who say we're going to run out of resources," Mr. Landsberg continued. "They plot our increasing demand for metals against known reserves, and it's like walking the plank; in a generation we go off the end.

"I can't argue with them because supply is less easily projected than demand, and each material is indeed available on this planet in finite amounts. But I'm satisfied that technology will continue to find new sources of raw materials, to devise substitutes, and to improve reuse techniques."

It is quite true that we depend heavily on raw materials from abroad. We import all of our tin and 90 percent or more of our asbestos, bauxite, chromite, manganese, and nickel. With only 6 percent of the earth's population, we absorb 35 percent of the world's annual output of energy and account for a similar percentage of its yearly consumption of other nonrenewable resources.

It is not easy to remain comfortable in the face of these statistics. Some economists and geologists visualize a specter of critical shortages as the developing nations of the world begin to step up their consumption of metals, fuels, and food.

In a report, *Resources and Man*, published in 1969, the National Academy of Sciences predicted that known and prospective reserves of tin, mercury, tungsten, and helium will be "nearly exhausted by the end of this century."

I already had learned that today we are mining ore that contains only .2 percent copper. When I was a college student, the average deposit in production contained at least ten times that much ore.

Dr. Barry Commoner, a widely quoted biologist at Washington University in St. Louis, blames the extensive use of the new technologies for the environmental crisis.

"Since 1945 synthetic fabrics, detergents, and plastics have replaced natural materials such as cotton, wool, soap, and lumber. But manufacturing nylon, Banlon, and Dacron pollutes the environment more than raising cotton and sheep. At the same time nature does not absorb or assimilate these synthetics, and they continue to accumulate as pollutants."

Other authorities cite fancy and superfluous packaging—polyethylene, paper, and cardboard which tax resources and fill dumps—and arbitrary design changes which create an artificial demand for goods.

Pressure of numbers

Are we to conclude, then, that population growth is of minor significance? Not in the view of many, including the embattled president of the National Parks and Conservation Association, whom I visited in his brownstone headquarters in the Nation's Capital. Anthony Wayne Smith spoke out forcefully.

"Yes, pressure for consumption is degrading the environment. But eventually the problem comes down to numbers of people. You can have only so many people and still preserve the beaches, mountains, and wetlands in anything like their natural state."

A lawyer, Mr. Smith led successful campaigns against a planned jetport in the Everglades and proposals which called for construction of a series of high dams on the Potomac River.

"The use of power," he continued, "may be increasing at a far faster rate than the population, but more people will consume just that much more. And the way we are operating, that means all the more pollution.

"The national parks probably can absorb substantially greater numbers of people, but they cannot take much more motor traffic. And traffic does not exist apart from people: the more people, the more traffic."

Visits to the parks have been increasing by nearly 8 percent a year over the last nine years, reaching 172 million in 1970. Should this rate continue, the number of park visits annually would reach 1.6 billion by the year 2000. I look back almost with disbelief to our first family camping trip in 1956, when we found the Balsam Mountain Campground in the Great Smoky Mountains in North Carolina two-thirds empty. On a big weekend today hundreds of families arriving to camp in such spots may be turned away. Accommodating the coming millions threatens the purpose for which the parks were created—to conserve "the scenery and the natural and historic objects and the wild life . . . by such means as will leave them unimpaired for the enjoyment of future generations."

Dick Scammon referred me to the co-author

of his latest book as one who made short work of population alarmists. Although Ben Wattenberg, a member of the White House staff of President Lyndon B. Johnson, believes that the United States probably could support twice, if not four times, its present population, even he concedes that growth obviously cannot go on forever. "It is wise to understand this fact now rather than a hundred years from now," Mr. Wattenberg said.

Moreover, even those who are not aghast at the prospect of our adding 130 million or more to our population in the next 50 years would declare all bets off if the more than 2.6 billion inhabitants of Asia, Africa, and Latin America continue to increase at the present rate.

But population is so controversial a field that no view goes unchallenged. A few years ago Karl Brandt, then director of Stanford University's Food Research Institute, considered most of the Southern Hemisphere as well as the United States "underpopulated." Recently I asked Dr. Brandt if he recognized any ecological limits to the carrying capacity of the earth.

"The world's available capacity of food, feed, and organic raw materials is so enormous," he replied, "that the prediction of famine caused by population growth in coming decades contradicts the facts."

Most demographers are not nearly so convinced. In their view the famines that Thomas Robert Malthus in 1798 believed would control population increases may yet become a harsh reality before children now in high school reach middle age. Malthus said that food production could not keep up with man's capacity to reproduce, but advances in agriculture and the vast fertile lands in the Americas eliminated the threat of mass starvation as population growth continued. Though for a time in the 1960's it looked as if Malthus would be proved right, the development of new so-called miracle grains has brought a reprieve.

But for how long?

"I always say 20 years when I am asked that question," replied J. George Harrar, president of the Rockefeller Foundation, as we sat at breakfast in a hotel not far from the White House. An eminent biologist who played a leading part in obtaining that reprieve, Dr. Harrar went to Mexico in 1943 to develop more productive varieties of corn and wheat to help meet the urgent need for grain there.

"We didn't know whether we could bring it off," he told me. "But by 1956 the improved types yielded twice as much to the acre, and the Green Revolution was born." And a few years later the International Rice Research

Laundry draped from balconies reflects the jammed existence of resettlement-housing dwellers in Hong Kong. Living five to seven in a room, many residents occupy as little as 30 square feet of space. Throughout the world, the migration from rural areas has placed heavy pressure on the urban environment. In the U. S., 70 percent of the people live on 2 percent of the land. Such crowding, sociologists contend, may result in increased sickness, stress, and aggressive behavior.

Institute in the Philippines bred a similarly productive miracle rice.

When agricultural scientist Dr. Norman E. Borlaug learned that he had been selected to receive the 1970 Nobel Peace Prize for his work on new varieties of wheat in the Rockefeller-supported program, he warned newsmen: "We have only delayed the world food crisis for another 30 years. If the world population continues to increase at the same rate, we will destroy the species."

Lester R. Brown, an energetic young man who grew up on a truck farm in New Jersey, has helped buy time to confront the population problem. As a Department of Agriculture executive from 1966 to 1969, he played a key role in exporting the Green Revolution to hungry nations. "But there is no painless way left to increase the food supply," he said. "The projected end-of-century population of 6½ or 7 billion is in my mind not sustainable. The Green Revolution has achieved a temporary victory over famine, but unless mankind makes better use of the time it has, the stork will outrun the plow once again."

Meanwhile, the statistics grow ever more staggering. For example, each year India adds the equivalent of almost twice the present number of people in New York City to the country's population. At this rate it will pass the billion mark by the year 2000.

How will such hordes of people affect the value attached to human life? I found an answer during World War II on arrival in India when my unit was taken east from Bombay by train. I saw the sympathy and concern of my fellow soldiers for the imploring, poverty-stricken throngs at the stations turn—within a hundred miles—to an appalled aversion.

Robert S. McNamara, president of the World Bank, addressing a meeting of the organization's board of governors in 1970, warned that ". . . the population problem will not go away. It will be resolved," he said, "in one way or another; either by sensible solutions or senseless suffering. . . . without a slowing down and control of the population explosion, the life awaiting millions upon millions of this planet's future inhabitants will be stunted, miserable, and tragic. . . ."

A man in the forefront of the struggle to achieve a worldwide reduction in births is Gen. William H. Draper, Jr., U. S. representative to the United Nations Population Commission. While heading a committee studying foreign aid for President Dwight D. Eisenhower, General Draper concluded that population growth was severely interfering with economic development in the countries that needed it most. Among his many other activities, he also serves on the board of the International Planned Parenthood Federation.

"Our aim," he told me, speaking of the work of the federation, "is to see that all couples everywhere have the information and service they need to exercise their right to have no more children than they want. We provide assistance in family planning through private clinics in more than 70 countries, but we need more research on better methods of preventing conception."

Family-planning programs often fail to cope with the problem created by people who desire too many children. Some authorities strongly feel that we must find a way to motivate families to want fewer offspring.

Centuries-old religious and social values are formidable obstacles to reducing family size. The Roman Catholic Church continues to ban the use of contraceptives. In some nations children are regarded as proof of virility, in others as insurance against want in old age. However, the governments of some 35 countries now have official population programs or are providing assistance in family planning.

Family-planning services

In the United States, Congress in 1970 authorized the expenditure of nearly 400 million dollars for population research and family-planning services over a three-year period. These services are designed to reach more than five million American women who reportedly lack the knowledge of ways to regulate the number of their offspring.

Demographers are waiting to see what the results will be. For most would agree that the United States has a real population problem— "not catastrophic, but serious," to use Robert Cook's words. In all four of the Census Bureau projections, the rate of population growth will inch upward into the 1980's before beginning to decline, and in all but the two lowest projections, the rate for the year 2000 will continue higher than it was in 1970.

Mr. Cook looks to common sense to resolve the problem. "On the average, each American woman now appears to be bearing about 2.5 children. This is not very far above the 2.1 figure that eventually would bring about zero population growth—the point at which the number of births equals the number of deaths.

"In less than a century—from about 1830 to 1920—the U. S. birth rate declined by one half. It continued downward in the halcyon days of the 1920's and reached a record low during the Great Depression. And though it spurted upward briefly after World War II, the birth rate today is lower than it was in the depths of the Depression. More and more people are realizing that small families are better for children and better for parents."

A Gallup Poll in January 1971 revealed that the percentage of Americans who favor families of four or more children has declined since 1967. And it appears that couples are marrying later and that the wife waits longer before the first child is born.

But what if this trend does not continue?

Zero Population Growth, an organization formed in 1969, offers one answer: governmental action. Professor Ehrlich, principal founder of Z. P. G., would provide bonuses to discourage or delay childbearing. If these incentives failed, he would impose "tax penalties and other sanctions against overbreeding."

Garrett Hardin, professor of biology at the University of California at Santa Barbara, makes similar proposals. He believes that if we defend the freedom to breed, we shall ultimately lose all other freedoms as a result of overcrowding. As a last resort he proposes sterilization of women who have borne a set number of children. A child, Dr. Hardin argues, is not the exclusive owner of genes handed down from generation to generation. The individual serves only as the temporary custodian of these genes, for in reality they belong to the species. Moreover, he says, bringing up children is costing society more and more; even less than in the past is childbearing a matter in the exclusive sphere of two parents.

Such views are far from universally accepted. Karl Brandt probably spoke for many in opposing what he called the "dictates of these tyrants who know too well what is good for other people."

Some persons feel that society has no business promoting contraception. They bitterly oppose liberalized abortion laws. "The human embryo is a human being from the moment of conception," they say in protest. "Legalized abortion is legalized murder."

I asked Dr. Edward V. Evarts, physiologist at the National Institute of Mental Health, to tell me at what age he believes a human fetus becomes a human being. "It's a question I don't think many doctors would try to answer," he replied.

"However, one can say that under six or seven months the fetus is not viable independent of the mother. Most physicians today believe that abortion should be a matter between a woman and her doctor."

Clouded though it may be with myriad, complicated questions, the problem of population growth poses a potentially crucial issue for the future. Hardly less crucial for us as an affluent Nation is an allied question: Can we afford an ever-expanding flow of homes and vacation cottages, television sets, cameras, stereo phonographs, automobiles, motorboats, airplanes, and products yet to be invented, *and at the same time bear the high costs of safeguarding our environment?*

I went back to Hans Landsberg of Resources for the Future with this question and got a firm no. "The rate at which volume and variety of such goods increase is bound to decline. We perhaps need a measure of how well our society is doing based not only on ingots of steel and board feet of lumber produced but also on the condition of our streams and landscapes and other things on which the survival of the species depends."

I found this view strongly held by others at Resources for the Future. "Too often we judge our performance by our gross national product," said Michael Brewer, the young vice president. "And we include in it not only smoke-belching factories but also the value of smoke-abatement devices, while omitting many valuable assets without price tags to individual consumers — pleasant vistas, rivers to swim in, land under natural cover, an unpoisoned biosphere. We need standards that give full value to what makes the world livable."

I have long felt that as we sacrifice nature, we shall find that not only has life lost its savor and excitement, but also that society is beset by mounting ills.

What will we choose? Will we adjust to a world filled with trash or drown in a sea of our own pollution? Will we have the resources to preserve the quality of our life?

I encountered a welter of opinions; everywhere people spoke emphatically about the effect of an increasing population on the environment. Does the present pace of population growth or the ever-expanding conquests of technology pose the greater peril? The answer would seem to be that each multiplies the damage done by the other. If it is technology that makes us ever more burdensome to the environment, then each additional person becomes ever worse news for the earth.

As a practical matter we probably cannot stop technological progress, but technology can be used to safeguard and restore the earth.

Few reasonable persons doubt that there is a limit to the carrying capacity of the planet. The only significant disagreement would seem to be over the imminence of the catastrophe that is being brought on by mankind's rapid rate of increase.

Community worker Elva Arce canvasses New York's East Side, distributing birth-control literature.

Inocencia Padilla shows an intrauterine device to members of the Luis Vega family. More than 30 nations now support wide-scale

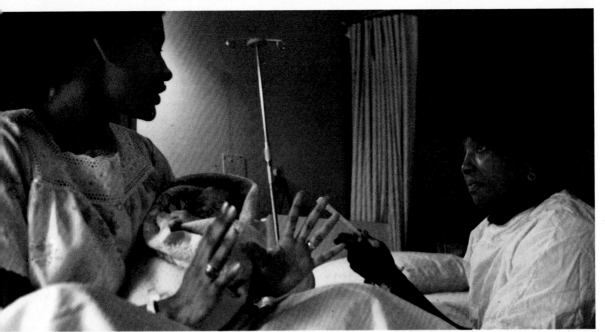

In Harlem's Sydenham Hospital, Pearl Benjamin explains contraceptive methods to a new mother.

birth-control programs.

Family planning gains converts

Three raven-haired children sit on the floor in a tidy Brooklyn flat, watching curiously as Inocencia Padilla, a neighbor, hands a small, convoluted object to their parents, Luis and Adriana Vega. "It's an intrauterine device —an IUD," she says. "When it is placed in the womb, it keeps you from getting pregnant." The Vegas receive a practical explanation of several other methods of birth control during the quiet, half-hour conversation. In a program sponsored by the Office of Economic Opportunity, some 1,600 neighborhood workers, centered at 450 clinics in economically deprived areas across the country, contact almost 500,000 women each year in homes, beauty shops, coin-operated laundries, and supermarkets.

"It's an overwhelming success," says Ella McDonald, director of New York City's 13 clinics. "The low-key approach really works." Liberalized abortion laws, voluntary sterilizations, and a trend toward later marriage also have played a part in lowering the U. S. birth rate by a third in 15 years; even so, births continue to exceed deaths by a ratio of 2 to 1.

Handmade poster urges planned births.

CONCERNED PEOPLE: KEY TO TOMORROW

By Haynes Johnson

Wading in an oil spill in San Francisco Bay, part of a volunteer army of thousands clears straw spread to absorb oil lost after a

"More than any other single issue, the environment has united Americans today. The evidence is all around us."

anker collision in January 1971.

Affluent America long ago bypassed Anmoore, West Virginia. For years the town slumbered in the backwash of the Appalachians, nestled in the rugged beauty of the hills and hollows and secure in the one industry that sustained it.

There were problems, to be sure. Anmoore's 960 citizens enjoyed few of the comforts common to other towns in other areas. In spring, people picked their way through streets clogged with mud. They had no adequate sewer system, no parks, no health clinic. The air they breathed was filled with grime and soot pouring forth around the clock from the seven factory chimneys that dominate the town. It wasn't the best kind of life, but the people of Anmoore tolerated it, for they had learned the old lesson: Don't bite the hand that feeds you.

Then one day one man rose up to challenge the system. He set in motion a chain of events that has made Anmoore a symbol of the long, hard struggle to halt the degradation of our environment. A few years ago Dale Hagedorn, a free-lance commercial artist, noticed an advertisement in a West Virginia newspaper: "A little bit of Union Carbide is in every house in West Virginia."

He got the message, but not quite the one the company intended.

"The grime and soot from Carbide's factory were not only in my house, but in my clothes, my air, and my lungs," Mr. Hagedorn told me. He immediately wrote to company headquarters in New York City complaining about pollution in his hometown. No results. But he did not give up. Slowly, a movement took form that eventually was to change the lives of everyone in Anmoore and become a focal point of national attention in the anti-pollution struggle.

Mr. Hagedorn was no crusader, nor was Anmoore a hotbed of citizens' action. Indeed, those are key parts of the story. Encouraged by his wife, he began his campaign to change the environment in which he lived—an effort he felt had little chance of success.

"I guess I thought all a citizen could do was to write a letter of protest," he said. "It was somewhat demoralizing. The feeling was that the town was going down, but everybody thought, 'What's the use?'"

Anmoore had been dependent on the Carbide carbon products division works for so long that it seemed unthinkable to question

Haynes Johnson *won a Pulitzer Prize in journalism in 1966. His columns in the* Washington Post *distinguish him as a keen observer of life in America.*

the side effects of air pollution. Carbide over-shadowed everything in town, and everything showed it. On the main street at a gas station near the plant, an attendant cleaned my wind-shield and launched into a monologue: "There's no clean air here. I'm a country boy myself, and I start hacking every morning I come down here. Sometimes I vomit."

In front of the post office alongside Danny's barber shop and Arlene's lunch-and-beer res-taurant, the American flag hung limply, be-draggled and begrimed. Up on the hill over-looking the pall of orange and black smoke shrouding the valley, a housewife sat in her small clapboard home and complained about "that black stuff": "The children, you know, I use scouring powder to scrub that black off their feet. And it's all over the drapes and the dishes. You can have an airtight house and it still seeps in."

For years no one had done any more than grumble. Pollution was a fact of life you ac-cepted. Until, that is, the citizens got angry—and organized.

I asked Mr. Hagedorn what caused him to take action.

"You know, you live under a smokestack and you endure so much dirt," he said, "but when it becomes excessive you say, 'Wait a minute, you're my neighbor and you shouldn't do that.' What finally got my back up was a feeling of frustration at being ignored. It was this big-me, little-you attitude on the part of the company. They said they couldn't do any-thing about it.

"Their excuse was always, 'Unfortunately, our product is black.'"

A campaign begins

In July 1967 Mr. Hagedorn and his wife began writing letters of protest: to local and state officials, to the West Virginia Air Pollu-tion Control Commission, to the governor, to their congressman, to a number of federal agencies. "Everybody was real nice," he said, "but nobody did anything."

He turned to the people of Anmoore, dis-tributing a newsletter called *Carbon Copy* in which he carried on his campaign against the company. A petition was circulated, town meetings organized, an Anmoore Citizens for Clean Air Committee established. Still no suc-cess. Then he branched out and started con-tacting local radio and television stations and newspapers across the state. The fight began to attract attention.

After an account of Anmoore's problems appeared in a Charleston, West Virginia, news-paper, Mr. Hagedorn contacted a group of public-interest attorneys. "We had been threat-ening to sue Carbide," he recalled, "but we didn't know how to go about it. The lawyers wanted to know if we were really serious and what resources we had. We said we were seri-ous, all right, but we had no resources."

John L. Boettner, Jr., of the Appalachian Research and Defense Fund became interested in the Anmoore situation and assisted Dale and Leonise Hagedorn in filing a $100,000 damage suit against Union Carbide and gov-ernmental pollution-control agencies, citing citizens' rights under the Fifth, Ninth, and Fourteenth Amendments. "I am real proud of the points of that suit," Mr. Hagedorn said, "that every American citizen has the right to private property and to enjoy it, that he has the right to breathe clean air."

Anmoore's citizens, casting off a history of apathy, joined the fight with a reckless kind of courage. Buck Gladden, a mayor with an eighth-grade education, publicly challenged Union Carbide and spoke of dealing what he called "a blow against corporate colonialism."

By then, Anmoore's battle was attracting national attention through the news media.

Another Carbide plant, at Marietta, Ohio, on the West Virginia line, also had a long his-tory of citizen discontent. A Clean Air Com-mittee in Vienna, West Virginia, across the Ohio River from Marietta, had been trying for years to halt the tons of pollutants raining down on the town.

The Federal Government had been investi-gating citizens' complaints of air pollution since 1965. At the first pollution abatement conference in 1967 the company refused to supply necessary data on emissions, but re-leased the information when the conference reconvened in 1969.

"At first they wouldn't even let us in the factory to look around," commented one U. S. official. Three years passed before the Gov-ernment called for a 40-percent reduction in sulfur dioxide emissions. The company coun-tered: It proposed to cut its emissions by 12.5 percent, and that only by December 1971.

In the meantime, something new had been taking place across America. The fight against pollution had become a national cause, and the Federal Government made Union Carbide a test case of its will to clean up the environ-ment. The Government's new Environmental Protection Agency entered the picture in a landmark show of strength, curtly rejecting Carbide's schedule for reducing pollutants from the Marietta plant. It was "not accept-able," the Government said. An "immediate commitment" was ordered, and the company immediately accepted a 40-percent reduction in sulfur dioxide emissions.

In Anmoore another signal action occurred. Early in 1971 the Union Carbide Corporation announced an 8½-million-dollar program to purchase air-pollution control equipment and rebuild furnaces at the Anmoore plant. The program was designed, the company said, to bring the plant within the requirements of the West Virginia Air Pollution Control Commission standards. Work began in mid-March 1971, with completion scheduled for three years later. Anmoore will have cleaner air.

"I'll have to say this," said Margaret Golden, a town council member who had become a vocal participant in Anmoore's antipollution fight, "It'll never be the same again for Union Carbide and the people."

No one took more pleasure than Dale Hagedorn. "It's been a thrilling thing for us," he said. "Indeed, the citizen does matter—he matters very much. He has freedom of speech, and by golly he can use it—and use it with tremendous impact. I've learned that little people can count if they don't lie down or quit."

Anmoore tells a story common to many American communities these days. The situation there goes to the heart of the questions that made pollution so difficult an issue, for it isn't a simple case of black or white, good versus bad.

The Anmoore story illustrates how the need for jobs coupled with a company's desire to maintain maximum production at the lowest cost, can cause a critical deterioration of the environment. It also shows how complex the problems are, how they touch virtually every aspect of American life, from economics to government to individuals. And it demonstrates that citizen action can bring change.

More than any other single issue, the environment has united Americans today. The evidence is all around us. After an oil spill in California's San Francisco Bay, a volunteer army of citizens flocked down into the slime and muck to try to save the wildlife and preserve the shoreline. They did not wait for the Government or industry to clean up the mess.

Society matrons, businessmen, hippies with long hair, college girls with short dresses, and other concerned citizens—all drawn by the same impulse—worked together in a common cause, spreading straw over the water to absorb the oil.

Already, the record is filled with notable victories that show how citizen action can triumph against what seem overwhelming odds. They testify to two profound facts about

Water bucket catches particulate pollution from a zinc-smelting plant (background) in Bartlesville, Oklahoma. The city's Jaycees began monitoring emissions as part of their clean-air survey, one of several projects for improving community life. "It is our responsibility," says Ken Warren, Jaycee president. "Unless organizations like ours attack these problems, they will never be met head on. After all, we will face the mess in the future unless we work now to clean it up."

American society today: grass-roots democracy does work, and the system is responsive to change.

Florida offered another case of national significance, a case of beauty—primitive, irreplaceable beauty—versus progress. Once no one would have doubted the outcome, for progress always triumphed. It had been the American way. Cut down the forests, drain the swamps, level the mountains, build the highways, make way for civilization.

But the outcome this time was different.

Since 1942 the U. S. Army Corps of Engineers had studied ways to carve an inland waterway across the heartland of Florida, connecting the Atlantic Ocean and the Gulf of Mexico. The Cross-Florida Barge Canal, its promoters said, would benefit shippers, landowners, and manufacturers. Solidly behind the project were the bulk of Florida's congressional delegation, the governor, powerful state legislators, and the President.

Construction began in 1964 and proceeded smoothly throughout the rest of the sixties. By early 1971, some 50 million dollars of public tax funds had been spent and nearly a third of the 107-mile waterway had been completed. It would cut a path 150 feet wide and 12 feet deep from Palatka on the St. Johns River down along the Oklawaha River and on toward the Gulf near Yankeetown, Florida.

The Oklawaha is one of the Nation's few remaining wild rivers. It twists through a mile-wide valley covered by a dense, subtropical hardwood forest. Construction of the canal was transforming part of the Oklawaha into two desolate, stagnant, weed-clogged ponds. Some of the trees in the great forest towering above the marshland stood bare and dead, and others were dying. Already the Corps of Engineers had begun to burn the huge hardwood logs, lighting the swamps with the glow of their blaze.

There had been opposition to the canal since its inception, but conservation groups historically had had little effect on such major projects. Still, a Gainesville-based citizens' organization called Florida Defenders of the Environment, which included a number of scientists from state colleges and universities, kept chipping away.

"Our whole approach was to find the actual information and then make those facts available to the public," recalled Mrs. Archie Carr, vice president of the organization. "The reason we all became so concerned about this is that the more we studied the facts, the more we were convinced the canal was wrong.

"There was no justification for it from a con-servation standpoint, or from an economic standpoint."

Although the Oklawaha had been regarded as one of the great natural scenic attractions of Florida for generations, people had been persuaded that progress in the form of increased economic benefits flowing from the canal outweighed any considerations of beauty. "We found out," Mrs. Carr said, "that a great many of these economic arguments didn't have much to back them up." Her group contended, instead, that a dollar value can be placed on a scenic river; money flows also from tourism. But what really turned the case around, she added, was something more specific—the willingness to use the law and go to court to fight a threat to the environment.

One day in 1969, members of the organization read about a group called the Environmental Defense Fund, Inc., a New York-based action group of lawyers formed to help citizens fight their pollution cases by filing damage suits. "We immediately picked up the phone and called New York," Mrs. Carr said. The Environmental Defense Fund joined the Florida Defenders of the Environment, filing suit against the Corps of Engineers to stop the canal construction.

Construction halted

The Corps answered that no one had the right to sue it, arguing that as an agent of Congress it was immune to such legal action. There the matter stood until January of 1971, when a U. S. district court rendered a stunning decision. Judge Barrington D. Parker put a stop to canal construction. He was doing so, he ruled, because irrevocable injury or harm might occur to the swamps and river.

The judge then addressed himself to a wider question: Congress was arguing that we must preserve our environment. Yet the same Congress was defeating that very purpose by approving projects that citizens believed were damaging or destroying the environment. "Maybe this is a good time to get an understanding and reach an accord so all of these things can be resolved," he said.

Four days after Judge Parker's ruling, President Nixon took action on his own. Ordering a halt to further construction, he stated, "The step I have taken today will prevent a past mistake from causing permanent damage."

That action of the citizens in Florida demonstrated clearly that people determined to lobby aggressively through the political process—and file damage suits if necessary—could win. And it showed *(Continued on page 228)*

ssage on Mary Ann Nagy's T-shirt conveys the notoriety of Steubenville.

The pall of industrial smoke hung more heavily than usual over Steubenville, Ohio, in the summer of 1970: The Government announced that Steubenville ranked as the Nation's dirtiest city, based on results from 16 testing stations. Steubenville's reaction? Headlines and recriminations, then back to normal.

In contrast, the citizens of Anmoore, West Virginia, plagued for years by grime from a Union Carbide plant— the town's only industry—took direct action. By writing letters, circulating a petition, electing effective town officials, and speaking out at clean-air meetings, they drew national attention to their plight, forcing the company to commit itself to installing antipollution facilities.

Geography and weather contribute to Steubenville's problem. The city sprawls along a narrow Ohio River valley, and weather systems trap industrial emissions, raising air pollution to breathtaking levels. The steel mills, power plants, chemical companies, and nearly 100 other industries of the surrounding area all add their effluence to Steubenville's air. Ohio standards allow 65 micrograms of suspended particulates—soot, smoke, and dirt—per cubic meter of air; samples taken at City Annex averaged almost four times that much.

Steubenville's smokestacks fill a bowl-like valley with soot, smoke, and dirt. Some parts of the Steubenville area receive as muc

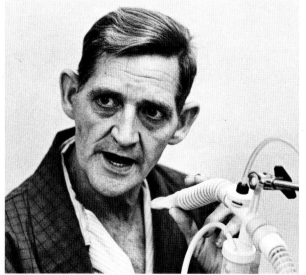

William B. Holmes: emphysema victim

Steubenville tolerates its grim

Industries in the Steubenville area employ thousand
most other businesses cater either to the industries
workers who depend on them. Few citizens will risk cha
lenging the steel companies that provide the city's ec
nomic base—officials estimate that 75 percent of loc
revenue comes from industry. William B. Holmes (left),
bricklayer for Wheeling-Pittsburgh Steel Corporation, h
lived near Steubenville all his life and has suffered fro
emphysema for several years. "They've been very go
to me," he says of his employers, and tells of co-worke
who take his place when "I'm too sick to work." Fred Tuc
er (right), vice president for environmental control f
National Steel Corporation, comments on Steubenville

30 to 40 tons of dustfall a month per square mile — the Federal Government specifies 15 tons as a livable limit.

toriety: "There hasn't been as much concern locally as
u'd expect. Most of the criticism has come from outside
e area." Paul Fabry of the Jefferson County Tuberculosis
d Health Association explains the lack of citizen
tion: "The schools felt it was too political, the business-
felt they'd be boycotted, the charitable organizations
pend on the steel companies for much of their income,
d everyone else works for the steel companies."
Political boundaries complicate the situation. About half
Steubenville's pollution comes across the Ohio River
m West Virginia; much of the remainder originates out-
e city limits, in Mingo Junction and Toronto. The divid-
line between federal air-pollution control districts also
ows the river, putting one regional director in Phila-
phia and the other in Chicago. In the spring of 1971
eubenville prepared for a primary city council election:
ne of the 11 candidates took a stand on air pollution.

Fred Tucker: steel company vice president

221

Slag heaps — dross of the steel industry — become backyard playgrounds. In Mingo Junction, near Steubenville, two girls walk acro

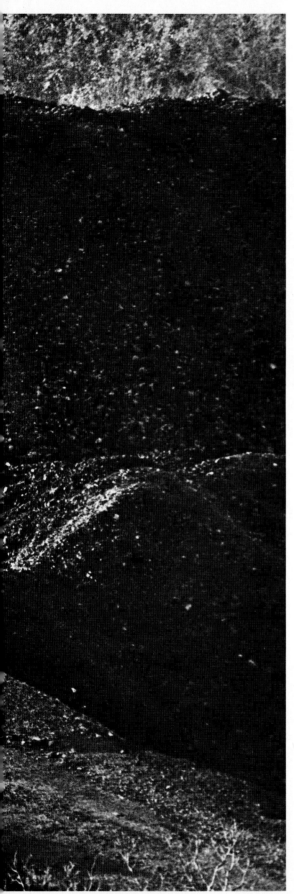

Smokestacks tower beyond Aetna Street in Mingo Junction.

Soot plagues a city

By-products of Steubenville's industries range from mountainous slag heaps to a gritty layer of particulates that coats old frame houses and modern motel windowsills alike. Coping with this continuous shower of pollution, residents pay an average of $85 a year more in cleaning bills and home repairs than other U. S. citizens. "I nearly despair of ever seeing Steubenville cleaned up," says Paul Fabry, as a dwindling population endures the grime.

mountain of waste from local furnaces.   Fingers gather a coat of grime from a windowsill.

Factory worker Sam Jermont: "Carbide's come a long way."

Children play during school recess in Anmoore, West Virgin

Cecil Winemiller: "It's better than it was a year back."

Anmoore: a time for dissent

Every hour, more than 800 pounds of oily black dust pa
ticles gush from seven chimneys, catch westerly wind
and drift across the town of Anmoore, West Virginia. T
dust settles in schoolyards, lunchrooms, homes—a
people's lungs. For years, Anmoore's 960 citizens endur
the soot and grime from Union Carbide's carbon produc
plant. A few people grumbled, but no one challenged t
company. Most of them accepted pollution as the pri
they paid for living and working in Anmoore. Directly
indirectly, they owed their livelihoods to the factory.

"We were an unsuspecting town that a big compa
took advantage of," explained Margaret Golden, a me

everal blocks away smoke and soot pour from factory stacks.

er of the town council. But finally, someone did take
ction. Dale Hagedorn, a free-lance commercial artist,
rote letters to Union Carbide headquarters in New York,
omplaining that "you are turning us into a grubby little
wn." The company never answered, and that further
rovoked Mr. Hagedorn.

He and his wife Leonise circulated a petition and began
letter-writing campaign that gained statewide and even
ational notice. Then, aided by lawyer John L. Boettner,
r., the Hagedorns sued the firm for $100,000 for violating
eople's constitutional right to breathe clean air and to
ve in a desirable environment. Most important, they
llied their fellow townspeople from apathy. The clamor-
g brought results: Early in 1971, Union Carbide an-
ounced an 8.5-million-dollar program to reconstruct its
rnaces and bring plant emissions within state standards.

Paint flakes from an Anmoore sign.

Councilwoman Margaret Golden speaks out for clean air.

Anmoore sixth-grader listens to an antipollution lecture.

Soot-covered door frame emphasizes the purpose of Anmoore

Mayor Buck Gladden presides at a town meeting.

Townspeople score a victory

From a grass-roots beginning — town meetings and unifie
community action — Anmoore citizens waged a successf
campaign against pollution. "It'll never be the sam
for Union Carbide and the people," said Councilwoma
Margaret Golden. Those people, the residents of A
moore — factory workers, merchants, and homemakers
discovered that ordinary citizens can improve their e
vironment. Mayor Buck Gladden, a laborer with an eight
grade education, headed the town council that he sai
delivered "a blow against corporate colonialism" by ta
ing the local factory's gross sales for the first time. Da
Hagedorn, who spearheaded the struggle, discovere
"that little people can count if they don't lie down or quit

...wn meeting. Citizen action triggered a move to force Union Carbide to regulate factory emissions.

...irculars urging Anmoore citizens to fight factory pollution hang to dry behind Dale and Leonise Hagedorn.

something more subtle, but equally significant. Attitudes about environmental questions were changing rapidly in America. After the battle was over, for example, Mrs. Carr talked about what "a great change in public attitudes" had occurred since her organization first began its work.

The Florida canal fight implied something else: The environmental issue was acquiring considerable political muscle. That political lesson was brought home even more sharply in another notable struggle, over appropriations for America's proposed supersonic transport airplane—the SST.

Before the SST political drama unfolded, many political strategists regarded the environmental issue as fashionable, but transitory. Among the things at stake in the SST battle were tens of thousands of highly skilled jobs and the international position of America's aerospace industry. Then environmental implications became a major issue.

The story properly begins at a small, private gathering in an upstairs room of a Washington restaurant, just a block from the White House. The time was spring of 1970. On hand were representatives of two conservation groups—the Sierra Club and Friends of the Earth—and four congressional aides who had assembled that night at the request of a young man named Laurence Moss.

An M.I.T.-trained engineer, Mr. Moss, at 35, had served as a White House Fellow assigned to the Department of Transportation and had developed an interest in conservation causes. He had attended a number of governmental sessions on the question of the SST. "I started out intrigued with the idea of flying at three times the speed of sound and crossing the ocean in three hours," he said, "but I changed my mind as I learned more about the SST. I hadn't been aware of the subtle economic and environmental issues."

Moss began the meeting by outlining what he felt were the problems involving the SST — the sonic boom, the added noise at airports, the unanswered questions of pollution in the stratosphere. To him all these represented threats to man's environment.

He and his associates agreed to organize a nationwide Coalition Against the SST, with Arthur Godfrey as honorary chairman. That was the start of a formal eight-month-long campaign that brought together a variety of citizens' and conservation groups.

Forlorn as its task first appeared, the coalition found grass-roots citizens' support across the country, eventually claiming to represent 39.5 million people, most of whom also opposed construction of the SST for economic reasons.

The coalition forces wrote letters to newspapers and congressional offices, raised money for a full-time staff, paid for advertisements in leading newspapers, magazines, and trade journals, and arranged for various delegations of 20 to 30 people to appear before Congress. The group also kept information flowing to its supporters.

"What we had to do," Moss said later, "was to change the political climate. We had to make each senator and congressman feel that unless he was on our side he might jeopardize his political support."

In 1971 the battle grew even more intense as the aerospace industry and organized labor fought back. But the House of Representatives and the Senate voted down any further money for the SST.

When the fight was over, a leading aerospace lobbyist said wearily, "The trouble is, everybody wants to go back to Walden Pond." He had singled out perhaps the most compelling reason for the defeat. The public rejected the notion that if something is technically possible, it is ethically justified. Citizens, and their elected representatives, were asking new questions about the way money should be spent, particularly for projects centering on serious environmental issues.

Whether the SST ever is built, or whether it should be, the environmental issue has become a power in its own right. With stiff new laws such as the Clean Air Act of 1970, and the EPA's will to enforce them, it seems certain that industry will never again be able to dismiss the pollution of the Nation's environment. Above all else, it has been demonstrated that determined citizens can solve the environmental problems confronting them.

While the great battles involving the Union Carbides and Florida canals and SST's have commanded the headlines, other less-heralded events have been taking place in the mainstreams and byways of American life. They have been managed by organizations with strange-sounding names in every part of the country—from GOO (Get Oil Out! Inc.) in Santa Barbara, California, to GASP (Group Against Smog and Pollution) in Pittsburgh, Pennsylvania.

A number of national organizations also stand ready to assist in environmental campaigns. There are the well-established ones, such as the Conservation Foundation, the National Wildlife Federation, the National Audubon Society, the Izaak Walton League of America, Inc., the National Recreation and Park Association, the Nature Conservancy, and the Wilderness Society. Other national groups with wide memberships and broad interests—the League of Women Voters and the National Association of Counties among them—have undertaken a series of major environmental efforts.

If these are not enough, citizens may write directly to antipollution control agencies in their state capitals, or to the Federal Government itself through the administrator of EPA.

Information for the asking

It is a formidable task to attempt to keep track of all the books, papers, laws, and organizations. An enormous number of new groups are being formed, offering a wealth of information. Environmental centers, created to provide basic scientific material on all environmental questions, have now been established in some 30 locations across the country.

"We found that by simply providing the physical facilities and an open atmosphere, all kinds of programs would develop," said Ray Balter, founder of the Ecology Center at Berkeley, California, one of the first such centers to open.

"Within six months," he told me, "we counted some 60-plus projects being carried out through the center. These involved dozens of staff volunteers and literally hundreds of occasional volunteers."

It was through the ecology centers that an army of 25,000 volunteers was organized swiftly to clean up the San Francisco Bay oil spill in 1971.

The Berkeley Center, for instance, operates an environmental bookstore and a switchboard to answer questions on pollution problems, and maintains liaison with dozens of conservation clubs, social action groups, scientific information agencies, and the 10,000 to 15,000 visitors coming to the office each year.

Millions of specific how-to-do-it citizens' action manuals have come from the presses and duplicating machines of organizations ranging all the way from the national to the local level. Even those persons preparing such documents are often amazed at the public response. Take, for example, Mrs. Howard W. Harrington of Palo Alto, California, who helped prepare a booklet for the local branch of the American Association of University Women entitled, *If You Want to Save Your Environment . . . START AT HOME!*

"The idea for doing such a handbook first came up when a group of members began discussing emerging issues," she recalled. "We realized that people, including ourselves, were asking, 'But what can I, an individual, do?' They were searching for specific ideas and suggestions about what to do in the environmental crisis. Our goal was to compile the most important information into a single, concise booklet, one that could be used as a reference and guidebook.

"So for a small group of us, our kitchens and living rooms became offices, reference libraries, and research centers. Our husbands lived with assorted piles of paper and three-by-five cards, our children quickly learned about recycling and reuse, and we gave up cooking gourmet dinners for the duration."

No sooner had the guidebook been published than requests for it began pouring in from 50 states and 15 foreign countries. The 52-page booklet, now in its fifth printing, has reached the kitchens of 100,000 women with advice such as, "Learn to cook from scratch. It tastes better, is less expensive, and you avoid those chemical additives."

Like others, she found a demand not just for information, but action.

And action—not just words—is what has been taking place. Local groups have banded together to fight pollution in Lake Erie, the filling in of San Francisco Bay, the damming of the floodplains and wetlands of the Neponset River in Boston Harbor. They have battled against air pollution in such widely distant places as Winston-Salem, North Carolina, and Butte, Montana. They have changed highway plans in San Antonio, Texas; they have saved a swamp in New Jersey, a marsh on the coast of Georgia, a wildlife sanctuary in Connecticut, and have begun clean-up campaigns in Manhattan and in the Los Angeles suburb of Culver City.

Helping these citizens achieve their goals has amounted to a legal revolution in America. Virtually overnight, new laws—federal, state, and local—dealing specifically with pollution problems have gone on the books. Until the antipollution struggle became a national issue, the right of the public to a decent environment had been generally recognized nowhere in the law. That has changed.

In 1970, for example, the Michigan Legislature passed what promises to become a model law for the Nation. The Michigan statute recognizes the public right to a decent environment as an enforceable, legal right; makes it possible for private citizens to sue as members of the public; and sets the stage for the development of a common law of environmental quality.

In California the Sierra Club filed suit against the U. S. Forest Service, charging that

Uncompleted canal slices through Florida wilderness.

Hardwood logs, crushed as construction

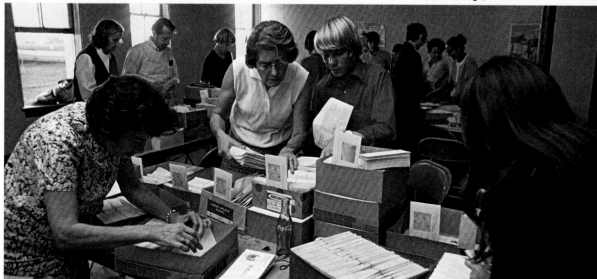

Florida Defenders of the Environment stuff envelopes with pleas for support in a lawsuit against canal builders.

...egan on the Cross-Florida Barge Canal, burn as members of the Florida Defenders of the Environment inspect the canal.

Citizens save a wilderness

Partially completed, the Cross-Florida Barge Canal cuts a 150-foot-wide swath through wilderness. Begun in 1964, the U. S. Army Corps of Engineers project appalled environmentalists who felt that the canal would destroy 45 miles of Oklawaha River forest and pollute the Floridan Aquifer, a major source of water for central Florida.

Protests got nowhere. Then a group of citizens and scientists formed the Florida Defenders of the Environment, conducted surveys, and published evidence to demonstrate the canal's adverse effects on nature. Also questioning economic benefits of the waterway, the group eventually swayed public opinion.

In 1971 the Defenders, aided by the Environmental Defense Fund, won a temporary injunction against further construction, and President Nixon halted the project.

Dr. David S. Anthony checks quality of the canal water.

it acted without public hearing in issuing permits for the building of a private ski resort on public land. Citizens' groups in New York went to court against the Department of Transportation, challenging the construction of an expressway alongside the Hudson River. In both cases the citizens sought court action to preserve natural, scenic, and wildlife resources. Other cases challenged the right to sell DDT, the oil pipeline now proposed for Alaska, a siting of a power station, and logging in the wilderness areas of Colorado, Michigan, and West Virginia.

Under the National Environmental Policy Act, every federal proposal must include an environmental statement describing in detail the impact the project would have on the environment. Public-interest groups are given 90 days to assess the statement, and their comments are made part of the final document submitted to Congress.

Perhaps the most encouraging aspect of these citizens' movements is the chain reaction they often create. It is possible to move from a small campaign to one that eventually encompasses an entire community. Take the example of Denver, Colorado.

All the elements in the American saga were there: the great dangerous trek to find a new place to fashion the good, free life; the building of the city amid the natural splendor of a mile-high plateau set against the backdrop of the Rockies; the progress, growth, security.

Then, inevitably, familiar problems developed: foul air and other forms of pollution. At the beginning of 1970 a small group of housewives, called the Educated Consumers Organization, began asking people to deposit their old automobile license plates to be melted down and reused, rather than contribute to the solid-waste disposal problem. "If Americans continue their use-once-and-throw-away philosophy, another range of the Rocky Mountains will be created consisting of solid waste, and we will then be mining that range of mountains for the natural resources deposited there," the group warned. As part of the drive, supermarkets agreed to provide containers to collect the plates.

By fall, supermarket chains were initiating their own antipollution campaigns, competing vigorously against each other. One chain of stores began the move by taking out full-page newspaper ads saying: "Some folks have commitments and some don't. We feel that *now* is the time to do something about our environmental problems! Let others wait for the 'easy' answers." Not to be outdone, another chain also began taking out antipollution ads.

The two firms started using biodegradable paper packing instead of plastics whenever possible. They encouraged the use of returnable bottles, installed antipollution devices on their trucks, and actively promoted community involvement in the national effort to improve the environment. Other stores soon followed their lead.

A far tougher kind of citizens' fight has been waged on the West Coast. It deals directly with one of the most difficult, and most fundamental, environmental questions: the use of the land. The issue reflects the conflict between private interests and the public good, between the present and the future.

Battle over shorelines

In Washington, a state that boasts magnificent shorelines, mountains, forests, lakes, and rivers, the waterfronts are being bought up by corporations and land speculators. Jack B. Robertson, president of the Washington Environmental Council in Seattle, calls these developments "ill-conceived and ill-planned. They have blighted large areas of our state's shores. And in our attempt to stop the move, we have witnessed an example of apathy on the one hand and private greed on the other."

As the council began building public support for its cause, citizens attending conservation meetings saw slides portraying developments taking place throughout the state. Many came away startled at the sight of shoulder-to-shoulder homes which would prevent the public from using beaches. At one meeting, Brock Evans, representative of the Western Federation of Outdoor Clubs, spoke of his gradual realization that 50,000 acres of trees were being logged yearly.

Camping areas and trails vanished from one summer to the next. Around Puget Sound, every river and lake was falling victim to the sprawl of urbanization.

"You don't win a battle because you're right," he told me. "You win because you work harder, day in and day out, than the other side."

The citizens worked hard. Three times in a three-year period, bills were introduced in the state legislature calling for a law regulating shoreline development. None passed. By 1971 the fight came down to another proposal, the Shorelines Protection Bill—a model of its kind. It declared the saltwater and freshwater shores of the state a valuable natural resource to be held in public trust for all citizens and their descendants. And it required the State Ecological Commission to adopt a plan to establish prohibitions on certain uses of the land. Among other things, it prohibited clear-cutting of timber along shores, oil drilling and exploration in Puget Sound, and the construction of high-rise buildings that block the view of nearby residents. It also provided strong enforcement provisions.

When that measure came up for a vote in the legislature early in 1971, it soon bogged down in political infighting, bureaucracy, and feuds. At this writing, it stands at a stalemate. A decision on the future of the shorelines and the orderly development of a land-use plan has been postponed.

It was the sort of action that would come as no surprise to the Dale Hagedorns, Mrs. Archie Carrs, and other Americans who have been fighting similar battles, often with similarly frustrating delays.

For every notable victory, the record shows a defeat or stalemate. The story abounds with confounding dilemmas: Block an SST, and many men are thrown out of work. Force a factory to install costly antipollution devices, and the company may fail or move away. Try to clean up a massive pollution problem, as Vermont officials and citizens have learned in their attempt to remove the sludge oozing across Lake Champlain, and you find pollution coming from another state beyond your legal jurisdiction. Mount the aggressive public education campaigns and witness the public nevertheless demanding more of the kind of goods that contribute to the pollution problems. Beyond these dilemmas, the old problems still exist: apathy, indifference, greed, and the human inclination to postpone the tough decisions—to let someone else do it, always some other day.

The environmental issue, after all, touches everything America represents, its strengths and weaknesses, its promise and imperfections, its failures and achievements, its legacy of a spendthrift past and its potential for tomorrow. For the future, one thing is clear: Americans are not succumbing to prophets of doom. In the end that is the most hopeful sign, for ultimately the question comes down not to technical knowledge, not to new fail-safe devices, not to new laws and instant remedies. None of them, individually or collectively, will be effective without one essential ingredient: the people themselves. It is, finally, their will and determination—their ability to ask the hard questions, to make the difficult sacrifices and adjustments, to ensure the proper choices and actions, to pay the price—that will fashion the future.

But it is my firm conviction that a profound awareness of the dimensions of the environmental crisis has been growing in all of us. I recall being vividly struck at this sense of change while traveling throughout the country looking at what citizens were doing to fight pollution in every region. But nothing made a more lasting impression upon me than my return home to Washington, D. C., to find my 9-year-old daughter suddenly asking sharp questions about pollution—in the Potomac, in the air we breathe, in the food we eat.

In elementary and secondary classrooms across the Nation, environmental education is becoming an integral part of the curriculum, according to a 1970 survey conducted by the National Education Association.

Earth Day on April 22, 1970, was supported by students in high schools, colleges, and universities from coast to coast. The fresh recruits banded together in cities and marched or held services. The largest group formed in New York City to displace traffic on 45 blocks of Fifth Avenue, from 14th to 59th Street, and to demonstrate the pleasure of walking in the street without the internal combustion engine polluting the air.

In an experimental program to involve urban youngsters in nature's laboratory, the public schools in the District of Columbia have taken fifth-graders on field trips to the Catoctin Mountains in Maryland. The man-and-his-environment course teaches the children about ecology in an outdoor classroom.

In the Shenandoah National Park, school children without textbooks or pencils walk mountain trails with park naturalists, pausing before boulders and clumps of bushes to observe the life of the forest. They are learning in the silence of the outdoors to understand what the poet Walt Whitman called "those inaudible words of the earth."

A statement in stone gives youngsters who visit New York City's Central Park a different message. Standing on a knoll in the park is Cleopatra's Needle, a tall granite obelisk, first erected in Heliopolis, Egypt, about 1500 B.C., and then moved to Alexandria in 14 B.C. There it stayed until the early 1880's when it was sent, in perfect condition, to New York as a goodwill offering. After some 90 years in the park, two of its four sides are still covered with hieroglyphics, but the south and west sides are now worn away. Those are the directions of New York's prevailing winds; the wind-driven chemicals in New York's air have eaten away the surface. In less than a century the needle has sustained more damage than in all its 3,500 years in Egypt.

It is a monument to man's ability to build. And to destroy.

Pounding surf and sculpted sand near Loleta, California, form the outdoor classroom of botanist Doris Niles. She hopes that a

A teacher holds a sprig of lupine.

Ecology: a life-style

Dr. Doris Niles communicates her infectious love of the natural world to groups of schoolteachers she often leads down a windswept beach in northern California. She identifies seaweed adrift in the surf, points out the variety of seashells patterning the shore, and summarizes relationships between forms of marine life.

A 67-year-old grandmother with doctorates in botany and marine biology, Dr. Niles shows educators an effective way to teach ecology: outside the classroom, wading among breakers and digging in sand. On the staff of the University of California at Davis, she offers such courses as "The Seashore Milieu" and "The Teaching of Science in the Elementary

School"—her classes meet most out of doors. She teaches 200 students in four cities each week, traveling 40,000 miles a year to spread simple philosophy: "Teach students how to look carefully at everything how to look at the world around them.

On weekends and during summer vacations, teachers flock to Dr. Niles home overlooking Humboldt Bay hear lectures, participate in group discussions, and accompany this vigorous woman on field trips. She help collect plants, shells, rocks, and fossils and shows how to display them in classrooms as an enticement interest children in the study of ecology. "The more students and adult begin to understand the delicate relationships between living things Dr. Niles says, "the more respect w will have for our natural environme and the more care we will take of it.

...nderstanding of ecology will lead citizens to a more widespread concern and respect for the environment.

...nergetic Dr. Niles (right) directs students on a field trip.

Ecology students discuss displays of marine algae.

INDEX

Illustrations references, including legends, appear in *italics*.

ACKNOWLEDGMENTS

The Special Publications Division is grateful to the people named or quoted in the text and to those listed here for their generous cooperation and assistance during the preparation of this book:

Dean E. Abrahamson, University of Minnesota; Perry L. Adkisson, Texas A&M University; J. T. Alexander, Atomic Energy Commission, Oak Ridge; Martin Alexander, Cornell University; Stanley Auerbach, Oak Ridge National Laboratory; Robert U. Ayres, International Research and Technology Corporation; Elso S. Barghoorn, Harvard University; Noel W. Beyle, Citizens' Advisory Committee on Environmental Quality; Donald Bliss, Environmental Protection Agency; Wallace Bowman, Library of Congress; Robert Cahn, Council on Environmental Quality; Robert H. Cannon, Jr., U. S. Department of Transportation; E. Lendell Cockrum, University of Arizona; Richard A. Copeland, Environmental Research Group, Inc.; Lawrence Cory, St. Mary's College; Donald Crane, Appalachian Regional Commission; Frank M. D'Itri, Michigan State University; Herbert W. Foster, National Coal Association; Norman R. Glass, EPA; Raymond G. Holmes, EPA; M. King Hubbert, U. S. Geological Survey; George W. Irving, Jr., U. S. Department of Agriculture; David Klein, Hope College; George A. Lacy, Chrysler Corporation; Ralph E. Lapp; Ron M. Linton, Linton, Mields, & Coston, Inc.; Paul Martin, University of Arizona; Arthur E. Merriman, U. S. Forest Service; Norman E. Nelson, Jr., Weyerhaeuser Company; Lamar Newkirk, Georgia-Pacific Corporation; William Osborn, Center for Study of Responsive Law; Connie Parrish, Friends of the Earth; James W. Plumb, American Forest Institute; C. T. Prout, Soil Conservation Service; Monroe Rabin, Lawrence Radiation Laboratory; Wayne D. Rasmussen, USDA; William H. Regan and William L. Richmond, Los Alamos Scientific Laboratory of the University of California; William K. Reilly, Council on Environmental Quality; Robert Reimold, University of Georgia's Marine Institute; Victor Reinemer, Office of Senator Lee Metcalf; H. T. Reynolds, University of California, Riverside; Robert F. Sawyer, University of California, Berkeley; Henry W. Setzer, Smithsonian Institution; Stanford Smith, Great Lakes Fishery Laboratory; William E. Stephenson, American Cyanamid Company; Philip N. Storrs, Engineering-Science, Inc.; Paul S. Taylor, University of California, Berkeley; William E. Towell, American Forestry Association; Joanna Underwood, Council on Economic Priorities; Etienne van de Walle, Princeton University; John R. Vosburgh, U. S. Department of the Interior; William A. Wallace, Rensselaer Polytechnic Institute; Shirley F. Weiss, University of North Carolina; C. M. Williams, Harvard University; John C. Witherspoon, American Forest Institute; William Woodin, Arizona-Sonora Desert Museum.

Composition for *As We Live and Breathe: The Challenge of Our Environment* by National Geographic's Phototypographic Division, John E. McConnell, Manager. Printed and bound by Fawcett Printing Corp., Rockville, Md. Color separations by Colorgraphics, Inc., Beltsville, Md., Graphic Color Plate, Inc., Stamford, Conn., The Lanman Company, Alexandria, Va., Lebanon Valley Offset Company, Inc., Annville, Pa., McCall Printing Company, Charlotte, N. C., and Progressive Color Corp., Rockville, Md.